The Beauty of the Eucharist

Dennis Billy, C.Ss.R.

The Beauty of the Eucharist

Voices from the Church Fathers

New City Press
Hyde Park, New York

Published in the United States by New City Press
202 Comforter Blvd., Hyde Park, NY 12538
www.newcitypress.com
© 2010 Dennis J. Billy

Cover design by Durva Correia

Library of Congress Cataloging-in-Publication Data:

Billy, Dennis Joseph.
   The beauty of the Eucharist : voices from the church Fathers / Dennis J. Billy.
      p. cm.
   Includes bibliographical references.
   ISBN 978-1-56548-328-6 (pbk. : alk. paper) 1. Lord's Supper—History of doctrines—Early church, ca. 30-600. 2. Fathers of the church. I. Title.
   BV823.B55 2010
   234'.16309—dc22   2009026400

1st printing: August 2009
2nd printing: November 2009

Printed in the United States of America

In memory of
Alfred C. Rush, C.Ss.R.
1911–2001

Contents

Abbreviations

ANF   *The Ante-Nicene Fathers*, 10 vols. (Grand Rapids, Mich.: Eerdman's Publishing Company, American reprint of 1885 Edinburgh ed., 1985–86).

CH   Karl Bihlmeyer, *Church History*, revised by Hermann Tüchle, 13th ed., trans. Victor E. Mills, 3 vols. (Westminster: The Newman Press, 1968).

CT   Jaroslav Pelikan, *The Christian Tradition: A History of the Development of Doctrine*, 5 vols. (Chicago/London: The University of Chicago Press, 1971–89).

ECF   *Early Christian Fathers*, ed. and trans., Cyril C. Richardson (New York: Macmillan Publishing Company, Inc., 1970).

EEC   *The Eucharist of the Early Christians*, trans. Matthew J. O'Connell (New York: Pueblo Publishing Company, 1978).

Eucharist   Daniel J. Sheerin, *The Eucharist*, Message of the Fathers of the Church, vol. 7 (Wilmington, Del.: Michael Glazier, 1986).

Eucharistie   *Dictionnaire de théologie catholique*, vol. 5, cols. 1121–83 (Paris: Librairie Letouzey et Ané, 1924), s.v., "Eucharistie (d'après les pères)," by G. Bareille.

FC   *The Fathers of the Church*, 84 vols. (Washington, D.C.: The Catholic University of America Press, 1962–91).

FEF   William A. Jurgens, *The Faith of the Early Fathers*, 3
               vols. (Collegeville, Minn.: The Liturgical Press, 1979).

FGC   Hans von Campenhausen, *The Fathers of the Greek
               Church*, trans. L.A. Garrard (London: Adam & Charles
               Black, 1963).

FLC   Hans von Campenhausen, *The Fathers of the Latin
               Church*, trans. Manfred Hoffmann (London: Adam &
               Charles Black, 1964).

HD   J. Tixeront, *History of Dogmas*, trans. H.L.B. (West-
               minster, MD: Christian Classics, 1984).

NPNF   *Nicene and Post-Nicene Fathers*, Second Series, 14
               vols. (Grand Rapids, MI: Wm. B. Eerdmans Publishing
               Company, American reprint of 1882– Edinburgh ed.,
               1982–83).

P   Berthold Altaner, *Patrology*, trans. Hilda C. Graef
               (New York: Herder and Herder, 1960).

Pat.   Johannes Quasten, *Patrology*, 3 vols. (Westminster,
               Md: Christian Classics, Inc., 1950; reprint ed. 1983).

Introduction

S omeone once called tradition "the living faith of the dead," not "the dead faith of the living."[1] This "living faith" has made the community of believers what it is today. If we cut ourselves off from this faith, we can easily forget our past and lose touch with what we are and where we are going. To ignore these distant voices would be like plugging up one of our ears with wax and acting as if we had perfect hearing. To hear God's Word today, we must listen carefully to what these voices from the past have to say. Merely listening to them, however, is only the first step. For the "living faith of the dead" to have a real impact on our lives today, we must also scrutinize, digest, and adapt what they say to our own circumstances. Either their faith lives on in us, or it does not live at all.

This book examines what some of the most prominent voices of Christianity's distant past have taught about the Eucharist. It focuses not on the Scriptures, where a wealth of material has already been made available for popular consumption, but on twenty-three sources from the late first century to the early seventh century C.E. that are commonly thought to have made substantial contributions to the Church's understanding of the Eucharist. While these sources do not exhaust the height, breadth, and depth of Christianity's venerable patristic heritage, their cumulative effect forms a sizeable (and quite representative) body of material for demonstrating the general contours of the Church's developing understanding of this important sacrament. Our goal here is to look at how the proponents of an emerging Christian orthodoxy understood, celebrated, and presented the Eucharist in the 500 years immediately following the end of the apostolic era.

These voices are each unique, with distinct characteristics and clearly recognizable styles. The themes they treat cover a wide variety

---

1. Jaroslav Pelikan, *The Vindication of Tradition* (New Haven/London: Yale University Press, 1984), 65.

of topics. Some, for example, demonstrate a deep concern for order in the liturgical assembly. Others display a strong Eucharistic realism. Some emphasize the sacrificial dimension of the Eucharist; still others refute the charges made against the Christian faith by their Roman persecutors. Some draw connections between the Eucharist and the witness of Christian martyrdom, while others combat false teachings such as Gnosticism, Docetism, and Arianism that had infiltrated and posed a serious threat to the integrity of the Christian community. All of these concerns were important issues for the emerging Christian orthodoxy of the post-apostolic age. Taken together, they reveal the changing face of the apostolic faith as it struggled for its own survival in the midst of immense and, at times, seemingly overwhelming internal and external pressures.

We present these voices from the past in chronological order and focus on what insights they give with respect to the Eucharist. Clement of Rome (c. 95/96), for example, considers the Eucharist from the perspective of proper Church order. Ignatius of Antioch, (c. 110) presents it in the context of Church governance, the fight against Gnosticism, and the meaning of discipleship. The mid-second-century work known as *The Martyrdom of Polycarp* (c. 156–67) focuses on the important link between martyrdom and the Eucharist. *The Didache*, a composite work put together in the mid-second century, looks at the prayer forms used during Sunday worship. Justin Martyr (c. 152–55) brings out the relationship between the Eucharist and the other rites of Christian initiation. Irenaeus of Lyons (c. 180–90) offsets Gnostic dualism by affirming the continuity of the worlds of spirit and matter in Eucharist. A little later in the second century, Clement of Alexandria (c. 190) draws out the relationship between the Eucharist and the Divine Logos. In the early decades of the third century, Tertullian of Carthage emphasizes the prophetic, sacrificial, and sacramental dimensions of the Eucharist. *The Apostolic Tradition* (c. 215), often associated with Hippolytus of Rome, provides one of the earliest extant versions of a Eucharistic prayer used in the ancient Roman liturgy, celebrated in Greek, the common language of time, although we only have Latin translations. Later in the early third century, Origen of Alexandria looks into the various spiritual meanings of the Eucharist. Still later, Cyprian of Carthage (c. 253) highlights the salvific significance of mingling water with wine at the Eucharistic celebration.

In the next three-and-a-half centuries, still other saintly voices proudly proclaim the centrality of the Eucharist for the Christian faith. Athanasius of Alexandria (295–373) presents the Eucharist as the means by which God's divinizing grace touches people throughout history. Cyril of Jerusalem (c. 313–387) sees the Eucharist as the last of the sacraments of initiation, whereby believers gain full participation into the life of the Church. Hilary of Poitiers (c. 315–67) finds the Eucharist a powerful tool in his efforts to curb the growing Arian influence in Poitiers and its environs. Ambrose of Milan (c. 339–87) focuses on the importance of the sacrament as a source of forgiveness and spiritual nourishment. Basil the Great (c. 330–97) affirms the underlying continuity existing between worship and life, liturgical celebration and action in the world. Gregory Nazianzus (329/30–c. 390) uses figurative language and the traditional "type/antitype" distinction to emphasize the centrality of the Eucharist for the faith. Gregory of Nyssa (c. 335–95) looks upon the Eucharist as a way of restoring the divine image in fallen humanity. John Chrysostom (c. 347–407) emphasizes the real presence, the change effected in the consecrated elements, and the sacrificial nature of the Eucharistic banquet. St. Jerome (347–420) looks upon the Eucharist as the central act of Christian worship, "the true Sacrament of the Passover." Augustine of Hippo (354–430), sees the Old Testament prophecies fulfilled in the Eucharist and calls it the sacrament of the New Creation. Leo the Great (d. 461) affirms the real presence of Christ in the consecrated elements and brings out the moral, spiritual, and even mystical dimensions of the sacrament. Gregory the Great (d. 604) describes the Eucharist as a mystical presentation of Christ's sacrificial death on Calvary.

All in all, these twenty-three voices come from different geographical locations around the Mediterranean basin (e.g., Rome, Jerusalem, Antioch, Alexandria, Carthage, Constantinople, Cappadocia), yet share a common cultural heritage made possible by the wide diffusion of Greco-Roman civilization. As such, they are representative witnesses of Christianity's first concerted and large-scale attempt at Gospel inculturation.

In conveying their message, these distant voices of the Church's Eucharistic faith employ a great variety of literary means: letters, prayers, dialogues, apologies, eyewitness accounts, Scripture commentaries, treatises — to name but a few. This great array of genres reflects the many ways in which the Eucharist had penetrated the consciousness of the emerging orthodoxy of the early Church. It also says something about the inventiveness with which the authors of these works sought to clarify their ideas and make them known. Today's believers, who live in a world where these and many other means can help promulgate the faith, should take heart from such efforts and seek to emulate them. They should also be inspired by the courage these voices display and the unflinching dedication with which they make their message known.

To highlight these connections between past and present, we have chosen to follow the same general format for each chapter. After some opening comments, we offer general remarks about the particular person or document under investigation (e.g., relevant biographical information, the work's audience, genre, and purpose). Our attention then focuses on what this particular voice reveals about the Christian understanding of the Eucharist. A series of observations follows which seeks to deepen these insights and apply them to today's believers in practical and relevant ways. Each chapter ends with reflection questions to help the reader both to delve more deeply into his or her own beliefs about the Eucharist and to draw practical conclusions about its role in his or her life.

Although each voice stands alone and can be appreciated as such, we are primarily interested in the harmony of sound resulting from their cumulative effect. One cannot listen to these distant voices, coming as they do from different geographical locations in the ancient Greco-Roman world and often separated from one another by sizeable lapses in time, without noting a series of similar themes and reoccurring leitmotifs. These voices of Christianity's emerging orthodoxy come together to form an inspiring and spirited chant extolling the centrality of Eucharist for the life of the believing community. They do so by highlighting the intrinsic connection between the Last Supper and Jesus' passion and death and by interpreting this central act of Christian worship in terms of table fellowship, bloodless sacrifice, and Jesus' real presence in the consecrated bread and wine.

Although these voices did not have refined theological terminology to clarify their innermost beliefs, their struggles with radically divergent strains of Christianity and their need to defend themselves against false accusations by imperial authorities enabled them to find a common message to interpret and to celebrate. Indeed, many of these witnesses to the faith paid the ultimate price for what they proclaimed. The blood they spilled for the sake of Christ and his body, the Church, adds strength to their voices and conviction to their words. Centuries later, they continue to encourage believing communities the world over to listen to their message, ponder it, apply it to their lives, and sincerely take it to heart.

Eucharist

Be careful, then, to observe a single Eucharist. For there is one flesh of our Lord, Jesus Christ, and one cup of his blood that makes us one, and one altar, just as there is one bishop along with the presbytery and the deacons, my fellow slaves. In that way, whatever you do is in line with God's will.

Ignatius of Antioch

Clement of Rome
Evolving Structures

Now that this is clear to us and we have peered into the depths
of divine knowledge, we are bound to do in an orderly fashion
all that the Maker has bidden us to do at the proper times he
set. He ordered sacrifices and services to be performed; and
required this to be done, not in a careless and disorderly way,
but at the times and seasons he fixed. Where he wants them
performed, and by whom, he himself fixed by his supreme
will, so that everything should be done in a holy way and with
his approval, and should be acceptable to his will.

Clement of Rome

Have you ever wondered where the Church's structures of
authority came from or how they developed? Contrary to popular
opinion, they were not written in stone from the very outset of the
Church's existence, nor did they suddenly appear out of nowhere at
some later date. Most scholars agree that they developed gradually
over time in response to practical questions concerning the proper
organization of the Church's affairs, especially those regarding the
liturgy. This evolution of structures took place through a communal
process of discernment that sought to respond to the promptings
of Christ's Spirit in the heart of the community. How exactly did
this process of development take place? Beyond the New Testament
writings, only a few early Church documents offer insights into what
actually happened. Our first voice from the past is one of the early
witnesses of these evolving Church structures.

Clement's Letter to the Corinthians

In the late first century C. E. (c. 95 or 96), a letter from the Church of Rome was sent to the Church of Corinth to deal with questions of Church order.[1] At the time, some presbyters at Corinth had been unceremoniously removed from office (44:6) and the Church of Rome used the occasion to intervene on their behalf (1:1). This letter has traditionally been attributed to Clement, the fourth bishop of Rome. It was greatly revered in the early Church and, in some locations, was even read aloud during the celebration of the Liturgy of the Word. For our present purposes, the letter reveals much about the Eucharistic celebration of the late-first-century Church in Rome, specifically regarding its sacrificial character, the role of authority, and the prayers used by those presiding. A look at these elements of Rome's late-first-century liturgical practice may help us to understand these elements better in our own Eucharistic celebrations.

Although the author of this letter cannot be positively identified, a highly tenable theory presents him as someone from the household of Titus Flavius Clemens, a Roman consul executed in the year 95 by his cousin, the emperor Domitian (81–96).[2] The charge against the consul was atheism, an accusation often levelled at Christians by the Romans. According to this theory, Flavius Clemens and his wife, Domitilla, the patroness of one of the earliest Christian catacombs in Rome, were either Christians themselves or Christian sympathizers, who kept a number of believers in their service. The author of the letter, a slave or freedman who was also named Clemens, possibly because of his connection with this noble Roman household, held a high position of leadership in the Christian community at Rome. It would be misleading, however, to think of him as a bishop in the traditional sense of the term, since this office was still undergoing development in the later part of the first century. The letter itself

---

1. The work is often referred to as *Clement's First Letter to the Corinthians,* in order to distinguish it from a second letter that was falsely attributed to the same author. This second letter is actually an anonymous Christian sermon, composed many years after Clement's death, sometime between the years 120 and 170 C.E. The English text of this letter comes from *ECF*, 33–73. The chapter builds on insights into the letter found in Georges Blond, "Clement of Rome," in *EEC*, 24–47.
2. See *ECF*, 37.

implies that a council of presbyter-bishops governed the Christian community of late-first century Rome, evidence which suggests that the presbyteral office had there (and elsewhere) not yet been fully separated from the episcopal (42–44).

The author may very well have been the senior presbyter-bishop of the Church of Rome and, given the nature of the letter, may also have been specifically charged with the task of overseeing Rome's relations with other churches. Because it contains many Old Testament themes presented largely within the conceptual framework of Hellenic thought, it is also thought that the author was a Hellenized Jew who, at the time of the writing, had probably long been established in Rome. As far as the occasion of the letter is concerned, it is not known if the Corinthian church had asked the Roman church to intervene in the case of the deposed presbyters or if the Roman church took the initiative itself. In any case, the letter provides firm evidence that the Church of Rome believed it had the authority to deal with such matters (1:1) and, as such, offers one of the earliest instances in Christian literature of an emerging concept of Roman primacy.

Eucharist as Sacrifice

One of the fundamental themes of Clement's letter is that the Christian Eucharist has replaced the many sacrificial offerings depicted in the Old Testament. In making this claim, Clement indicates that the Eucharist itself is a sacrificial offering with Jesus Christ as its one high priest: "This is the way, dear friends, in which we found our salvation, Jesus Christ, the high priest of our offerings, the protector and helper of our weakness" (36:1). Jesus is the person who brings our offerings to the Father. In doing so, he heals our iniquities and shields us from the overwhelming power of God's transcendent light.

In his function as high priest, Jesus mediates for us on our behalf and allows us to touch the threshold of the divine: "Through him we fix our gaze on the heights of heaven. In him, we see mirrored God's pure and transcendent face. Through him the eyes of our hearts have been opened. Through him, our foolish and darkened understanding springs up to light. Through him the Master has willed that we should taste immortal knowledge" (36:1–2). Jesus' action on our behalf permits us to enter God's presence. Our experience of God is always mediated in and through the person of Christ (7:4–7).

Clement makes it clear that Jesus' bloody death was an offering of sacrificial love (49:1–6). Sacrifice, for him, represents the main action of the Eucharistic celebration. To make his point, he draws many parallels between the Christian Eucharist and cultic actions of the Old Testament, showing how this one sacrifice has replaced the sacrificial practices of the Mosaic Law (40:1–44:6). Although Clement never uses the word "Eucharist" (*eucharistia*) to refer specifically to the weekly ritual of Christian worship and never develops an extended teaching on the meaning of Christian sacrifice, his stylish rhetoric and heavy use of Old Testament themes clearly present the worship of the Christian community as the fulfillment of the Mosaic dispensation.

The Role of Authority

Closely related to the sacrificial understanding of the Christian Eucharist is the role of Church authority, the specific function of which was to offer spiritual oblations to God through Christ on behalf of the believing community. As mentioned earlier, the Church of Rome in the late-first century seemed to have been ruled by a council of presbyter-bishops, a clear indication that the structure of authority there was still in the process of development. The emergence of the monarchical episcopacy in later decades came from a combination of internal and external pressures that made it important for the local churches to have a strong internal cohesiveness rooted in a single ecclesiastical office. The heterodox threat from Gnostic dualism, already a growing presence in the Roman world, helped bring this need to the fore and contributed to the evolution of Church structures.

Clement's letter reflects a strong concern for performing the liturgical rites according to the order ordained by God (40:1–2). The Church's structure of authority, he believes, has been divinely established to guarantee such order (40:3–4). He draws a clear distinction, moreover, between those in authority and the rest of the faithful and points to the three-tiered division of bishop, presbyter, and deacon that would soon emerge: "The high priest is given his particular duties; the priests are assigned their special place, while on the Levites particular tasks are imposed. The layman (*laikos*) is bound by the layman's code" (40:5). Clement's letter represents the first time the term *laikos* appears in Christian literature. He uses it as a way of referring to those with no specific liturgical function in the community of God's People. While this use of the term must be taken in the context of the idyllic picture of ecclesial order that Clement is painting for the factious Corinthian community, it is clear that the distinction exists in the late-first-century Church of Rome and is well on its way to becoming firmly rooted in the theological mindset of the believing community.

For Clement, this structure comes from God and is rooted in the authority of the apostles, who appointed overseers and ministers to take their place and who also instructed that, even when these die, others should be selected to succeed them (44:1–2). Because this authority enjoys both divine institution and the full weight of apostolic authority, Clement strongly disagrees with the way the Church at Corinth has removed its presbyters from office (44:3). The tone of Clement's letter suggests that a group of charismatic figures may have attempted to and eventually succeeded in upsetting the established order in the Christian community at Corinth by deposing those presbyters in charge and putting themselves in their place (47:6). Clement challenges these actions through a series of injunctions against jealousy (4–5), the need for repentance (7–8), and the importance of obedience, humility, and other Christian virtues (9–23). His interest here is to re-establish the community's traditional liturgical celebrations so that, from there, right order might also flow into the teaching and governance of the entire Christian community.

Liturgical Prayer

Clement's letter also contains an example of late-first-century liturgical prayer at Rome. While integrated into the letter in a carefully crafted, practically seamless manner, chapters 59–61 stand out by virtue of their eloquent poetic style. The language of these chapters resembles the kind one would normally find in a liturgical setting rather than in a letter seeking to resolve controversy in another Church. Since they do not contain an Institution narrative or the words of consecration, the chapters cannot be strictly identified as a Eucharistic prayer. Their content evokes more the sentiments of thanksgiving and petition that one would find in general intercessory prayers offered elsewhere during the celebration.

The prayer can be divided into four parts. The first (59:3–4) praises God's greatness and omnipotence and asks him to help the lowly and afflicted. The second (60:1–4a) offers homage to God the world's Creator and asks him for forgiveness. The third (60:4b–61:2) asks God for the help to be obedient not only to his name, but also to temporal authorities, whose power ultimately stems from divine providence. The fourth (61:3) ends the prayer with an affirmation of God's power and goodness and his willingness to grant not only what has been asked of him, but countless blessings more. Taken as a whole, the prayer presents the Christian God as someone who sides with the poor and oppressed of the world, shows mercy and compassion toward those who repent of their sins, works in history through the established temporal order, and answers our prayers in a way beyond our wildest dreams. Since it alludes several times to the problems at the Church in Corinth, it may represent a liturgical text that was composed specifically with them in mind. In this case, Clement presents the Church of Rome as a community not only trying to resolve a thorny issue in another Christian community, but also actively praying for a solution.

It must be remembered, however, that Christian liturgical practice during the late-first century retained a high degree of flexibility. Even in the Church of Rome, a community noted for its emphasis on proper order at all levels of life and worship, the presider was given a considerable amount of leeway over the composition of the prayers said during the Eucharistic worship. Such a tendency exists even half a century later when Justin Martyr observes that the one presiding at the liturgical assembly at Rome gives thanks on behalf of the community "to the best of his ability" (*First Apology*, chap. 67). In such a liturgical atmosphere, Clement's prayer may very well represent an original composition that took account of the troubles of the Church at Corinth and into which the Instituted narrative and words of institution could be inserted, possibly after chapter 59. In such a scenario, chapters 59–61 of Clement's letter would represent a substantial part of a Eucharistic canon from the Church of Rome, one that reflects the flexibility and initiative of the presider (possibly Clement himself) in bringing the troubles of the Corinthian Church into the very heart of its liturgical worship.

Observations

Clement's letter to the Corinthians provides us with important information about the Christian Eucharistic worship of late-first-century Rome. When examined with care, it also offers many relevant insights about the meaning of our own present-day Eucharistic celebrations. Five in particular come to mind.

1. *Lex orandi, lex credendi, lex vivendi*. It should not surprise us that the earliest evidence pointing at least to the beginnings of the theory of Roman primacy has to do with a controversy concerning the proper order in the liturgical assembly. For Christians, the liturgy lies at the very heart of their belief and practice. It shapes the community's self-understanding, its way of seeing God, and its relationship to the world. In the late-first century, the Church of Rome saw the importance of sound liturgy for the life of the entire community and was willing to take concrete steps to resolve conflicts even when they arose beyond its borders. It did so out of a sense of the universal scope of the liturgy, sensing that discord in any local community affected the life of the entire Church. Today, many Christian communities have lost this sense of the role liturgical worship plays in shaping their faith and providing them with their moral bearings. As in the case of the Church of Corinth, it sometimes takes an interested but outside onlooker to rekindle an appreciation of the central role the Eucharist plays in this regard.

2. Given the liturgical focus of the letter, Clement's focus on the life of virtue in the early part of the letter should come as no surprise. In nourishing the Christian community through both Word and sacrament, the Eucharist enables those participating to share more deeply in Christ's Paschal Mystery. In doing so, they gradually become conformed to the mind of Christ and exhibit in their own lives the

very same virtues that Jesus embodied in his. Clement hints that the troubles in the Church at Corinth stem from a failure to see the close interconnection between the proper liturgical ordering and growth in the spiritual life. The divisions they are experiencing, moreover, go beyond the confines of their local community and redound throughout the whole Church. Awareness of this important continuity between a community's Eucharistic worship and its growth in the life of virtue needs to be emphasized today with greater rigor. In too many communities liturgical worship is still understood merely as an obligation to be met rather than a source of nourishment for growth in the Spirit. True Eucharistic worship opens the human heart to God and effects a gradual transformation in the community as a whole and in the individuals who take part.

3. Clement's letter emphasizes the sacrificial nature of the Eucharist by virtue of its intimate connection with Christ's death on the cross. This teaching, while deeply rooted in the Christian tradition, has become increasingly difficult for Catholics to understand and, in today's environment of spiritual consumerism, even harder to accept. The crux of the matter revolves around a single question: Why would a loving and compassionate God make a sacrificial blood-offering a requirement for the forgiveness of humanity's sins? Because of the strong emphasis on sacrifice in both Jewish and Gentile culture at the birth of Christianity, such a question would hardly have occurred to Christians of the late-first century such as Clement. For today's believers, however, such a requirement fails to convince and, to some, seems even barbaric. When faced with the notion of sacrifice, today's Christians react in various ways. Some ignore it, some reject it, some accept it without reflecting upon it, and some try to interpret the concept in a way that has relevance and meaning for their lives. With its strong emphasis on the sacrificial nature of the Eucharistic celebration, Clement's letter challenges us to examine our own attitudes toward Christ's sacrificial death and to elaborate a new language that will be continuous with the concept of sacrifice yet also help us to transcend it.

4. Clement's letter gives us a glimpse into the developing hierarchical structure of the Church at Rome. When it was written, the Christian community there was governed by a council of presbyter-bishops;

within the next few decades, however, the three-tiered structure of bishop, presbyter, and deacon would be well in place and widely accepted as the fundamental governing structure of the Church at Rome and throughout most of the Christian world. These developments were a response to the changing needs of the Christian community: the growing Christian population and the need for multiple sites of Christian Sunday worship; the need for new and diversified ministries to match the emerging requirements of the Christian population; the need to have a single voice centered in a strong monarchical episcopacy to offset the threat of heterodox movements both within and without the confines of Church membership — to name but a few. When read today, Clement's letter encourages us to imagine what new ministries the Spirit might be asking the Church to develop as a response to the present needs of the believing community and how they will relate to the Church's existing structures of authority. The role of the laity in these new ministries and the degree of authority they can share with the governing structure of the Church must also be examined and taken carefully into account.

5. Clement's letter is primarily concerned with proper liturgical order. The liturgical prayer embedded in Clement's letter, however, hints at the considerable degree of flexibility given to presiders when they led the assembly during its Eucharistic worship. As such, the letter maintains a careful balance between structure and personal initiative that prevents the liturgy from being overly rigid, on the one hand, or overly spontaneous (and possibly disruptive), on the other. While difficult to maintain, keeping such a balance is very important for the spiritual well-being of the liturgical assembly. Moving to either extreme can have grave consequences for the way the Christian community relates to God and others. As they go about planning their weekly liturgies, pastors need to be sensitive to the importance of maintaining this balance. Too much control over the details of the liturgy can stifle the Spirit and prevent people from having a genuine experience of God in their lives. Too much spontaneity, however, can undermine the communal nature of the celebration by allowing certain individuals to impose their own agenda on the worshiping community (cf. 47:6–7). The flexibility needed should be of the type

that holds structures in place but allows them to be adapted to the needs of the community that has gathered. At all times, the focus of the Eucharistic celebration should be on helping worshipers to give honor and glory to God.

Conclusion

Clement's letter to the Corinthians emphasizes the importance of proper order in the liturgical assembly and highlights the Eucharist's role in the spiritual growth of the Christian community. For today's readers, it raises challenging questions concerning their understanding of the sacrificial nature of the Eucharist, the developing role of the hierarchy, and the flexibility needed in making the liturgy a locus of conversion and growth for the entire community.

The letter also offers us a sense of the Church's growing universal (i.e., "catholic") consciousness. In coming to this awareness, the Church at Rome came to see that whatever befell a single Christian community ultimately affected the entire body. It intervened in the affairs of the Church at Corinth because it understood the grave consequences that divisions on the local level could have for the Church throughout the world. In the late-first century, the Church at Rome began to assume the role of arbitrator and peacemaker in the wider community of the faithful. Its response to this call reflected a desire on its part to serve local Christian churches in the name of the Church universal. While this ministry has undergone considerable development over the years, it remains, in essence, a call to service to the universal body of believers.

For today's readers, Clement's letter offers a chance to reflect on the nature of the Eucharistic celebration and the role it plays in their walk of Christian discipleship. It challenges us to look at our liturgical celebrations in connection with the wider body of believers and to find ways of steering a middle course between an exceedingly rigid and an overly lax application of liturgical prescripts. It also encourages us to work to overcome divisions, of whatever kind, in our own local communities and to pray for the universal ministry of the Church of Rome in its service to the people of God and its efforts to help bring about the reconciliation of the Christian churches.

Reflection Questions

1. To what extent does liturgical worship shape your faith and moral bearings? A great deal? A little? None whatsoever? Do you think it should? If so, how should it do so? What are the benefits to there being a continuity between worship, faith, and moral conduct? Are there any liabilities?

2. Do you consider the lack of unity among Christians a result of failure of taking seriously the close interconnection between proper order in worship and growth in the spiritual life? If so, what practical steps can you take to emphasize this important relationship within your own Church on the local, regional, and universal levels? What can you do to promote this important relationship with Christians from other denominations?

3. How do you respond to the Church's teaching on the sacrificial nature of the Eucharist and its relationship to Christ's suffering on the cross? Ignore it? Reject it? Accept it on face value? Reinterpret it? Why, in your opinion, would a compassionate God make a sacrificial blood-offering a requirement for the forgiveness of humanity's sins?

4. What is your attitude toward the hierarchical governing structures of the Church? Are they divinely inspired? Purely man-made inventions? A mixture of both? Do they form part of the essence of the Church? Can they continue to undergo development and change? What benefits do they bring to the Church? What are their liabilities? Where do you see the Church's governing structures heading?

5. What is your attitude toward the manner in which the Church's public worship should be conducted? Are you in favor of strict regulation? Creative and spontaneous invention? Something in between? Should those participating be given a certain amount of flexibility in the way they implement the Church's guidelines? Where does one draw the line between what is essential and non-essential in the Church's public worship? Who has the authority to draw that line?

Voice Two

Ignatius of Antioch
Real Discipleship

I am God's wheat and I am being ground by the teeth of wild
beasts to make a pure loaf for Christ. I would rather that
you fawn on the beasts so that they may be my tomb and no
scrap of my body be left. Thus when I have fallen asleep, I
shall be a burden to no one. Then I shall be a real disciple of
Jesus Christ when the world sees my body no more.

Ignatius of Antioch

Do you look up to your local bishop? Is he a charismatic figure,
a real disciple, someone willing to speak the truth in the face of hostile
adversaries? Does he locate the source of the Church's unity in the
celebration of the Eucharist? Does he live for this sacrament and, if
necessary, would he even be willing to die for it? Ignatius of Antioch,
our next voice from the past, was one such figure. Bishop of Antioch
lived during the early years of the second century; he was arrested by
the Roman authorities around the year 110 during a brief but particularly severe persecution under the emperor Trajan. On his way from
Syria to Rome, where he was to be tried, convicted, and eventually
executed, he wrote seven letters to the Christian communities of Asia
Minor and Rome. These letters offer a first-hand look at the tensions
within the developing Church of the early second century and the
way Christians within those communities sought to resolve them. For
Ignatius, the Eucharist was central to the life of the believing community. It was the source of the Church's unity, an ongoing remedy
for sin, and a continuation of Christ's redemptive action in the world.

The Eucharist in Ignatius' Letters

Ignatius' letters are passionate and intensely personal. They are concerned with topics very close to him, such as Church governance, the fight against heterodox teaching, and martyrdom for Christ. His teaching on the Eucharist touches each of these concerns and integrates them in the office of the monarchical episcopacy.

1. *Church Governance.* Ignatius' letters offer the first historical evidence of the presence of a strong episcopal structure within the developing Christian communities of the early second century. Prior evidence presents a more fluid apparatus of Church governance that varied from one region to another. Some churches were governed by a council of elders; others by charismatic prophets or teachers; still others by combined presbyteral and diaconal ministries.

With the lack of a central authoritative figure, such structures were vulnerable to the influence of heterodox Christian movements that introduced members to teachings that ultimately undermined the apostolic teaching. Although Ignatius probably was not the first to espouse the idea of a monarchical episcopacy, his letters are the earliest surviving evidence directly pertaining to the office. The brand of leadership found in his letters concentrates authority in the person of the bishop who, as the visible representative of Christ, holds responsibility for the doctrinal, moral, and liturgical life of the community.

Because of its great success in dealing with both internal and external threats to Church unity, this model of Church leadership would grow in popularity during the course of the second century and eventually become the mainstay of nearly all Christian communities in the ancient world. When combined with the notion of apostolic succession and a hierarchical ordering of the clergy (bishop, presbyter, deacon), it provided the Church with the basic structure of governance that would serve it well for centuries to come.

The bishop's authority was especially manifest at the Eucharist. No celebration was valid unless the bishop performed it or delegated someone to take his place. As he tells the members of the Church at Philadelphia: "Be careful, then, to observe a single Eucharist. For there is one flesh of our Lord Jesus Christ, and one cup of his blood that makes *us* one, and one altar, just as there is one bishop along with the presbytery and the deacons, my fellow slaves. In that way whatever you do is in line with God's will."[1] The close connection between episcopal authority and the Eucharistic celebration gave the bishop unique control over the spiritual and moral life of the community. Ignatius' teaching on the subject demonstrates the clear use of a principle that later came to be known as *lex orandi, lex credendi* ("the law of praying is the law of believing"). By exercising tight control over the worship of the believing community, the bishop would strongly influence what it believed and how it acted.

2. *Offsetting Heterodoxy.* One of the greatest problems of the Church in the early second century concerned the purity of the faith and the struggle against false teaching. In Ignatius' day, this conflict mainly involved a dangerous mixing of Gnosticism — a metaphysical dualism identifying the material world with evil and the spiritual world with good — with the external trappings of the Christian faith.

Gnosticism was a parallel religious movement to Christianity that grew up in the ancient world at roughly the same time. Its malleable and syncretistic tendencies enabled it to exist in many forms that could exist independently with a separate belief system and mythology or adapt to another religion's language, infiltrate it, and eventually take it over. In this way, Gnosticism was not only a competing religion with Christianity, but represented an internal threat to it as well.

This internal threat to Christianity was particularly difficult to deal with. In one form it manifested itself in a teaching about the nature of Christ known as "docetism," a doctrine that undermined the belief in the Incarnation by stating that God only *appeared* to have become human in the person of Jesus. The underlying Gnostic presumption in this teaching comes from the refusal to allow the world of spirit to have any contact whatsoever with the evil world of matter. For the Docetists, God was not born into this world, he did not walk this earth, and he did not suffer and die on the cross. God only *seemed* to do these things in Jesus of Nazareth. The reason for this illusion was so that the God could impart a secret knowledge that would awake the divine spark within believers and cause them to leave the material world behind and ascend with Christ to the world beyond.

---

1. *Letter to the Philadelphians*, 4.1 (*ECF*, 108–9).

Ignatius combated this teaching with a strong Eucharistic realism that emphasized the real presence of Jesus' body and blood in the consecrated bread and wine of the Eucharistic celebration. As he states in his letter to the Church at Smyrna: "Pay close attention to those who have wrong notions about the grace of Jesus Christ ... and note how at variance they are with God's mind.... They hold aloof from the Eucharist and from services of prayer, because they refuse to admit that the Eucharist is the flesh of our Savior Jesus Christ, who suffered for our sins and who in his goodness the Father raised from the dead."[2] By insisting on Jesus' real presence in the bread and wine, he affirms the mystery of the Incarnation; by presenting the Eucharist as the very source and expression of the Church's unity, he is able to counteract the influence of Docetist teachers and undermine their authority.

3. *Martyrdom for Christ*. As he wrote his letters to the churches of Asia Minor and Rome, Ignatius knew that, once he reached Rome, he would mostly likely be thrown to the wild beasts. Martyrdom was very much on his mind and something for which he deeply yearned.

This desire came from a deep conviction that death by martyrdom was the ultimate witness one could give to Christ and that it constituted a participation in Christ's redemptive action. For these reasons, Ignatius pleaded with the members of the church at Rome not to put any obstacle in the way of his making this ultimate sacrifice. As he tells the Christian community there: "I plead with you, do not do me an unseasonable kindness. Let me be fodder for wild beasts — that is how I can get to God. I am God's wheat and I am being ground by the teeth of wild beasts to make a pure loaf for Christ."[3] Ignatius longs for martyrdom, because he believes it will lead him to God. He willingly embraces death in order to unite himself to the passion of Christ.

For Ignatius, being a "real disciple" meant sharing in the sufferings of Christ.[4] Martyrdom was the supreme way to imitate and hence share in the Passion of God. Christ entered the world, gave of himself completely, to the point of dying for humanity, in order to become its nourishment and source of hope. By spilling their blood for the sake of the Lord, Christians united themselves to Christ's sacrificial

---

2. *Letter to the Smyrnaeans*, 6.2–7.1 (*ECF*, 114).
3. *Letter to the Romans*, 4.1–2 (*ECF*, 104).
4. Ibid., 4.2.

offering on the cross. In doing so, they manifested Christ's redemptive activity in the world and affirmed their belief in the resurrection. They embraced suffering and death not as ends in themselves but as a means to achieving their hearts' deepest and most ardent desire.

For Ignatius, this spilling of blood is also closely associated with the sacrificial offering of the Eucharist. His use of Eucharistic imagery to describe his martyrdom highlights the close bond between the two. Both martyrdom and the Christian celebration of the Eucharist represent a sharing in the passion, death, and resurrection of Christ. The first does so through spilling of one's blood as a witness to Christ; the second, by the offering of self in an act of liturgical worship. Martyrdom and the Eucharist both come from a deep hunger and thirst for God: Eucharist plants the seed of martyrdom; the latter extends the offering of self to Christ that takes place at the Eucharist and brings it to fruition.

In Ignatius' mind, each of the above themes — Church governance, offsetting heterodoxy, and martyrdom — was intimately linked to the Eucharist. For him, there was little difference between Jesus' presence in forms of bread and wine and his historical body and blood. As a continuation of Christ's incarnational and redemptive activity on earth, the Eucharist preserves the Church's unity and offers to those receiving it the hope of eternal salvation. It is in this context that he refers to the Eucharist as the "medicine of immortality" and "the antidote which wards off death but yields continuous life in union with Jesus Christ."[5] The Eucharist, for Ignatius, is God's gift of his Son to humanity in the form of bread and wine. Those who eat and drink it participate in Jesus' suffering, death, and resurrection and, by allowing Jesus' actual flesh and blood to flow through their veins, likewise become witnesses or martyrs to his cause.

Observations

Ignatius' teaching on the Eucharist challenges us to look at our own beliefs and underlying presuppositions about the sacrament. The

---

5. *Letter to the Ephesians*, 20.2 (*ECF*, 93).

following remarks take up this challenge and seek to present a mature Christian reflection on the role the Eucharist plays in our lives.

1. One word that comes to mind in relation to Ignatius' teaching on the Eucharist is "passion." When going through his letters, we immediately sense that we are in the presence of a committed Christian whose life centers around Jesus' sacrificial offering and presence in the Eucharist. For Ignatius, the Eucharist holds the Christian community together, preserves it, protects it, and keeps it going. His passion for the Eucharist is the same as his passion for Christ. It propels him to model his life after Christ and, ultimately, to give his life for him. Ignatius' authentic and all-consuming passion for the Eucharist inspires us, but also challenges us.

2. Another word that comes to mind in relation to Ignatius' teaching on the Eucharist is "realism." For Ignatius, Jesus' presence in the Eucharist stands in close continuity with the flesh and blood of his historical personage. The consecrated bread and wine are not mere metaphors or symbols of Christ's body and blood, but the actual presence of his transformed historical existence. Because of the Resurrection, Jesus' body and blood are able to become present to us in the form of bread and wine. When we gather for Eucharist, we thus celebrate the great Christological truths of salvation history: the Incarnation, Christ's passion and death, his Resurrection, our ongoing Redemption.

3. Still another word that comes to mind in relation to Ignatius' teaching on the Eucharist is "authority." Ignatius' letters are the earliest recorded writings depicting the sovereign authority of the bishop in areas of faith and morals. In Ignatius, the bishop exercises that authority in a special way during the celebration of the Eucharist. Only the bishop or someone delegated by him has the right to celebrate the Eucharist for the Christian community. The bishop's close ties to the Eucharist make him the guarantor of the community's faith and the guardian of its actions. He represents Christ to his people, serves them and, through the Eucharist, enables them to celebrate Christ's presence and redemptive action in their lives. The close bond between bishop and the Eucharist endures to this day and is important for the life of the believing community.

4. Another word that comes to mind in relation to Ignatius' teaching on the Eucharist is "unity." The Eucharist, for Ignatius, was the prime

unifying force of the Christian community. It created that unity and was not a mere expression of it. It did so because it was the extension of God's incarnational and redemptive activity in the world. Ignatius recognized Church unity as a manifestation of Christ's real presence and ongoing salvific action. This emphasis on the Eucharist as the source of Church unity makes us take a hard look at our own efforts to overcome the divisions that separate us from other Christians.

5. Another word that comes to mind in relation to Ignatius' teaching on the Eucharist is "orthodoxy." The early second-century churches in Asia Minor were seething with controversy over the meaning of the Eucharist and its relationship to the Christ event. The most basic tension was between the proponents of Eucharistic realism, with their close connections to the emerging Christian orthodoxy, and those of Gnostic dualism, with their strong docetic tendencies. Ignatius champions the Eucharist's links with the Incarnation and Christ's passion, death and Resurrection. By binding the sacrament so closely to these Christological mysteries, he makes participation in the Eucharistic celebration a true test of orthodoxy.

6. Yet another word that comes to mind in relation to Ignatius' teaching on the Eucharist is "martyrdom." Ignatius depicts his upcoming martyrdom in Eucharistic imagery because he firmly believes in the close, intimate connection between the self-offering of Christ on the cross and the Eucharistic sacrifice. By offering his life for Christ, Ignatius sees himself more deeply incorporated into the mystery of Christ's passion and death, an event that enters our world anew in the mystery of the Eucharist. The word, "martyr," comes from the Greek word for "witness." When celebrating the Eucharist, we affirm our willingness to give witness to Christ.

7. A final word that comes to mind in relation to Ignatius' teaching on the Eucharist is "mysticism." For all his passion and realism, Ignatius is a mystic at heart. He presents the Eucharist not as an abstract, intellectual doctrine to be analyzed and speculated upon, but as a mystery that the Church must experience in the depths of its communal being. The Eucharist affected Ignatius deeply. It made him yearn for Christ and moved him to offer himself to the church in a life of dedicated service. It also ignited in him a thirst to be one with Christ's passion so that he could draw closer to his Lord and ulti-

mately experience him face-to-face. Ignatius offers us a Eucharistic mysticism that inspires us to model our lives after Christ's passion, death, and Resurrection. He forces us to look at our attitudes toward the sacrament and to ask ourselves if we experience Christ's life in our own. Karl Rahner once wrote that "[t]he devout Christian of the future will either be a 'mystic,' one who has 'experienced something,' or he will cease to be anything at all."[6]

Conclusion

Ignatius of Antioch's letters offer us many important insights into the life of the early second-century Church. These powerful testaments of faith of a man on his way to martyrdom highlight the essentials of the Christian faith at a time when the churches of Asia Minor (and beyond) were involved in controversy and experiencing a great deal of inner tension.

In dealing with these tensions, Ignatius saw in the Eucharist a way to explain how Christ's saving activity made its way into the present historical moment. The Eucharist, for him, was an extension of Christ's Incarnation, one which affirmed the presence of God in our midst and which brought the sacrifice of the cross to the altar. It offered the real body and blood of Christ. It was a source of unity, a test for orthodoxy, and a witness to authority. It offered Christians an intimate experience of Christ and inspired them to give their lives for Christ — and to do so with passion and courage.

Ignatius' teaching on the Eucharist has much relevance for those of us today who are pondering its meaning for our lives and the role it should play in our life of faith. When we examine what he says, we see someone with a deep passion for God and an even deeper desire to follow Christ in every aspect of his life. Ignatius focuses his eyes on Christ and never takes them off him. The Eucharist, he firmly believes, helps him to do so. If the same is to be said of us, we, like Ignatius, must allow the mystery of this freely given gift to open our minds and thoroughly penetrate our hearts.

---

6. "Christian Living Formerly and Today," *Theological Investigations*, vol. 17, trans. David Bourke (London: Darton, Longman & Todd, 1971), 15.

Reflection Questions

1. Ignatius of Antioch had a passion for the Eucharist. Do you? If so, how would you describe it? Would you be willing to die for your beliefs about the Eucharist? Do you see Jesus' own passion reflected in it in any way? Does the Eucharist in any way reflect divine passion for you? For believers? For the world?

2. Ignatius of Antioch was a Eucharist realist. Are you? Do you believe that the bread and wine at the Eucharist become the body and blood of Jesus? If so, how would you describe the way this transformation takes place? Do your beliefs coincide with Catholic teaching? If not, how do they differ? What makes you believe what you do? Does your personal experience of God have anything to do with it?

3. Ignatius of Antioch was a figure of authority for the early Church at Antioch and beyond. What, in your opinion, are the most important characteristics of good Church leadership? Would you prioritize them in any way? Are those characteristics present in your present leaders? How should Church leaders be chosen?

4. Ignatius of Antioch was concerned about orthodoxy or "right teaching." Are you concerned about this important dimension of faith and morals? Who should be empowered to make decisions concerning them? Are the present structures within the Church adequate? What are their strengths and weaknesses? How can they be improved?

5. For Ignatius of Antioch, the Eucharist was the prime unifying force of the Christian community. Do you think the Eucharist is a unifying force for today's Christians? Does it serve the same function on the local level as it does on the diocesan and universal levels? What steps need to be taken for the Eucharist to effect unity among the various Christian denominations?

Voice Three

The Martyrdom of Polycarp
Dying for Christ

> For the fire made the shape of a vaulted chamber, like a ship's sail filled by the wind, and made a wall around the body of the martyr. And he was in the midst, not as burning flesh, but as bread baking or as gold and silver refined in a furnace. And we perceived such a sweet aroma as the breadth of incense or some other precious spice.
>
> *The Martyrdom of Polycarp*

Would you be willing to die for your faith? Most of us will never know the answer to this question, because we will never be in a situation where we either must renounce our belief in Christ or be put to death. Those who have found themselves in such situations and who do not waver when confronted with death offer the ultimate testimony of their faith. Polycarp of Smyrna, our next voice from the past, was one such person. The mid-second century account of his death is the oldest surviving record of Christian martyrdom outside the New Testament. Written in the form of a letter from the Church of Smyrna to the Church of Philomelium in Asia Minor, this document offers an eyewitness account of the circumstances leading up to and including the death of one of the most important second-century witnesses to the apostolic faith. *The Martyrdom of Polycarp,*[1] as scholars usually refer to it, offers important insights into the way many Christians of the mid-second century understood their relationship to the passion and death of Christ and their Eucharistic faith. Even today, the story it tells never ceases to inspire.

---

1. All references to this work come from *ECF*, 141–58.

Polycarp's Life and Death

According to the account, Polycarp had already reached the ripe old age of 86 when he was taken prisoner by the proconsul of Smyrna during a severe outbreak of persecution sometime in the early part of the second half of the second century. Questioned about his allegiance to Caesar and the religion of the state, he was found guilty of being a Christian and sentenced to death (9.1–3). By that time, he already was renowned among Christians both in Smyrna and beyond for his holiness of life (13.2) and as an important spokesman for the apostolic faith (16.2).

Polycarp was a disciple of John the Apostle at Ephesus and was directly appointed by him to head the church at Smyrna. He was also a friend of Ignatius (d. c. 110), the renowned bishop of Antioch, who was dragged in chains to Rome and thrown to the wild beasts at the Coliseum during the time of the emperor Trajan. Irenaeus of Lyons, the great theologian and Christian apologist of the late-second century, records fond memories of learning at the feet of Polycarp when he was young.

According to Irenaeus, Polycarp wrote many letters to churches and individuals in order to exhort them and advise on issues of the day. Of those letters, only one survives, an epistle to the Church at Philippi, written shortly after Ignatius of Antioch had made his way through Asia Minor to his martyrdom in Rome. Whatever other scant knowledge there is of Polycarp's life has been gleaned from the writings of Ignatius, Tertullian, Irenaeus, and Eusebius, the Church historian.

Some might say that more is known about Polycarp's death than about his life. Although *The Martyrdom* is the only known evidence of his death, it contains first-hand evidence of the details surrounding his capture, interrogation, and execution. That is not to say that the account does not expound strong theological views about the purpose and nature of Christian martyrdom. A close examination of the document shows that a skilled editorial hand surveyed the eyewitness accounts and consciously shaped them to fit the story of Polycarp's suffering and death to the pattern of Christ's own walk to Calvary.

Although the day and month of Polycarp's martyrdom are provided in the account (22 February; cf. 21.1), the precise year has itself been the subject of debate. Possible dates range from as early as 156 to as late as 167 A.D, and could easily fall somewhere in between. Whatever the year, the account of Polycarp's martyrdom has a universal message to all Christians. During the age of persecution, it inspired Christians to remain steadfast in their faith without counting the cost. Presented as "a martyrdom conformable to the gospel" (1.1), it shows how someone totally consumed by the love of Christ could profess his faith to the very end. It reminds Christians of all ages that they can find life in the midst of death, because Jesus their Lord did so and promised never to abandon them.[2]

Martyrdom and the Passion of Christ

The account presents Polycarp as someone who lived in close, intimate communion with the Lord. It says he had always been honored for his holy life and had shown himself to be "… an apostolic and prophetic teacher and bishop of the Catholic Church in Smyrna" (16.2). Polycarp, we are told, imitated Christ in both life and death. Because of this close communion, the Lord conversed with him, strengthened him, and suffered with him.

The account presents Polycarp's martyrdom as one closely reflecting the Lord's own passion and death. Like Jesus, Polycarp retreats to a quiet place to pray (5.1–2). Like Jesus, his persecutors actively seek him out (3.2). Like Jesus, one of his disciples betrays him (6.2). Like Jesus, he desires only to do the will of God (7.2). Like Jesus, a Roman magistrate interrogates him (9.2). Like Jesus, he remains silent at first, but then responds with calm and unflagging courage (8.2–12.1). Like Jesus, he suffers a brutal death (13.1–16.2). Like Jesus, a great amount of blood flows from his pierced side (16.1). Like Jesus, he gives his life as a living sacrifice, "a burnt offering ready and acceptable to God" (14.1). Although the details of Polycarp's death do not *exactly* match those of Jesus' (e.g., he is stabbed to death after an unsuccessful attempt to burn him alive [16.1]; his body is not

---

2. The above biographical and other historical information comes from Ibid., 121–26, 141–48; *FC*, 1:131–50; W.H.C. Freund, *The Rise of Christianity* (Philadelphia: Fortress Press, 1984), 182–83.

released immediately after death [17.1]), the similarities are enough to demonstrate the close correlation between the two.

To emphasize the close resemblance between the two deaths even further, the author weaves into his narrative many allusions to the Gospel accounts of Jesus' passion and death (e.g., Jn 7:1; 8:59; 10:39; 12:28; 18:37; 19:19, 31; Mt 3:12; 6:10; 10:36, 38–39; 26:55; Mk 9:43; 14:61; Acts 9:7; 13:51; 16:20–21; 17:14; 19:3–31; 21:14). These references tie the narrative of Polycarp's passion and death even more closely to that of Jesus and affirm for us the reason why Christians hold the martyrs in such high regard: "… we love the martyrs as disciples and imitators of the Lord, deservedly so, because of their unsurpassable devotion to their own King and Teacher. May it be also our lot to be their companions and fellow disciples!" (17.3).

Martyrdom and Eucharist

The account of Polycarp's martyrdom represents a polished literary reworking of eyewitness accounts of the holy bishop's final hours. As such, it contains sound historical evidence of what happened along with literary interpretation of how those events are to be understood in the light of Jesus' passion and death. The same also holds true for the insights the account of Polycarp's death gives to the early Christian understanding of the Eucharist.

Just as Polycarp is about to be burned at the stake, he looks up to heaven and utters his final words:

> Lord God Almighty, Father of thy beloved and blessed Servant Jesus Christ, through whom we have received full knowledge of thee, "the God of angels and powers and all creation" and of the whole race of the righteous who live in thy presence: I bless thee, because thou hast deemed me worthy of this day and hour, to take my part in the number of martyrs, in the cup of Christ, for "resurrection to eternal life" of soul and body in the immortality of the Holy Spirit; among whom may I be received in thy presence this day as a rich and acceptable sacrifice, just as thou hast prepared and revealed beforehand and fulfilled, thou that art the true God without any falsehood. For this and for everything I praise thee, I bless thee, I glorify thee, through the eternal and Heavenly Priest, Jesus Christ, thy beloved Servant,

through whom be glory to thee with him and the Holy Spirit both now and unto the ages to come. Amen. (14.1–3)

While there is no reason to suspect that these words do not reflect the genuine sentiments of the saint as he is about to make the ultimate sacrifice, one cannot overlook its rather obvious liturgical orientation. The references to "the cup of Christ," "sacrifice," and Jesus the "High Priest" would appear to indicate that Polycarp identified his approaching death not only with the passion and death of the Lord, but also with the Holy Eucharist. His entire speech, moreover, resembles in both content and form the Eucharistic prayers in the Church of mid-second century Smyrna.[3]

Since Polycarp, as bishop of the Church at Smyrna, was the usual presider over the community's Eucharist celebrations, it makes perfect sense that his final statement would reflect those very words that connected both him and his community so closely to Christ's paschal mystery. It is more than likely that he would have had these words committed to memory and that he would have adapted them, if necessary, to fit the circumstances of his approaching death. It is also highly possible that the author of the account, seeing Polycarp's underlying intent, further developed this connection with the Eucharist by consciously shaping Polycarp's speech to fit into a more fixed liturgical pattern.

Regardless of how Polycarp's words were composed, the link they make with the Eucharist would appear to be beyond question. This link is even more strongly established by the description of what happens directly afterwards:

> And when he had concluded the Amen and finished his prayer, the men attending to the fire lighted it. And when the flame flashed forth, we saw a miracle, we to whom it was given to see. And we are preserved in order to relate to the rest what happened. For the fire made the shape of a vaulted chamber like a ship's sail filled by the wind, and made a wall around the body of the martyr. And he was in the midst, not as burning flesh, but as bread baking or as gold and silver refined in a furnace. And we perceived such a sweet aroma as the breath of incense or some other precious spice. (15.1–2)

---

3. *ECF*, 141.

In this passage, Polycarp's experience in the fire is likened to baking bread and burning incense. This connection between nourishment, sacrifice, and death reflects the close connection made by the early Christians between the Last Supper and Jesus' death and dying. When placed in the fire, Polycarp's flesh is like oven-baked dough and gives off "a sweet aroma as the breath of incense or some precious spice" (15.2).

Observations

The above presentation of the major themes in the account of Polycarp's martyrdom offers some unique insights into the faith of Christians at the Church of Smyrna in the mid-second century. The following remarks will focus specifically on what the account reveals about their attitude toward the Eucharist.

1. In the first place, *The Martyrdom of Polycarp* shows that the Christians of Smyrna saw a close connection between the Last Supper and Jesus' passion and death. This connection is so close that, when describing Polycarp's martyrdom, the author of the account felt free to embed vivid Eucharistic imagery within a narrative dedicated to portraying the saint's death as a reflection of Jesus' own. This connection goes to the very heart of the Christian message. Christ suffered for the salvation of the world, and offered himself to his disciples in the form of bread and wine so that they do have access to this saving power. The Eucharist points to Calvary — and vice versa. The two cannot be separated without doing serious harm to Jesus' message and the integrity of the faith.

2. The account also shows that the Christians of Smyrna understood Christ's passion and death as a *sacrificial offering*, the presence and power of which were made manifest at the celebration of the Eucharist. In his death, Polycarp is described as "... a noble ram out of a great flock ready for sacrifice, a burnt offering ready and acceptable to God" (14.1). He himself asks to be received "as a rich and acceptable sacrifice" (14.2). Such descriptions are possible only because Polycarp's union with Christ is so intimate that the power of God's love is able to shine through his frail human frame. The Christians of Smyrna understood that the ultimate giving of oneself comes

through the spilling of one's blood for the sake of others. They saw Christ offering his blood from the cross and distributing it through the Eucharistic cup. They also saw this sacrificial offering of self manifesting itself in the life and death of the holy bishop Polycarp.

3. The account also gives some strong indications about why martyrdom was held in such high esteem by the Christians of mid-second century Smyrna. The account of Polycarp's death makes a number of references to the "imitation of Christ" (1.2; 19.1). Martyrdom was considered the most authentic way in which a person could pattern his or her life after Christ. This imitation was not considered a sterile repetition of Jesus' actions, but a dynamic participation in his life. By following Jesus along the way of martyrdom, Christians entrust their lives totally to Christ. By following him in death, they hope to share in the fullness of life they have already tasted while at the Eucharist. Martyrdom and the Eucharist go together by virtue of the eschatological witness they give to the kingdom. They proclaim that this kingdom is, in some way, already here and yet, in another way, still to come. They are also united by the faith they require, the hope they engender, and the love they instill in the hearts of others.

4. The author of the account uses the images of bread and wine to describe Polycarp's martyrdom. In his final words before his death, Polycarp himself addresses the Father and offers to share in "the cup of Christ" (14.2). A few moments later, when his persecutors attempt to burn him at the stake, a miraculous vaulted chamber forms and he is depicted as "bread baking" and giving off "a sweet aroma" (15.2). By placing these images of bread and wine at the very moment of Polycarp's martyrdom, the author draws a close connection between the death of the saintly bishop, the Eucharistic banquet, and Jesus' own passion and death. His martyrdom, in other words, is a reflection of the martyrdom of Christ and the sharing in it made possible by the Eucharistic banquet.

5. The drama surrounding Polycarp's death draws strength from its being patterned after Christ's passion and death and is sustained by the liturgical language that has been woven in the text by an expert editorial hand. By instilling this sense of drama, the author of the account makes Polycarp's martyrdom come alive for his readers and encourages them to make that drama a part of their own lives. By

way of association, it also imparts a deeper sense of drama to the Eucharistic celebration. The author clearly states that Polycarp's bones have been collected and kept in a suitable place so that the community could "... gather together in joy and gladness to celebrate the day of his martyrdom as a birthday" (18.2–3). In all probability, the account was read to the Christian assembly that gathered for the Eucharist on that very day. In this way, Polycarp's death was even more intimately connected to Jesus' sacrificial offering. In this liturgical setting, moreover, the account of his death invited those partaking of the bread and sharing in the cup to reflect on their own following of Christ in a more personal way.

6. At the very outset of the account, the author acknowledges the hand of Providence in Polycarp's martyrdom. It states that, through Polycarp, the Lord is seeking to show again "a martyrdom conformable to the gospel" (1.1). Later, when Polycarp enters the arena, he hears a voice from heaven saying, "Be strong, Polycarp, and play the man" (9.1). Still later, he is saved from the fiery flames by a miracle "to whom it was given to see" (15.1). These references to Divine Providence demonstrate that Polycarp's martyrdom is, above all, a work of Christ. This emphasis on Christ's providential action is something else that martyrdom shares with the celebration of the Eucharist. Although both involve human participants, they are primarily manifestations of Christ's redeeming love. By participating in the Eucharist, Christians everywhere are nourished by this love and, like Polycarp, inspired to model their lives after Christ.

7. The purpose of hagiographical literature is to edify the faithful. The account of Polycarp's martyrdom does so not only by deepening our respect for the noble martyr-bishop of Smyrna, but also by increasing our appreciation of the ideal of Christian martyrdom itself. That ideal was nurtured in Polycarp's life through his participation in the Eucharistic mystery. It is meant to do the same for the lives of all the faithful. The account reminds its readers that Polycarp was martyred along with twelve other Christians (19.1). Their anonymous witness to the faith shows that the aim of martyrdom is to give glory not to oneself, but to God alone. The fact that others that day recanted when they came face-to-face with death (4.1) strongly suggests that Christians should not actively pursue martyrdom of their own accord.

The strength to make this ultimate sacrifice comes from the power of Christ alone and his action in the life of the faithful.

While in no way exhaustive, these insights into the Eucharist from the account of Polycarp's martyrdom highlight its central role in the lives of Christians of the mid-second century Church at Smyrna. As such, they remind today's readers of the place this sacred celebration should have in their own lives and in their understanding of the meaning of Christian discipleship.

Conclusion

As the earliest surviving account of a Christian martyrdom outside of the New Testament, *The Martyrdom of Polycarp* throws a great deal of light on the early Church's attitude toward Jesus' passion and death and its relationship to the Eucharist. It also offers many insights into the ideal of Christian martyrdom and the revered place it holds in the imagination of the believing community.

This account makes both historical and theological claims. It faithfully preserves the eyewitness accounts of Polycarp's death, but consciously shapes them after the Gospel narrative of Jesus' passion and death. By weaving the story of Polycarp's martyrdom into that of his Lord and master, the account demonstrates in a very vivid and concrete way what it means to imitate Christ and be his disciple.

Jesus' disciples follow the way of the cross and nourish themselves on his body and blood. The account presents Polycarp as a noble teacher, an able bishop, and a distinguished martyr. He is the faithful disciple, someone who professes his faith in Christ and is willing to give up his life for what he believes. Polycarp imitates Christ in both life and in death; his whole being has become closely intertwined with Christ. The account encourages its readers to follow his example. It presents Polycarp as a model martyr (i.e., witness) for the faith and inspires it readers — both past and present — to follow in his path and do the same.

Reflection Questions

1. *The Martyrdom of Polycarp* shows that, like the Christians of the apostolic era, those of the mid-second-century church at Smyrna saw a close connection between the Last Supper and Jesus' passion and death. Do you see such a connection? Do you believe in it? How would you explain it? Would you be willing to die for it?

2. *The Martyrdom of Polycarp* shows that the Christians of Smyrna thought of Christ's passion and death as a sacrificial offering closely connected to the celebration of the Eucharist. Do you think of the Eucharist as a sacrificial offering? Is this belief important to you? Does your faith in Christ make sense without it?

3. Martyrdom was held in very high esteem by the Christians of Smyrna and beyond. Do you think martyrdom is held in such high regard today? From where does Polycarp draw his strength? Where do today's martyrs get it? Do you see a connection between martyrdom and the imitation of Christ? Do you see a connection between martyrdom and the celebration of the Eucharist?

4. *The Martyrdom of Polycarp* acknowledges the hand of Providence at work in Polycarp's death. Do you believe in Providence? What does it mean (or not mean) to you? Does God intervene in your life? Does God act on your behalf? Does God offer you guidance? Does God help you make decisions? Where is the hand of Providence operative in your life?

5. The purpose of literature about the saints is to edify the faithful. Does *The Martyrdom of Polycarp* challenge you in your faith? Does it help you to reflect upon how you yourself walk the way of discipleship? Does it make you think about the kind of witness to Christ that you give to others? If someone wrote the story of your life, would it edify the faithful or embarrass them? What more can you do to turn your life over to God?

Voice Four

The Didache
Church Order

As this piece [of bread] was scattered over the hills and then was brought together and made one, so let your church be brought together from the ends of the earth into your Kingdom.

The Didache

When instituting the Eucharist, Jesus broke bread and gave it to his disciples and gave them a cup of wine and said, "Do this in memory of me." Ever since that moment, Christians have gathered around the table of the Lord to celebrate his presence in their midst through some form of commemorative meal. While remaining faithful to Jesus' words, the way they have done so has evolved over time, sometimes considerably. Apart from the New Testament accounts, we have relatively little historical evidence of what the Church's Eucharistic worship was like for Christians in the early generations of the Gospel's spread. To gain some insight, we need allow the available sources to speak and spark our imagination. Our next voice from the past, *The Didache*, or *The Teaching of the Twelve Apostles*, gives us some important information in this regard.

A Manual of Church Order

Discovered only in 1873, this document has given rise to a variety of opinions about its origin and purpose.[1] While a definitive answer remains elusive, most scholars think it is a mid-second-century com-

---

1. The English text of *The Didache* comes from *ECF*, 171–79. For details and references concerning the various theories presented in this chapter, see *ECF*, 161–70 and Willy Rordorf, *"The Didache,"* in *EEC*, 1–23.

pilation of two earlier texts: a moral catechism known as "The Two
Ways" (chaps. 1–5) and a manual of Church order (chaps. 6–15). The
first of these works was an independent catechism, possibly of Judaic
origin, with roots going back to the first century; the second, by way
of contrast, probably reflects the situation of the church in Syria at
roughly the same time. The compiler, who has been variously identified as coming from Palestine, Syria, or Alexandria, brought these two
texts together and introduced other material for his own purposes.

We are interested in the treatment of the Eucharist given in the
manual of Church order, specifically in chapters 9, 10 and 14. While
it is difficult to distinguish the original material from the final edited
version, these chapters still offer a rare view of the developing liturgical practice of the sub-apostolic Church.

Some information about the content and origin of the chapters
forming this early manual of Church order may be helpful. Scholars
have maintained a variety of opinions concerning its composition.
Some claim that the compiler of *The Didache* himself was the author; others emphasize the manual's Montanist origins; still others
think it is an artificial construct meant to recall the second-century
Church to its apostolic origins. For a variety of reasons, which we
cannot explore at present, none of these theories seems particularly
convincing. Much more likely is the possibility that the compiler of
The Didache incorporated an earlier document into his work with
some slight revisions.

The content of chapters 9, 10, and 14 needs to be read in the
light of the rest of the material treated in this ancient Church manual.
Taken as a whole, the treatise covers such issues as food offered
to idols (chap. 6), baptism (chap. 7), fasting and prayers (chap. 8),
the treatment of traveling teachers, apostles, and prophets (chaps.
11–12), dealings with other traveling Christians (chap. 12), what to
do with traveling prophets who desire to remain with the community
(chap. 13), the appointment of bishops and deacons (chap. 15), and a
warning that the end is at hand (chap. 16). It discusses a wide variety
of issues related to proper Church order and treats the Eucharist, not
in a comprehensive manner, but as a single (albeit significant) piece
of a much larger concern.

The manual is a directory of sorts that offers general guidelines for the organization and proper functioning of the late-first-century Christian community. When seen against this backdrop, the material dealing with the Eucharist reflects a time when the monarchical episcopacy had not yet fully emerged as the dominant form of church governance and when the celebration of the Eucharist was still related in some way to the celebration of a meal. A look at these chapters provides a rare view of the liturgical practice of an early Christian community.

Chapters 9–10

Chapters 9 and 10 of *The Didache* contain a series of prayers over bread and wine that very much resemble the Hebrew tradition of blessings normally said after meals. The text reads as follows:

> Now about the Eucharist: This is how to give thanks: first in connection with the cup: "We thank you, our Father, for the holy vine of David, your child, which you have revealed through Jesus, your child. To you be glory forever." Then in connection with the piece [broken off the loaf]: "We thank you, our Father, for the life and knowledge which you have revealed through Jesus, your child. To you be glory forever. As this piece [of bread] was scattered over the hills and then was brought together and made one, so let your Church be brought together from the ends of the earth into your Kingdom. For yours is the glory and the power through Jesus Christ forever." You must not let anyone eat or drink of your Eucharist except those baptized in the Lord's name. For in reference to this the Lord said, "Do not give what is sacred to dogs." (Chapter 9)

> After you have finished your meal, say grace in this way: "We thank you, holy Father, for your sacred name which you have lodged in our hearts, and for the knowledge and faith and immortality which you have revealed through Jesus, your child. To you be glory forever. Almighty Master, 'you have created everything' for the sake of your name, and have given men food and drink to enjoy that they may thank you. But to us you have given spiritual food and

drink and eternal life through Jesus, your child. Above all, we thank
you that you are mighty. To you be glory forever. Remember, Lord,
your Church, to save it from all evil and to make it perfect by your
love. Make it holy, 'and gather' it 'together from the four winds'
into your Kingdom which you have made ready for it. For yours is
the power and the glory forever. Let Grace come and let this world
pass away. Hosanna to the God of David! If anyone is holy, let him
come. If not, let him repent. Our Lord, come! Amen." In the case
of prophets, however, you should let them give thanks in their own
way. (Chapter 10)

Since these moving prayers do not contain words of Institution,
it is not certain they were intended for the Eucharist itself or for
the ordinary meals of the community. Some scholars believe they
evolved from ordinary blessings used by Christians before and after
their meals. Others see them as prayers meant to be said at some
point during the Eucharist, possibly as prayers to be said before and
after the words of Institution. Still others see them as prayers to be
said during a special meal of fellowship (i.e., an *agape*) that anticipated the Eucharist itself. Others still envision two different kinds
of Eucharist in the Christian community of the time: one celebrating
fellowship in Christ and anticipating the messianic banquet (chaps.
9 and 10); the other using the words of Institution to focus on the
sacrificial offering of Christ's body and blood (chaps. 14).

Whatever their intent, these prayers offer us some of the most
beautiful words of thanksgiving ever produced by the early Church.
It should also be noted that the term "Eucharist" (*Eucharistia*) was
itself adopted from the Judaic tradition of giving thanks to God for
the countless blessings that he has given his people. The reference
to the prophets at the end points to a certain flexibility in the use of
such prayers. The text thus appears to have been written to provide
a concrete formula to be used in the absence of those capable of
giving more spontaneous expressions of thanks.

Chapter 14

Following the prayers of chapters 9–10, instructions come in chapters 11–12 on how to deal with traveling teachers, prophets, apostles, and other Christians. These, in turn, are followed in chapter 13 with further instructions on those wishing to remain with the community. At first sight, this material seems to have little to do with the eloquent prayers of thanksgiving immediately preceding them. When we remember, however, that chapter 10 ends with an exhortation to allow prophets to give thanks in their own way, the relevance of the material becomes clear. Only true prophets, teachers, and apostles should be allowed to offer prayers of thanksgiving as they wish. The material in these chapters offers concrete ways of distinguishing true prophets, teachers, and apostles from false ones. Once these criteria have been presented, the author returns to the topic of the community's Eucharistic celebration.

> On every Lord's Day — his special day — come together and break bread and give thanks, first confessing your sins so that your sacrifice may be pure. Anyone at variance with his neighbor must not join you, until they are reconciled, lest your sacrifice be defiled. For it was of this sacrifice that the Lord said, "always and everywhere offer me a pure sacrifice; for I am a great King, says the Lord, and my name is marvelled at by the nations." (Chapter 14)

Our conclusions about the presentation of the Eucharist in *The Didache* depend on how we construe the relationship between chapters 9–10 and chapter 14. The opinions on this relationship span a wide spectrum, and there seems to be little movement toward a consensus.

For our present purposes, it is enough to say that chapter 14 specifically identifies "The Lord's Day" (i.e., Sunday) as the time when Christians gathered for the Eucharist and places great value on reconciliation and the communal confession of sins. The reference to the Eucharist as a "sacrifice," moreover, can just as easily mean a "sacrifice of thanksgiving" as it could Christ's death on the cross. The quotation from Scripture comes from the prophet Malachi (11:14) and places the Eucharistic celebration in continuity with its Jewish origins. Since nothing in chapter 14 openly contradicts the material found in chapters 9–10, an argument can be made that they are referring to the same ritual, or at least to different stages in an evening Eucharistic celebration. One possible point of contact, however, is the reference after chapter 14 to the importance of electing bishops and deacons. The mention of these offices immediately after an exposition of the community's Sunday worship parallels the emphasis on discerning true prophets, teachers, and apostles following chapters 9–10. The author of *The Didache* makes it clear that their ministry is identical with that of the prophets and teachers (15:1). This information supports our earlier observation that the structure of Church governance at the end of the late-first century had not yet developed into the typical three-tiered hierarchical offices of bishop, presbyter, and deacon that, starting in the early part of the second century, would take root and eventually spread throughout the entire Church.

Observations

Whatever position one takes on the scholarly debates, chapters 9–10 and 14 encourage us to look at our own celebration of the Eucharist and to ask serious questions about its meaning, purpose, and relevance for our lives. A number of observations come to mind.

1. The author of *The Didache* puts together two documents from the sub-apostolic period and edits them to meet the needs of his community. He does so not out of mere antiquarian interests, but to address the various concerns of his own community. In similar fashion, we too are called to look to the texts of the Christian tradition and use them in a way that will help us examine our lives as Christians and take the necessary steps to deepen our commitment to Christ. Such an examination will necessarily involve taking a look at how we celebrate the Eucharist and looking for ways to improve it.

2. The author of *The Didache* combines two very different works— a moral catechism known as "The Two Ways" (chaps. 1–5) and a manual of Church order (chaps. 6–15) — in a single document. By placing these documents together, he emphasizes, among other things, the strong continuity between a community's worship and its

moral life. For Christians, the "way of life" is rooted in the person of Jesus Christ, whose Paschal Mystery is celebrated by the Christian community in its Eucharistic worship. The quality and care with which we celebrate the liturgy says a great deal about the values we cherish and act upon in our relations with ourselves, others, and God.

3. In chapters 9–10 of *The Didache*, the author preserves for posterity some early Christian prayers of thanksgiving that are based upon the typical Jewish post-meal blessings. These prayers bring out the Christian community's continuity with its Jewish past, by dialoguing with it and adapting it to its own particular needs. Because the fathers of emerging Christian orthodoxy went to great pains to preserve their Jewish legacy, an appreciation of this heritage should continue in today's liturgical assembly. The anti-Semitism which has scarred Christianity for so much of its history must be positively offset by conscious efforts to bridge the distance that separates Jews and Christians and emphasize the common ground upon which they stand.

4. Chapter 9 of *The Didache* offers a heartfelt prayer for Christian unity. It asks God, the Father, to gather the Church from all the ends of the earth into his kingdom. However and whenever it was offered, this prayer was an integral part of the Christian community's life and worship. While much progress has been made in the efforts to promote Christian unity, still more needs to be done to make this urgent need a permanent feature of the prayer and worship of the believing community. Rather than being set aside for special occasions, such prayers should be highly visible, ordinary occurrences in the daily life of the community.

5. Whether or not they directly pertain to the Eucharist itself, chapters 9–10 of *The Didache* convey to the reader a strong sense of the fellowship and close personal intimacy that existed within the early Christian community. As the prayers themselves suggest, these qualities did not simply happen, but were actively fostered through the formulation of proper Church ordinances. Efforts are needed to construct an atmosphere where such experiences of close personal fellowship can be fostered in today's Christian communities. Whether this takes place in the Eucharist itself or through some other structures supported by the Church, a deep sense of belonging to one

another is central to a community's efforts to work for the coming of the Kingdom and to realize its presence in their midst.

6. Chapter 14 of *The Didache* reveals the underlying communal context required for confession and for the proper reception of the Eucharist. Closely connected to this emphasis is the need to be reconciled with one another before one approaches the altar for the breaking of the bread. Although today's Eucharistic celebration addresses this need for confession and personal reconciliation through the opening penitential rite, efforts need to be made to raise awareness in the worshiping community of the significance of this ritual and its intimate relationship to what follows. When repeated often (almost by rote) and with little forethought, rituals can lose sight of the motivating force and spiritual effectiveness that originally gave rise to them. In such cases, they can hide just as much as (if not more than) they reveal. Those involved in planning the liturgy need to find ways of highlighting the importance of the penitential rite so that it becomes a locus for the way the believing community connects its worship with the concrete circumstances of daily life.

7. Chapter 14 of *The Didache* emphasizes the sacrificial dimension of the Church's Eucharistic worship. This emphasis can be taken to mean Christ's "sacrifice on the cross," the community's "sacrifice of thanksgiving" — or both. The two notions of sacrifice are not contradictory and have, in fact, been purposely juxtaposed to convey a deeper sense of the mystery that takes place in the worship of the Christian community. The Eucharist (or "Thanksgiving") of the believing community is deeply rooted in Christ's total offering of self. A "sacrifice of thanksgiving" is the response of the worshiping community to the Paschal Mystery which it celebrates in the breaking of the bread. This foretaste of the messianic banquet is made possible by Christ's passage from death to life. For Christians, the table of the Last Supper has become the altar upon which Christ offers himself for the members of his body and where they, in turn, offer praise and thanksgiving to the Father.

Conclusion

The Didache has much to teach us about the intimate relationship between Christian life and the worship of the believing community. By bringing two disparate works of an earlier time together, the author challenges his second-century readers to examine the link between the way they act and the manner in which they worship. Since the connection between the two works is calculated and purposeful, the author should be considered more than a mere compiler of ancient texts.

When it comes to the Eucharist, the offerings of *The Didache* are much more difficult to ascertain. The precise relationship between chapters 9–10 to chapter 14 remains controversial and will most likely continue to stir debate. The wide range of theories regarding the nature of this relationship, however, should not deter us from using the texts as a means for a critical examination of our own Eucharistic celebrations. We too are called to dialogue with the classic texts of the Christian tradition and to use them in relevant ways as an important point of departure for improving our worship services.

Reflection Questions

1. *The Didache* is composed of a moral catechism and a manual of Church order with special emphasis on liturgical practice. How would you describe the relationship between worship and moral conduct? Does worship influence your moral outlook on life? If so, in what ways? Can you point to specific examples? Does your moral outlook on life influence the way you worship? If so, in what ways? Can you point to specific examples?

2. The prayers of *The Didache* are modelled on Jewish mealtime blessings. How do you understand Christianity's relationship to its Jewish heritage? Is it something to be embarrassed by? Something to be ignored? Something to overcome? Something to celebrate? How does *The Didache* present this relationship? Have you learned anything from it? What does Christianity gain by celebrating its Jewish heritage?

3. *The Didache* offers a heartfelt prayer for Christian unity. In your opinion, what is the root cause of disunity among Christians? What can be done about it? Does disunity among Christians bother you? Have you ever done anything to try to change it? Do you pray for Christian unity? Privately or with others? Do you ever do so while at the Eucharist? In what way is the Eucharist the source of Christian unity? In what way is it an impediment to it?

4. *The Didache* reveals the underlying communal context required for confession and for the proper reception of the Eucharist. What is your understanding of the relationship between the penitential rite at the beginning and all the rest of the Eucharistic celebration? What is your understanding of the relationship between sacramental reconciliation and receiving the Eucharist? What is the relationship between the penitential rite at the Eucharist and sacramental reconciliation? Does one replace the other or are they complementary?

5. *The Didache* emphasizes the sacrificial dimension of the Church's Eucharistic worship. Do you believe that the Eucharist makes present in an unbloody way Jesus' sacrifice of Calvary? Is this connection absolutely necessary? Do you think it would be possible to have a complete Christian understanding of the Eucharist without including this sacrificial dimension? What, in your opinion, is the relationship between "the sacrifice of the cross" and the community's Eucharistic "sacrifice of thanksgiving"?

Voice Five

Justin Martyr
Explaining the Faith

> ... this food is called among us the Eucharist, of which no one is allowed to partake but the man who believes that the things which we teach are true, and who has been washed with the washing that is for the remission of sins, and unto regeneration, and who is so living as Christ has enjoined.
>
> *Justin Martyr*

H ave you ever been called upon to explain your faith to others? Have you ever been called upon to defend it? Apologetics, as it is sometimes called, has very deep roots in the Christian tradition and involves providing rational explanations of the meaning of the faith to non-believers. Because of the unusual claims of the Christian liturgy, these explanations often focused on the nature and meaning of the Eucharist. Justin Martyr (d. c. 165), our next voice from the past, was one of the great Christian apologists of the second-century Church.

Justin's First Apology

In his *First Apology* (c. 152–155),[1] Justin provides the earliest extant description of a Eucharistic service held in Rome. Born in Samaria of Gentile parents sometime in the early second century, he was converted to Christianity sometime between 132–135, came to Rome around 150, and in the pursuing years until his martyrdom in 165 wrote some of the greatest apologetic works of the early Christian

---

1. The English text of Justin's *First Apology* comes from *ANF*, 1:159–87.

faith. In his *First Apology*, Justin provides details of a post-baptismal Eucharist (chaps. 61, 65) and a Sunday liturgy (chap. 67). He also offers important commentary on the meaning of the Eucharist for the second-century Church of Rome (chap. 66). A look at these accounts will help us appreciate the central role held by the Eucharist in the early Church at Rome. It should also help us to look at our own celebration of the Eucharist and to ask relevant questions about its meaning and purpose for our lives.

Before doing so, however, it would be important to have an idea of the work's literary genre and the audience it addresses. Justin was an educated man who, after his conversion to Christianity, took to wearing the philosopher's garb. His decision to do so reflects his intellectual stance toward his newfound religion. Steeped in Greek philosophy, especially the thinking of Socrates and Plato, Justin considers Christianity "the one true philosophy." To demonstrate this conviction, he takes great pains to defend Christianity's astonishing claims against its many, often hostile, detractors.

Justin's writing is apologetic in nature and employs rational argument as a principal means of persuasion. Although he probably had a much wider audience in mind, he addresses his *First Apology* specifically to the Roman emperor, Antoninus Pius, his son Verissimus, and his adopted son Lucius, all three of whom he recognizes for their deep love of learning. Justin makes his case for Christianity before the most powerful people on earth, the rulers of the Roman Empire. He writes with boldness and a confidence that Reason will bring the truth to light and convince the opponents of the Christian faith to retract their unfounded charges.

Justin's *First Apology* is the earliest surviving example of Christian apologetic literature. He uses Reason as a tool to sway the emperor and his sons away from the false accusations made against Christians. Justin seeks a fair hearing for the Christian cause: "… we have come not to flatter you by this writing, nor to please you by our address, but to beg that you pass judgment, after an accurate and searching investigation" (chap. 2). His goal is "… to afford to all an opportunity of inspecting our [the Christian] life and teachings, lest, on account of those who are accustomed to be ignorant of our [Christian] affairs, we should incur the penalty due to them for mental blindness" (chap. 3). To accomplish these aims, he presents the Christian cause clearly and succinctly. His presentation of the Eucharist is a case in point.

A Post-Baptismal Eucharist

Justin's first depiction of the Eucharistic celebration comes in the form of a post-baptismal liturgy (chaps. 61, 65). Those who accept Christ and set out to live according to his teachings are instructed to fast and pray for the remission of their sins. The entire Christian community fasts and prays with them. At an appropriate time, they are brought to a place where there is water so that they can be made anew. This regeneration is necessary since, as Christ himself asserts, "No one can see the reign of God unless he is begotten from above" (Jn 3:3). Justin concurs: "Since at our birth we were born without our own knowledge or choice," we must be born a second time through the waters of baptism so that we might become "children of choice and knowledge" (chap. 61). In keeping with his presentation of Christianity as the "one true philosophy," he emphasizes the enlightened understanding given to the newly baptized. Baptism, for Justin, is the "sacrament of illumination" and takes place, "in the name of God, the Father and Lord of the universe, and of our Savior Jesus Christ, and of the Holy Spirit" (chap. 61). Jesus Christ is the Light of the world; through baptism, we share in that Light as members of his body.

The newly baptized Christians are then brought into the presence of the assembly of the brethren where heartfelt prayers are offered for the community, for those just baptized, and for all others. This is done so that the faithful might put into practice what they have learned with the hope of receiving a share in the rewards of everlasting life. When their prayers have come to an end, the members of the community salute each other with a holy kiss. Some bread and a cup of wine mixed with water is then given to the president of the assembly who, in turn, gives praise to the Father, Son, and Holy Spirit, and offers thanks at considerable length. At the conclusions of these prayers, all those present express their consent by saying "Amen." At this point, the deacons distribute the bread and wine mixed with water to all present. A portion is set aside and carried away to the absent members of the assembly.

Justin's account contains four distinct moments: (1) the celebration of baptism itself, which ends with a procession to the place where the brethren have assembled; (2) a period of prayer for the entire community, which ends with a kiss of peace; (3) the celebration of the Eucharist, during which time the president of the assembly gives glory, praise, and thanks to God, and the faithful express their assent through the Great Amen; and (4) the distribution of the Eucharist by the deacons to those who have gathered and then to the community's absent members. The account highlights the intrinsic unity of the celebration and its centrality to the life of the Christian community. One gets the distinct impression that all of the faithful are involved in welcoming the newly baptized into their midst. The Eucharist is depicted as the food which nourishes and binds them together. It not only holds them together as a believing community, but also represents a concrete, living reminder of their baptismal promises.

Sunday Worship

A little later in his *First Apology*, Justin offers a description of a typical Sunday liturgy (chap. 67). On Sunday, the day of the Lord's resurrection, all Christians, regardless of whether they live in the city or the country, gather in one place. They begin their celebration by reading the memoirs of the apostles or the writings of the prophets.

When the reader has finished the lessons, the president of the assembly instructs the people and exhorts them to follow the way of goodness. After his teaching, the entire community rises together in prayer. When this time of prayer has drawn to a close, bread and wine are produced, and the presider offers prayers and thanksgivings according to his ability. When he has finished, the people demonstrate their assent by saying, "Amen." The distribution of the Eucharist to those assembled follows, and deacons are sent off with portions of it for those who are absent.

After the distribution of the Eucharist, a collection is taken up. Those who are willing and able give what they think appropriate.

The collection is given to the presider of the assembly, who uses it to help orphans and widows, the sick, the imprisoned, strangers, and all in need. Sunday, Justin asserts, is the day on which Christians everywhere hold their common assembly. They do so because that is the day Christ rose from the dead. Behind this there is the suggestion that, just as Christ brought about a change in the world through his death and his glorious resurrection, Christians share in his transforming work through their almsgiving and works of kindness.

This description of Justin's gives us some interesting insights into the Christian community of second-century Rome. There is a strong emphasis on gathering in one place for Sunday worship, as well as a clear distinction between the Liturgy of the Word and the Liturgy of the Eucharist. The Eucharist is sent out to those who cannot be present, while great stress is placed on taking care of the needs of the poor. Justin depicts the Eucharistic celebration as something that overflows the confines of the place where it is celebrated. By bringing it to those who cannot be physically present and by making a concerted effort to meet the material and spiritual needs of those in need, the Christian community affirms its responsibility to all the members of Christ's body, whatever their situation is and wherever they may be. Christians, Justin says, stay together and continually remind themselves of their duties to one another. The wealthy among them help the needy, while everyone blesses God the Father through his Son Jesus Christ, and through the Holy Spirit, for all the gifts they have received.

Justin's Commentary

Between his depiction of the post-baptismal liturgy and the Sunday Eucharistic worship, Justin makes some important observations that apply to both (chap. 66). He tells us that the faithful refer to the bread and wine they share as *Eucharistia*, a word in Greek meaning "Thanksgiving." To receive this food, Justin says, three things are required: (1) a person must believe that the things taught by the Christian community are true; (2) he or she must have received the remission of sins and regeneration through the waters of baptism; and (3) he or she must be living as Christ has instructed. Faith, baptism, and a moral life are necessary for admission to the sacrament. Without them, the Eucharist is not received worthily.

The bread and wine, Justin goes on to say, are not common bread and common drink. As Jesus Christ gave up his body and blood for the salvation of the world, Christians have been taught that the food which is blessed by the prayer of his Word is the very flesh and blood of Christ himself. The Gospels themselves attest "... that Jesus took bread, and when he had given thanks, said, 'This is my body. Do this in memory of me'; and that, after the same manner, having taken the cup and given thanks, he said, 'This is my blood'; and gave it to them alone" (chap. 66). By including them at this point in his commentary, Justin reminds us that these words of institution are central to the Eucharistic celebration.

As an apologist, Justin passes on to his readers the very tradition upon which every Eucharistic celebration rests. He is well aware that, without this special witness of the apostles, the true teaching on the Eucharist would be greatly diminished or perhaps completely lost. Conscious that he is writing to a pagan audience, Justin contrasts the Eucharist with certain false imitations as found, for example, in the mysteries of Mithras. The Christian Eucharist, Justin maintains, comes from Christ himself and rests on the testimony of the apostles. The pagan mystery cults, he asserts, are inspired by demons and have no such witnesses to assert the authenticity of their claims.

Observations

Justin's description of and commentary upon the Eucharistic celebration in mid-second-century Rome allow for some interesting observations about our present-day outlook toward the sacrament. Five in particular come to mind.

1. In this work of apologetics, Justin builds toward his presentation of the Eucharist, placing it at the end of his work as a climactic conclusion to his arguments. In trying to defend the faith and present it to others as clearly and succinctly as possible, he is not afraid to point out similarities and differences with other religions. One is never in doubt, however, about where he stands. Justin is a Christian, a fervent adherent to the "one true philosophy." A relevant parallel to

our own time arises. As in the time of second-century Rome, we too live in a world of pluralism and syncretism. In our attempts to explain our belief to others, however, we must be careful not to "explain them away" and fall into the trap of religious relativism. Like Justin Martyr, a man who died for his faith, we must be willing to let people know where we stand. When applied to the Eucharist, this means not only letting people know that it lies at the center of our lives, but also explaining to them in plain, simple language how and why this is so. Because of the secular nature of Western society, such explanations may even be necessary for Christians themselves, many of whom do not understand the underlying reasons for their faith and can be easily swayed by the allures of a consumer culture.

2. Justin is very clear about the prerequisites of one's full participation in the Eucharistic celebration. Reception of the Eucharist presupposes that a person has been baptized, believes the fundamental tenets of the Christian faith, and is striving to live a moral life. These same basic requirements need to be emphasized today. How this is to be done depends on the pastoral prudence and the needs of the believing community. Care must be taken to present the Eucharist as a sacrament which, when taken seriously, is carefully prepared for and dutifully received. At the same time, care must also be taken to present the Eucharist as God's gift to the believing community, one which must be received with great eagerness and joy. Participation in the Eucharist is meant to strengthen one's commitment to a life of Christian discipleship. Today's faith communities need to bring this dimension of Eucharistic worship to the forefront of their awareness. If we are willing to receive the Eucharist, we must also be willing to open our hearts to God. Doing so will have concrete consequences for what we profess in faith and how we live our lives.

3. Justin places a great emphasis on the community gathering for its weekly celebration "in one place." The effect of this gathering was to force the members of the Christian community to encounter their Lord in the context of their prior encounter with one another across a variety of ethnic backgrounds and socio-economic factors. This "spirituality of place" enabled the community — at least for a time — to cross the barriers separating them and envision a society entirely transformed by Gospel values, those which in Justin's words,

represent "the one true philosophy." In a world increasingly divided by ethnic, sociological, and economic factors, creative efforts are needed within the believing community to use the Eucharistic celebration as a way of healing divisions both within itself and within the world. In doing so, the Eucharist will become an even more visible sign of the new creation made possible by Christ's redemptive action and the in-breaking of the Kingdom.

4. Related to the above insight, special efforts are made to bring the Eucharist to those not able to attend. The result of these efforts is a stronger sense of connectedness within the believing community. The Eucharist, as Justin emphasizes, is what holds the believing community together; even those who are not physically present have a right to be nourished from the table of the Lord. In Justin's day, this need was met through the ministry of the deacons, who brought the Eucharist to the sick and infirm immediately after those present at the celebration had received. In like manner, creative efforts are needed today to shore up the intimate relation between the celebration of the Eucharist itself and its later distribution. Deacons and extraordinary ministers of the Eucharist must play a proactive role in this endeavor (i.e., personal availability, recruiting others, drawing up communion lists, etc.). It is appropriate, moreover, that they be given a prominent role in the weekly Sunday liturgy when, just after the faithful have received, they are sent out to carry the Eucharist to the infirm, housebound, and those in need. As a result, those receiving the Eucharist elsewhere will have a deeper sense of the care of the entire community and a greater understanding of their participation in the celebration from which the Eucharist has come to them.

5. Finally, Justin devotes a large part of his description of Sunday worship to how the Christian community meets the material needs of the poor. He does so by giving a detailed list of how the weekly collection is taken and how it is parcelled out. This connection between the Eucharistic celebration and the material care of the needy goes to the heart of the Christian message. Scripture tells us that "God is love" (1 Jn 4:8). The Christian community's dedication to serving the needs of the poor validates the Eucharistic celebration which, as the "sacrament of love" (*agape*), must concentrate its resources

on those in need with the hope of alleviating suffering, of whatever kind, so that God's love may be made manifest in the present. This call to the service of the poor and the oppressed is an integral part of the Eucharistic celebration. Christians gather for worship in order ultimately to be sent out on mission. In the Church today creative efforts are needed to heighten the awareness of the faithful to responsibilities that accompany their participation in their Sunday worship. A broader interpretation of Justin's insights would want these efforts not only to stress traditional avenues of charitable service such as tithing and volunteer work, but also look to ways in which the very causes of poverty and oppression themselves can be confronted and overcome.

Conclusion

Justin Martyr's *First Apology* gives us a close, inside look at Eucharistic worship in second-century Rome. It also offers us an opportunity to examine our own attitudes toward the Eucharist and to look at ways of improving our liturgical practice. While the above observations in no way exhaust the ways in which Justin's descriptions can help us to ponder the Eucharist's relevance for our lives, they offer a good point of departure for our own creative reflection on future directions we may wish to travel. For Justin, the Eucharist holds the Christian community together through the dynamic power of Father, Son, and Holy Spirit. It is meant to do the same for Christian communities today. Justin's descriptions of the Eucharist put us in touch with the wellspring of a vibrant Christian community intent on following in the footsteps of its master — no matter what the cost. By looking at these descriptions we can see a faint reflection of what we ourselves are called to strive for and embody in our own lives.

Reflection Questions

1. For Justin Martyr, Christianity is the "one true philosophy." What do you think he meant by this description? That Christianity can be explained in purely natural terms? That it provides a compre-

hensive explanation of human existence? That it can withstand
rigorous rational scrutiny? Do you look upon Christianity as a
philosophy? The one true philosophy? What is the relationship
between faith and reason? Which has precedence?

2. Justin Martyr is very clear about the prerequisites for full participation in the Eucharist: baptism, belief, and striving to live a
moral life. Do you agree with him? Is there anything you would
like to add or take away? Are these three elements given enough
emphasis for today's believers? Are they given too little emphasis? Too much? If someone asked, how would you explain what
a Christian must do to be admitted to full participation in the
Eucharistic celebration?

3. Justin Martyr emphasizes the importance of the community
gathering each week in one place for the Eucharistic celebration. What are the underlying values of such a practice? Given
the impracticalities involving a single gathering for today's local believing community, can you think of any other practices
that would convey the same or similar values today? If so, how
practical are they and how would you implement them?

4. Justin Martyr emphasizes the importance of making the Eucharist accessible to the community of believers, especially to the
sick and infirm. Do you think the Church is doing enough in this
area? Can you think of any groups within your local community
for whom the Eucharist is not being made available? If so, what
practical steps can be taken to meet their needs?

5. Justin Martyr emphasizes the importance for the worshiping
community to meet the material needs of others. Does your
local worshiping community reach out to the poor and needy?
How does it do so? Does it make it a priority? Is there anything
more it can do to help them? How do you share in this outreach?
Is there anything more you can do to contribute to it?

Voice Six

Irenaeus of Lyons
Correcting Error

But vain in every respect are they who despise the entire dispensation of God, and disallow the salvation of the flesh, and treat with contempt its regeneration, maintaining that it is not capable of corruption. But if this indeed does not attain salvation, then neither did the Lord redeem us with His blood, nor is the cup of the Eucharist the communion of His blood, nor the bread which we break the communion of His body.

Irenaeus of Lyons

H ave you ever thought of the Eucharist as a sacrament that regenerates the body and frees it from the powers of corruption? Irenaeus of Lyons, our next voice from the past, was certainly of such a mind. For him, the Eucharist was the food of salvation that strengthens humanity's flesh, sinews, and bones with the body and blood of Christ. He roots his teaching on the Eucharist in a sweeping cosmic vision of the history of salvation. He developed this vision as a way of defending the apostolic tradition against the threat of Gnostic dualism. He presents his teachings against this "false gnosis" in the five books of his *Against Heresies*,[1] a collection of treatises written in Greek from 180 to 190 and preserved in Latin translation from roughly the year 300. This highly successful work of apologetics has earned him the title, the "Father of Catholic Dogma." His teaching on the Eucharist is but one example of his strong defence of orthodoxy

---

1. The English translation used in this article comes from Irenaeus of Lyons, *Adversus Haereses* in *ANF*, 1:309–567. Dates, biographical information, relevant themes in the first section have been gleaned from: *CH*, 1:180–81; *Pat.*, 1:287–313; and Adalbert Hamman, "Irenaeus of Lyons," in *EEC*, 86–98.

and his deep desire to preserve the tradition handed down through the teachings of the apostles.

The Man and His Teaching

Irenaeus was born in Asia Minor between 140 and 160. A disciple of St. Polycarp of Smyrna, he left his homeland in 177 for the Roman Province of Gaul, where he was elected bishop of Lyons in 180. Irenaeus was a missionary and evangelizer at heart. His writings reflect his deep concern for authentic teaching and the spread of the faith. These concerns led him to refute the proponents of Gnosticism, the false doctrines of which presented the greatest threat to the apostolic faith in the latter part of the second century.

Irenaeus' knowledge of Gnosticism came from his own reading of Gnostic sources and earlier Christian refutations of it. His *Against Heresies* offers a history of the origins of Gnosticism (Book I). Next come refutations of it based on reason (Book II), the teachings of the Church (Book III), and the sayings of Jesus (Book IV). It concludes with a defence of the resurrection of the flesh, a doctrine explicitly rejected by the Gnostics (Book V). What these treatises lack in style and cohesive structure Irenaeus makes up for with his passion for the refutation of heresy and defence of the faith. What is more, he focuses on real problems facing the Church of Lyons during his time in office, ones that threatened the very existence of the Church of the late-second century.

During his tenure as bishop, Gnostics in the area of Lyons were leading Christians astray by pitting the God of the Old Testament against the God of Jesus Christ. The material world, they asserted, was the creation of an evil Demiurge, who sought to imprison souls in matter and thus bring them under his control. The God of Jesus Christ, by way of contrast, was a God of Light, who sent his Word to impart a secret knowledge that would enable people to recognize their hidden divinity and rise above the flesh. Even though these Gnostics were using Christian symbols and language, their underlying assumptions about the nature of Christianity were strongly dualistic: the material world was evil; the spiritual world was good. Each had its own God who struggled with the other for cosmic prominence.

Irenaeus perceived this Gnostic assimilation of the Christian narrative as a distinct threat to the existence and future growth of the Church. He countered it by devising a view of history that was rooted in the unity of faith and the unity of God's plan of salvation. For Irenaeus, the material world represented not a cosmic devolution into evil, but an act of divine creation that was pre-eminently good. The Old and New Testaments were not opposed to one another, but closely interwoven into a single economic plan of creation, redemption, and sanctification.

For Irenaeus, each Person of the Holy Trinity had a specific role to play in shaping humanity: "…the Father planning everything well and giving His commands, the Son carrying these into execution and performing the work of creating, and the Spirit nourishing and increasing [what is made]."[2] Human beings were the pinnacle of creation and the glory of God. Drawn by Christ and the power of the Spirit, their calling was to move toward fulfillment by overcoming their evil tendencies so that they could live in full communion with God and one another.

Central to Irenaeus' theology is his theory of recapitulation. According to this theory, God had intended Christ, from the very beginning, to recapitulate all of creation in himself. Although Adam and Eve had spoiled this plan by their unhappy fall from grace, Christ's Incarnation brought it once again to the fore. Christ is the new Adam and Mary, the New Eve. Together, they herald the establishment of a new creation, one that does not eradicate the old, but transforms it so that it could reach new heights. Irenaeus puts it this way: "When he [Jesus] became incarnate, and was made man, he commenced afresh the long line of human beings, and furnished us, in a brief, comprehensive manner, with salvation; so that what we had lost in Adam — namely, to be according to the image and likeness of God — we might recover in Christ Jesus."[3]

---

2. Irenaeus of Lyons, *Against Heresies*, 4.38.3 (*ANF*, 1:521–22).
3. Ibid., 3.18.1 (*ANF*, 1:446).

Irenaeus on the Eucharist

For Irenaeus, the Eucharist is the sacrament par excellence of this new creation. Prefigured in the miracles of Christ's multiplication of the loaves and fishes and in his changing water into wine at the Wedding of Cana, it represents God's power to transform the material world from within and to raise it to new heights.

For this reason, the Eucharist is also very closely bound to the miracle of Christ's resurrection. The Father, for whom all things are possible, raised Jesus from the dead and planted in his mortal remains the seeds of the new creation: "... our bodies, when they receive the Eucharist, are no longer corruptible, having the hope of the resurrection to eternity."[4] Jesus does not disdain the material elements of bread and wine, but affirms their fundamental goodness and uses them to raise the present creation to another dimension. In so doing, he affirms the continuity between the world of matter and the world of spirit. The Eucharist affirms the intimate union of these realms: each forms a part of God's original creation; each has a place in the new.

In this way, Irenaeus uses the Eucharist to combat the pessimistic and dichotomizing tendencies of his Gnostic adversaries. To celebrate the Eucharist is to affirm one's hope in the redemption of the whole person: body, soul, and spirit. Unlike the Gnostics, who refused to accept the ability of the body to receive God's grace, Irenaeus glories in God's power to transform the corruptible into something incorruptible. He uses metaphors from nature to make his point: "... as a corn of wheat falling into the earth and becoming decomposed, rises with manifold increase by the Spirit of God ... becomes the Eucharist ... so also our bodies, being nourished by it, and deposited in the earth, and suffering decomposition there, shall rise at their appointed time."[5]

The Eucharist, for Irenaeus, is both the hope and the reality of the new creation. By nourishing ourselves on this food, we look forward to that distant time when we will share in the fullness of God's life. The Eucharist offers us food for our long pilgrim journey to God. As we eat and drink of this food, we gradually prepare ourselves for life in the kingdom.

---

4. Ibid., 4.18.5 (*ANF*, 1:486).
5. Ibid., 5.2.3 (*ANF*, 1:528).

Observations

Irenaeus' teaching on the Eucharist has much relevance for us today. The following remarks offer some insights into how this "sacrament of the new creation" might help us in our journey through life and our long walk to fulfillment.

1. Although Irenaeus does not devote an entire treatise to the Eucharist, the sacrament holds a central place in his theological vision. His teaching on it permeates much of his writing and plays a major role in his refutation of his Gnostic adversaries. In a similar way, the gift of the Eucharist should hold a central place in our own understanding and practice of the faith. Although we do not need to refer to it at all times, it should underlie all our beliefs and practices. In one way or another, everything we do should flow from it. In one way or another, everything we do should be oriented toward it. The integrated way in which Irenaeus writes about the Eucharist challenges us to look at the way we ourselves have integrated it in our own lives.

2. Irenaeus also looks upon the Eucharist as a catechetical tool. He uses it to teach the faithful of Lyons the true meaning of their faith and to help them to detect any false interpretations of it that might creep in through Gnostic dualism. Such an approach to the Eucharist also has great relevance for us. We should be conscious of what the Eucharistic liturgy tries to teach us and be constantly evaluating whether we communicate those teachings successfully in our celebration of the sacrament.

3. Irenaeus' struggle against Gnosticism has much in common with the Church's suspicion of much of today's New Age mysticism. Like Gnosticism, New Age cults have a strong individualistic and esoteric quality about them. Like the Gnostics, their doctrine is extremely malleable; they tend toward dualism; they deny the need for humanity's redemption from sin; and they are very suspicious of organized religion. Irenaeus bids us to examine our own position toward these present-day Gnostic movements.

4. Unlike the Gnostics, Irenaeus believed that Jesus came to save the whole human person: body, soul, and spirit. He embraces an anthropological vision of the human person based on the in-

tegration of various dimensions of our experience. Jesus came to redeem every aspect of human existence. For Irenaeus, nothing was beyond the reach of God's redeeming grace. His comprehensive vision invites us to examine our own assumptions about the scope of redemption.

5. Irenaeus connects the Eucharist to the unity of the faith. He ties the apostolic tradition so closely to it that the sacrament becomes a universal symbol of the Church's unity of belief and practice. This close connection between the sacrament and the faith of the Church bids us to look at our own understanding of the relationship between our celebration of the Eucharist and the faith we proclaim.

6. For Irenaeus, Christ poured himself into bread and wine so that the Church could offer a fitting sacrifice to God in his name. When he asked his disciples to celebrate the breaking of the bread in memory of him, he was offering them a way in which they could participate in his forthcoming suffering and death. Irenaeus saw the Eucharist as the sacrifice of the new covenant. Just as Jesus recapitulated all things in himself, so has he gathered all the sacrifices of the world into a single offering of self. At the Eucharist, Jesus' sacrifice on the cross becomes present to us in a mysterious and bloodless way. Each time we celebrate the sacrament, his sacrifice of self to the Father becomes our own. For this reason, we must contemplate the sacrificial dimension of the Eucharist and offer our lives to God through it.

7. For Irenaeus, the Eucharist nurtures in us a hope in our own resurrection. It gives us Christ's transformed existence to eat in the form of bread and wine and, in doing so, helps us to see how closely and intimately bound our destiny is with his. This hope in the resurrection touches the very core of Christ's redemptive mystery. It reminds us of why we gather and where we are going both individually and as a people.

8. Because Jesus recapitulates all things in himself, Irenaeus believed that humanity's redemption was the first fruit of a new creation. Foreshadowed by Jesus' multiplication of the loaves and

fishes and by his changing water into wine at Cana, the Eucharist was a concrete, visible manifestation of this new creation. For Irenaeus, this new creation transformed the first creation and raised it to new heights. He believed that God, who made creation out of nothing, could also shape a new creation out of what already existed.

9. Irenaeus uses the metaphor of a long, arduous journey to describe the process of humanity's redemption. That journey involves a movement of gradual growth that leads to maturity and communion with God. Irenaeus' presentation of redemption entails our active involvement in our journey to God. Christ draws us toward him, but never against our will.

10. Irenaeus also connects the Eucharist to the unity of God's universal plan of salvation. That unity is rooted not in humanity's feeble powers of perception, but in the intimate life of the Trinity. It affirms a fundamental continuity between the Old and New Covenants and sees God's plan for humanity as underlying the whole of history. Irenaeus' understanding of salvation history challenges us to explore our own views toward it.

Conclusion

Irenaeus of Lyons' teaching on the Eucharist revolves around his understanding of the unity or integrity of God's plan for salvation. It reminds us that, through his passion, death, and resurrection, Christ has drawn all things to himself and that the sacrament of his body and blood is the first fruit of a new creation. By participating in this sacrament, we receive food for the journey that will culminate in the healing of our souls and the transformation of our lives.

Irenaeus uses the Eucharist as a way of handing on the apostolic tradition. Through it, he affirms the fundamental goodness of the material world, the continuity of the New Covenant with what went before it, and the hope in the resurrection for all who believe. Although he did not write a separate treatise on the Eucharist, the sacrament holds an important place in his understanding of salvation history. At the Eucharist, the power of the Spirit transforms elements of the visible world so that God can dwell in them and even become them. Those who receive the Eucharist share in this redemptive process and are gradually transformed by it.

The Eucharist, for Irenaeus, is the sacrament of the new creation par excellence. It offers a concrete sign of God's redemptive grace at work in our hearts and in the world. It offers us food and nourishment for our long, arduous journey to God. It reminds us that redemption takes place in us through a slow, gradual process. It points out the way we should walk, and, in Jesus' life, death, and resurrection, offers a model for us to imitate. For Irenaeus, the Eucharist embodies the mysteries of our creation, redemption, and sanctification. It keeps alive in us the hope in the redemption of every dimension of our human makeup. It roots us in God as individuals and as a people. Without it, we would fail to appreciate the wonderful gifts we have received from God. We would lose both our sense of direction and sight of our goal. We would not know where to turn, which light to follow, or how to give glory, honor, and praise to the living God.

Reflection Questions

1. The Eucharist held a central place in Irenaeus' theological vision. Does it hold a similar place in yours? How would you describe its importance to you? Can you envision Christianity without the Eucharist? Would such a religion be missing anything significant?

2. For Irenaeus, the Eucharist was an important catechetical tool. Do you look upon this sacrament in this way? What doctrinal and moral teachings does it convey? What values does it affirm? What values is it meant to offset? Is the Eucharist an adequate catechetical tool for today's Christians? What can be done to make it more effective?

3. Do you see any similarities between Gnosticism and New Age mysticism? Has any of this arcane spirituality influenced your own outlook on life? If so, in what ways? Has it influenced your attitude toward Christianity in any way? Toward the Eucharist?

In what ways does the Eucharist contradict the teachings of Gnostic dualism?

4. For Irenaeus, Jesus came to save the whole person: body, soul, and spirit. Do you believe in such a message of salvation? Do you believe that the Eucharist has anything to do with it? To what extent does the Eucharist nurture in us the hope of our own resurrection? What, in your opinion, will such a transformed existence be like?

5. Irenaeus connects the Eucharist with both the unity and integrity of the faith and God's universal plan of salvation. What role does the Eucharist play in our journey to God? What role does it play in God's providential plan for humanity? Do you believe that the whole of human history is centered around the person of Jesus Christ? What does it mean to say that all things will be recapitulated in Christ?

Voice Seven

Clement of Alexandria
Christian Gnosis

This Eucharistic feast of ours is completely innocent, even if
we desire to sing at it, or to chant psalms to the lyre or lute.
Imitate the holy Hebrew king in his thanksgiving to God: "Re-
joice in the Lord, O ye just; praise becometh the upright," as
the inspired psalm says: "Give praise to the Lord on the harp,
sing to Him with the lyre" ... "Sing to Him a new canticle."

Clement of Alexandria

How do you look upon the Eucharist as a celebration? Do
you think of it as a time when you can gather with the rest of the
believing community to open the Scriptures, listen to God's Word,
chant psalms, break bread together, pass the cup, and offer hymns
of praise to God? Clement of Alexandria (c. 150–c. 215), our next
voice from the past, was one of the most creative thinkers of the
early Church and presented the Eucharist in such a way. For him,
Eucharistic worship was a festive sacrificial meal, a time when the
Divine Logos entered the world to mingle with the believing community and make it holy. Thoroughly immersed in the Greek culture
and literature, Clement used his knowledge to probe the truths of
the Christian faith and to make them understandable to the educated
classes of his day. His teaching and writings contributed greatly
to the Christianization of Hellenic culture, the first of many such
cultural adaptations that would accompany the Christian religion on
its historical journey.

Clement's Life Work

Titus Flavius Clemens was born in Athens of wealthy Greek parentage.[1] He converted to Christianity from paganism during his travels as a youth in search of a liberal education. In time, he found himself in Alexandria, the second largest city of the empire and the great seat of learning of his day. While at Alexandria, he attended the Christian Academy, the famous catechetical school founded by Pantaenus, a Stoic philosopher turned Christian. This school aimed its curriculum at the educated classes of Alexandria. Meetings took place in private homes and were opened to adult men and women, the majority of whom were recent converts of Greek heritage. After Pantaenus's death at the turn of the third century, Clement took charge of the catechetical school at Alexandria. He left Alexandria in 202, however, during the persecution of Sulpicius Severus, going first to Cappadocia and then to Antioch, where he died around the year 215.

A layman with a strong contemplative bent, Clement dedicated himself to expounding the mysteries of the Christian faith, using the tools of Greek philosophy to decipher the meaning of the Scriptures. He did this at a time when there were few precedents to follow or to look to for guidance. Influenced heavily by the principles of Platonic and Stoic philosophy, he combed the Scriptures and pondered their deeper spiritual meanings. The allegorical method he employed when interpreting the Scriptures resonated with both pagan philosophy and exegetical principles of the Jewish scholar Philo of Alexandria (d. 40 C.E.). This approach was highly esteemed in its day and had a great impact on the history and development of Christian exegesis.

Generally speaking, Clement followed a threefold approach to Christian learning: to persuade, to educate in morals, and to unfold the mysteries of the faith. His three greatest works, *An Exhortation to the Greeks* (c. 189), *Christ the Educator* (c.190), and the unfinished *Stromata* (i.e., a tapestry or colorful collection, c. 202 f.), implements this plan exceedingly well. Once he had convinced his hearers of the truth of the Christian faith, he proceeded to teach them how to live the

---

1. Most of the biographical and other historical information in this section depends on Simon P. Wood, "Introduction," in *Clement of Alexandria, Christ the Educator*, trans. Simon P. Wood in *FC*, 23:v–xviii.

moral life, and then expound for them the deeper spiritual meanings of the Christian faith. His aim was to promote a true and authentic Christian Gnosis, one that would counteract the heretical tendencies of the various Gnostic sects that were prevalent in his day. Although his insights were often enigmatic and, at times, even seemed to go beyond the limits of orthodoxy, Clement's intention was always to remain loyal to the Church and the teachings of Christ. His literary corpus has been affirmed for its attempt to relate Christianity to the whole of human thought. He has been described as "… the first systematic teacher of Christian doctrine, the formal champion of liberal culture in the Church."[2]

The Eucharist and the Divine Logos

It is very difficult to ascertain Clement's meaning in the texts where he seems to be referring to the Eucharist. Of the roughly forty times where such references occur, only four are generally held to be genuine references to the Eucharistic banquet — and even those, after close scrutiny, have been questioned by some.[3] Part of the difficulty comes in Clement's highly symbolic way of writing, one that enables him to use extended Eucharistic imagery when talking about matters other than the liturgy itself. His interest in Christian Gnosis, moreover, generally leads his thinking away from the rituals of Christian worship to areas of a more speculative, spiritual nature.

When approaching Clement's teaching on the Eucharist, it would not be fair to pose questions that presuppose doctrinal insights arising much later in the Church's reflection on the meaning of the sacrament. His understanding of the Eucharist must be studied from within his own mindset, using his concepts and his way of approaching the meaning of the breaking of the bread and the sharing of the cup. To this end, it will be useful first to discuss Clement's general understanding of the Christian life and then look at the particular way in which the Eucharist helps to support it.

---

2. J. Patrick, *Clement of Alexandria* (London, 1914), 13. Cited in *FC,* 23:v.
3. Most of the historical and scholarly data in this section depends on André Méhat, "Clement of Alexandria" (*EEC*, 99–129).

a. *The Purpose of Christian Living.* For Clement, the goal of the Christian life is to participate in the life of God and his Divine Word. His understanding of the Word, that is, the Logos, comes from Greek thought, largely through Platonic and, even more importantly, through Stoic influences. Logos, for Clement, stands for the Reason that brings order and harmony to every aspect of reality, the small-scale world of the human heart, as well as the unbounded scale of the cosmos. The goal of the Christian teacher is to help the faithful get in touch with this divine, universal, ordering Word. Once that happens, the Logos itself becomes the teacher and nourishes the faithful with its calming, harmonious presence. It will help them to root out the various vices and passions that get in the way of their leading a life of virtue. Even more importantly, it will reveal to them the true knowledge (or Gnosis) of the divine mysteries that will eventually lead to their own divinization.

Since, for Clement, the Word is the most important source of nourishment for the Christian life, it is not surprising that he would use Eucharistic imagery to describe it:

> What a holy begetting! What holy swaddling clothes! The Word is everything to His little ones, both father and mother, educator and nurse. "Eat My flesh," He says, "and drink My blood." He is Himself the nourishment that he gives. He delivers up His own flesh and pours out His own blood. There is nothing lacking His children, that they may grow. What a mysterious paradox! He bids us put off the former mortality of the flesh and, with it, the former nourishment, and receive instead this other new life of Christ, to find place in ourselves for Him as far as we can, and to enshrine the Savior in our hearts that we may be rid of the passions of the flesh.[4]

In this passage, Clement uses Eucharistic imagery to expound his Logos theology. The Logos (Word) is father, mother, teacher, and nurse. The Logos says, "Eat my flesh and drink my blood." The Logos represents that paradoxical mystery that enables us to destroy the passions of the flesh and eventually to live a life of virtue. Only by having a thorough grasp of Clement's strong emphasis on the

---

4. Clement of Alexandria, *Christ the Educator* 1.6. 42–43 (*FC*, 23:40–41).

divinizing role of the Logos in the Christian life can we understand the approach he takes to the Eucharist.

  b. *The Role of the Eucharist.* For Clement, believers gain eternal life by coming into contact with the Divine Logos. But how do they go about doing so? Ever the teacher, Clement certainly places a high priority on catechetical instruction. He dedicated so much of his life to reconciling the Christian faith with Hellenic culture precisely because he believed that both had genuine insights to contribute to the well-being of all of humanity. His many years at the Christian Academy in Alexandria illustrate the depth of his dedication to this goal. Clement, the teacher, wished nothing more than to lead others to Christ, the True Teacher. His work, *Pedagogus* (*Christ the Educator*) emphasizes this very important theme.

  A presentation of Clement's theology would not be complete, however, if his Eucharistic realism was not also taken into account. For Clement, the believer gets in touch with the Logos not only through catechetical instruction, but also at the Eucharistic banquet. At this festive sacrificial meal, the Logos becomes heavenly food for the entire believing community. When receiving it, the faithful become mingled with the Logos and their lives divinized. Clement expresses this thought allegorically:

> … the blood of the Lord is twofold: one corporeal, redeeming us from corruption; the other is spiritual, and it is with that we are anointed. To drink the blood of Jesus is to participate in His incorruption. Yet, the Spirit is the strength of the Word in the same way that blood is of the body. Similarly, wine is mixed with water and the Spirit is joined to man; the first, the mixture, provides feasting that faith may be increased; the other, the Spirit, leads us on to incorruption. The union of both, that is, of the potion and the Word, is called the Eucharist, a gift worthy of praise and surpassingly fair; those who partake of it are sanctified in body and soul, for it is the will of the Father that man, a composite by God, be united to the Spirit and to the Word.[5]

The notion of mingling of water and wine referred to by Clement comes very close to the Stoic concept of the penetration of the cosmos

---

5. Ibid., 2.2.19–20 (*FC*, 23:110–111).

by the divine Spirit (or Pneuma). The analogy Clement is making hinges on his presentation of the two bloods of Christ: one corporeal, the other spiritual. The Eucharist represents a coming together of the material world and the world of Pneuma which, for Clement, represents the very strength of the Logos. When Christians partake of the Eucharist, they come into close contact with the divinity. In doing so, they receive the opportunity to delve deeper into mysteries of Christian Gnosis. When seen in this light, the Eucharist is very important for growth in the Christian life. Without it, it would be that much more difficult for the faithful to calm their passions, to overcome their vices, and to lead a life of virtue. Without it, it would be that much more difficult for them to delve into the mysteries of Christian Gnosis and complete the process of their own divinization. The Eucharist, for Clement, leads all the way to a face-to-face encounter with the divine. It lies at the very heart of an authentic Christian mysticism and is something that Christians cannot do easily without.

Observations

The above presentation of Clement's understanding of the Eucharist, while by no means exhaustive, offers an appreciation of his approach to the sacrament and the role it plays in his overall thought. The following remarks will focus on these insights and seek to find relevant parallels for today.

1. Clement was deeply involved in what can be termed Christianity's first encounter with a foreign culture, i.e., Hellenic civilization. He represents the forces within Christianity that tried to interpret the faith to the predominantly pagan world of the Greco-Roman culture. To carry out this process of inculturation, he used concepts from Greek philosophy, most notably Platonism and Stoicism, in order to come up with ways of understanding Christian doctrine that would be both understandable and palatable to his readers and listeners. His teaching on the Eucharist represents a single (albeit important) part of this process of translation. Like Clement, today's Christians need to be ready to enter into dialogue with other cultures and to formulate new ways of presenting the faith in a way that will be both interesting and readily

understandable. While the historical and revelatory nature of their religion warrants that they must not simply discard the formulations that served them so well in the past, they must be able to recognize the way in which these presentations were themselves conditioned by time and historical circumstances and be able to propose new ways of explaining the mystery of Christ's body and blood to interested Christians and non-Christians alike.

2. For all of Clement's emphasis on Greek philosophy, he was first and foremost a commentator on Scripture. One does not have to read his works very long before realizing how much the Scriptures permeated his thought. Allusions and references to the sacred authors abound on every page. What is innovative in Clement's approach to the Word of God, however, is the allegorical way he interprets the Scriptures. While he was not the originator of this hermeneutical approach to the sacred texts, he is the first Christian theologian to apply it to them in a systematic way. His presentation of the Eucharist is also heavily influenced by this approach. The catechetical school at Alexandria was in the forefront of applying this method of interpretation to Holy Writ, and Clement was one of that school's greatest teachers. In similar fashion, Christians today, especially theologians (regardless of their field of expertise) should make great efforts to place the Scriptures at the very heart of their theological reflection. Otherwise, they run the risk of losing touch with the narrative of salvation history and distancing their reflections from God's providential plan. Like Clement, they should also not be afraid to try innovative types of exegesis that will offer relevant and meaningful insights into the Word of God for people today. In its day, the allegorical method was an important exegetical tool for translating the insights of Christianity to the Hellenic world. Christians today need to find similar tools that will translate the riches of the Scriptures and the Eucharist to their world.

3. As a layman, Clement offers one of the most creative and innovative presentations of Christian theology of his day and possibly even of the entire patristic era. He does so at a time when clergy and laity were still emerging as identifiable classes within the Church and when the boundaries between orthodoxy and heterodoxy were

much more porous than previously thought. Clement's theology in general and his presentation of the Eucharist in particular represent a bold attempt on his part to make sense of the faith in a way that all Christians could understand it. Unlike his Gnostic counterparts, his Christian Gnosis was not meant for a spiritual elite, but for Christians everywhere. His threefold program of persuasion, education, and initiation into the mysteries of the faith represented a walk that everyone could follow. When seen in this light, the Eucharist takes on even greater significance in Clement's thought. This celebration was not some esoteric mystery cult intended for a select few, but a sacrificial means celebrated by the entire community. Following Clement's example, today's clergy and laity alike should be encouraged to explore creative and innovative ways of probing the depths of their faith and sharing it with the wider believing community.

4. In line with the above, Clement's innovative theology comes not from a hierarchically organized diocesan structure, but a loosely organized school that emphasized both the desire for learning and the love of God. The Christian Academy at Alexandria held a prominent place in ancient Christianity. Although similar schools existed in Caesarea in Palestine, and in Antioch, it was by far the most prestigious, largely on account of the teachers who taught there (e.g., Pantaenus, Clement, Origen), the great Alexandrian libraries it had at its disposal (e.g., the Serapeion, the Museum), and the theological method developed there. While this school had a definite approach to Christian learning, it resembled more an informal study group rather than a tightly organized institutional curriculum. While the lecture (and not the Eucharist) was its central activity, Clement's writings indicate a deep appreciation for the Eucharistic celebration and its importance for the life of the Christian faithful. Today, centers of Christian learning may wish to foster a similar appreciation for Church worship and emphasize the strong links that exist between worship, the world of thought, and Christian action.

5. A contemplative at heart, Clement explains the Christian faith in terms of the acquisition of deeper and deeper insights into the nature of the divine. This Christian Gnosis lies at the heart of his theology and colors nearly everything in its path. His teaching

on the Eucharist is no exception. Clement explains the Eucharist as
an important means through which Christians can have direct access to the Divine Logos, the living Word of God who orders all of
reality according to the principle of divine reason. At the same time,
Clement's Gnosis is a rational mysticism, but one that denigrates the
affective side of human existence in the course of extolling the role
of "holy indifference" (*apatheia*) in the spiritual life. Christians today
would do well to develop Clement's link between the Eucharist and
contemplation, an important emphasis in a world hungering for a
sense of spiritual well-being. It would probably not be wise for them,
however, actively to promote a spirituality that downgrades the role of
human affectivity in the spiritual life. While control of the passions is
important for spiritual growth, their repression or even the complete
elimination is not. Today's Christians can learn from the particular
approach to Christian mysticism taken by Clement and the way he
relates it to Eucharist.

These observations are just some of the relevant ways in which
Clement's presentation of the Eucharist could influence the approach
today's Christians ought to take to the sacrament. While in no way
complete, it demonstrates not only the importance of an innovative
thinker such as Clement for his own time, but also how his insights
might be adapted to speak the needs of believers and non-believers
alike in the world today.

Conclusion

In his teaching and in his writings, Clement of Alexandria
sought to reconcile two very different worlds: the Christian and
the Greek. In doing so, he made great efforts to translate the key
concepts of the Christian faith into a form that would be understandable and palatable to Greek tastes, while remaining staunchly
loyal to apostolic tradition. Although he did not always succeed in
this attempt (nearly every translation falters), he was not afraid to
risk innovative thinking for the sake of the Gospel.

In a similar way, Clement's attempt to promote an authentic
Christian Gnosis shows his desire to counteract the heterodox Gnos-

tic movements that were making strong inroads into the religious mindset of his day. One way he was able to offset these unhealthy influences was through the strong sacramental realism he brought to his Eucharistic teaching. While Gnostics would never allow elements from the material world such as bread and wine to mediate an experience of the divine, Clement used an understanding of how God works through them to lead believers into an ever deeper and deeper experience of the Logos. To explain how this process took place, he borrowed concepts from Platonic and especially Stoic philosophy to describe the mingling of human and divine that initiated a process of humanity's divinization.

When seen in this light, Clement's teaching on the Eucharist represents not only a tool against heterodox Gnostic movements, but also a means of translating authentic Christian belief for the predominantly Hellenistic mindset of his day. His teaching on the Eucharist, in other words, served not only to counter the Gnostic distaste for the material world, but also to translate the Christian faith to Greek culture. As such, it served as a touchstone of orthodoxy and as a tool of inculturation. Although today's Christians live in a world very different from the one inhabited by Clement, they can learn a great deal from the approach he took to the Eucharist and the way it can be used both to preserve and promote the integrity of the faith.

Reflection Questions

1. Clement sought to express Christianity in the Hellenistic culture of his day. Is something similar needed today? How would you describe the relationship between Christianity and the culture in which you find yourself living at present? What role does the Eucharist play in this relationship?

2. Although Clement emphasizes Greek philosophy in the presentation of the faith, Scripture still permeates most of his thought. What is your understanding of the relationship between philosophy and Christian revelation? Which do you rely upon more?

To what extent do you use Scripture in your presentation of the faith? In your presentation of the Eucharist? How does it differ from Clement's?

3. Clement develops a Christian Gnosis that is meant not for some spiritual elite, but for everyone. Do you accept the idea of a Christian Gnosis? If so, what are its essential ingredients? What value do you find in it? Where does the Eucharist fit into it? How would you present it to your fellow Christians? How would you present it to non-believers?

4. Clement develops his theology not in the setting of an organized local church, but in the context of a loosely structured school. What is your understanding of the relationship between academic thinkers and the Church's teaching office? Are they parallel? Confrontational? Complementary? How do the educational roles of each differ? How are they the same? What service does each give to the life of the Church? What contributions can each make to the theology of the Eucharist?

5. Clement offers a contemplative understanding of the Eucharist. Can you think of any other ways of emphasizing the contemplative dimensions of the Christian faith? Can you think of any other ways of emphasizing the contemplative dimensions of the Eucharist?

Voice Eight

Tertullian of Carthage
Emerging Concepts

[W]hen He established the covenant sealed with His blood by speaking of the cup, He also proved the reality of His body, for blood can belong to no other body than one of flesh. For even if some type of body other than one of flesh should be brought forward in argument against us, unless it be of flesh, it surely will not have blood. Thus, the proof of the body will stand on the testimony of the flesh, and the proof of the flesh will stand on the testimony of the blood.

Tertullian of Carthage

Have you ever sought to probe the depths of the Eucharist in a systematic way? Although Tertullian of Carthage (160-220), our next voice from the past, was not an organized thinker of this kind, he developed much of the Latin terminology that would eventually make such deep theological reflection possible. Tertullian was a prolific author (some thirty-eight of his tracts survive), as well as a man of great wit and creativity. Although he never wrote a work dedicated solely to the Eucharist, his teaching on the sacrament has great relevance for the insights it offers us into the faith and practice of the early third-century African Church. It also raises some important questions about our own understanding of the sacrament and the way we should celebrate it.

General Insights

A gifted lawyer from Carthage, Tertullian became both a Christian and a presbyter during his late thirties (c. 197). For reasons due largely to questions of Church order and personal temperament, he eventually switched his allegiance to the rigorist Christian sect of Montanism (c. 205). Even though Tertullian took questionable, even heterodox, positions in his later years, his contribution to Latin theology was still by no means small. Because he developed many of the key words and concepts of the emerging Latin theology, he is considered one of the greatest and most influential of the early third-century Christian writers. Tertullian's thought on the Eucharist is dispersed throughout his writings. He uses many terms and phrases when referring to it: "God's feast," "the Lord's Supper," and "the *sacramentum* of the bread and the cup," to name but a few.[1]

One of Tertullian's more interesting descriptions comes in a brief account of its relation to the sacraments of baptism and confirmation:

> The flesh, indeed, is washed, in order that the soul may be cleansed, the flesh is anointed, that the soul may be consecrated, the flesh is signed (with the cross) that the soul too may be fortified; the flesh is shadowed with the imposition of hands that the soul also may be illuminated by the Spirit; the flesh feeds on the body and blood of Christ, that the soul likewise may fatten on *its* God.[2]

In this brief description, he makes a clear reference to the material and spiritual dimensions of the sacraments. What happens externally to the flesh also has internal, spiritual effects. The soul is purified and cleaned through the washing of the body at baptism. It is consecrated, fortified, and enlightened through the anointing, the signing of the cross, and the imposition of hands at confirmation. It is nourished when we eat the body and blood of Christ at the Eucharist.

The Eucharist, for Tertullian, offers us both bodily and spiritual nourishment. His emphasis, however, is clearly on the latter. The Eucharist fattens the soul on God, giving it the necessary strength and spiritual muscle it needs to walk the way of the Lord Jesus.

---

1. The English terms come respectively from *On the Games* (*De spectaculis*), 13 (*ANF*, 3:85); *To My Wife* (*Ad Uxorem*), 2.4 (*ANF*, 4:46); and *Against Marcion* (*Adversus Marcionem*), 5.8 (*ANF*, 4:445). For a summary of Tertullian's Eucharistic teaching and a fuller list of the Latin terms he uses to designate the sacrament, see *Pat.*, 2:335-36. See also Victor Saxer, "Tertullian" (*EEC*, 132-55).
2. *On the Resurrection of the Dead*, 8 (*ANF*, 3:551).

Three Key Concepts

Since Tertullian does not give us a systematic presentation of his teaching on the Eucharist, it would be a mistake to project later understandings of the sacrament onto his own. In general, he presents the Eucharist as: (1) a prophetic prefiguring of Christ's passion, (2) a spiritual sacrifice and oblation, and (3) a *sacramentum* of the real presence. With these concepts, he is breaking new ground in Latin theology. He does not prioritize these insights or discuss how each of them relates to the others. Nor does he deal with possible tensions or explain seeming contradictions. His innovative thinking will be tested and further refined by later thinkers.

1. *Prophetic Prefiguring.* In his refutation of the followers of the Docetic teacher Marcion, Tertullian refers to the bread and wine of the Eucharist as a "figure" (*figura*) of the body and blood of Christ.[3] His use of this term has sparked sharp debate among Protestant and Catholic commentators, who interpret it respectively along symbolic or realistic lines. When one recognizes that Tertullian is arguing against Gnostic dualism and Docetism, and that he combats these heresies by affirming the strong continuity between the New and Old Testaments, as well as the unity of God's salvific action, yet a third possibility arises. Tertullian points out many prophetic prefigurings of the Eucharist in the Old Testament (e.g., Gn 49:11; Jer 11:19). In the same way, the bread and wine of the Eucharist are themselves a prophetic prefiguring of Jesus' passion and death on the cross.[4] When seen in this light, the use of the term "figure" underscores the prophetic element of the Eucharistic celebration. Since a prophetic utterance effects what it signifies, there is thus a close, intimate bond between the celebration of the Eucharist and Jesus' paschal mystery.

2. *A Spiritual Sacrifice.* Tertullian also underscores the sacrificial dimension of the Eucharist. Even if they are unable to receive communion because they have not been able to keep the Eucharistic fast,

---

3. *Against Marcion*, 440 (*ANF*, 3:417-19).
4. See *Against Marcion*, 3.19 (*ANF*, 3:337-38); 4:40 (*ANF*, 3:417-19). For an explanation, see Saxer, "Tertullian," 141-45.

he encourages his readers to "stand at the altar" and "participate" in this "sacrificial prayer."[5] He depicts the Eucharist as a "new sacrifice," and an "eternal sacrifice."[6] For Tertullian, the sacrifice of the New Covenant was prefigured in the sacrifices of the Old, especially in those involved in Jewish temple worship. He underscores both the ecclesial dimensions of the Eucharistic sacrifice and promotes its primary spiritual significance for his readers. For Tertullian, whenever it celebrates the Eucharist, the community of believers offers Jesus' sacrifice on the cross on Good Friday in a real, yet spiritual, way. Intimately bound up with the event of Calvary, this sacrifice is more than a mere symbol, yet not the actual historical event itself. Because it prefigures Jesus' sacrificial death it embraces what happened there, yet also points beyond it. The Eucharist points to Jesus' sacrificial death—and vice versa. Tertullian distinguished between the two, yet also bound them closely together.

3. *The real presence*. At the same time, Tertullian is very much a realist when it comes to interpreting the presence of Jesus in the consecrated bread and wine. Jesus' body and blood, he held, were truly present in the consecrated species. He uses this Eucharistic realism to combat the strong dualistic and docetic tendencies of the Marcionites, who rejected both the fundamental goodness of the material world and belief in the Word of God become flesh. He maintained that those who participated unworthily in the Eucharist offended the body of Christ itself: "Once did the Jews lay hands on Christ, these mangle his body daily."[7] He also maintained that at the Eucharist Jesus "represents his own proper body."[8] The person receiving the Eucharist, he maintained, "feeds upon the fatness of the Lord's body."[9] When discussing the meaning of the words, "Give us this day our daily bread," in the Our Father, he said that Jesus included his own body in this request and not merely the required daily sustenance.[10]

---

5. *On Prayer*, 19 (*ANF*, 3:687).
6. *Against the Jews*, 6 (*ANF*, 3:157).
7. *On Idolatry*, 7 (*ANF*, 3:64).
8. *Against Marcion*, 1.14 (*ANF*, 3:281).
9. *On Modesty*, 9 (*ANF*, 4:83).
10. See *On Prayer*, 6 (*ANF*, 3:683).

In Tertullian's unsystematic teaching on the Eucharist, he did not integrate these insights of the prophetic prefiguring it offers, its sacrificial character, and the real presence. At this stage of the development of Latin theology, he is still trying to find the terms and expressions that will do justice to this important act of Christian worship. As it stands, his teaching is one of the earliest surviving Latin sources on the topic and, for this reason alone, offers invaluable help for our understanding of Eucharistic belief in the early third-century African Church.

Observations

Nonetheless, the above description does not exhaust all that Tertullian has to say with respect to the Eucharist. The following remarks will fill out his teaching and offer some comments about its relevance for Christian belief and practice today.

1. It is important to note that Tertullian's switch to Montanism in his later years did not seriously affect his Eucharistic teaching, much of which comes from that period of his life and which was itself oriented mainly against false Gnostic and Docetic teachings. He turned towards Montanism largely because of the strong puritanical and rigorist bent of his personality and his deep desire to maintain the purity and zeal of the apostolic faith. His disagreement with the Church of Rome stemmed largely from questions of order and discipline rather than the fundamentals of sacramental doctrine. His Eucharistic teaching stands at the beginning of Latin theology and was considered reliable and orthodox in its day. Although his emphasis on the Eucharist as a prophetic prefiguring of Christ's passion and death fitted well with the Montanist emphasis on prophetic utterances, when properly understood, it fell squarely within the bounds of the emerging Catholic orthodoxy. Tertullian's life and teaching raise parallel issues for us about our belonging to the Church. It makes us wonder how much we feel we belong to the Church and what is the basis of our belonging. Our belonging may be because we believe the Church's doctrines or for some other reason, for instance that we feel it meets our needs or fits our

personality. Such questions of belonging ask us to face the question as to where we draw the line between orthodoxy and heterodoxy.

2. The Church at Carthage in the first decade of the third century was engaged in a heated struggle against Gnostic dualism and its Docetic corollary that the Word of God only appeared to take on human flesh. Tertullian was in the forefront of that struggle, writing several treatises against the Marcionites, the main heretical threat to the Church at the time. He uses the Eucharist as a way of impressing upon the minds of the Catholic faithful the importance of the Christian doctrine of the incarnation. If Christ's body and blood are truly present in the consecrated bread and wine, it is only because Christ himself was already truly present in the flesh. The followers of Marcion had a low estimation of the Eucharistic celebration and rejected this teaching of the real presence. According the Gnostic doctrine, the material world was fundamentally evil and could not be a vehicle of the divine. Tertullian turns this Gnostic logic on its head. Because Christ himself asked his followers to celebrate the breaking of the bread in his memory, the material world was fundamentally good. This goodness acts as a vehicle for the divine to reach out and touch human experience. This teaching on the Eucharist asks us today about our attitude towards the material world. It can be unnerving as well as exciting to think of matter as a vehicle for our encounter with the divine. Such a possibility is challengingly illustrated by the notion that Jesus' body and blood are truly present in the consecrated bread and wine.

3. Tertullian puts the Eucharist in relationship to the other sacraments of initiation. Baptism cleanses the soul; Confirmation strengthens and illumines it; the Eucharist feeds it. In his description of these functions, he emphasizes the material nature of the sacraments and the spiritual effects they convey. The order in which he lists these sacraments is significant. He does not depict the Eucharist as a sacrament that necessarily precedes Confirmation (the common practice of many Roman Catholic dioceses today), but as one the function of which is simply to provide the soul with nourishment for its journey to God. Although he does not specifically say it, Tertullian's strong anti-Gnostic tendencies would also probably lead him to assert the bodily nourishment of the sacrament. The point being made here is

that Tertullian emphasizes the specific role that the Eucharist plays in the life of the believer and does so by emphasizing its relationship to the other sacraments of initiation. His teaching offers some light upon how we may see the relationship between the Eucharist and the larger sacramental teaching of the Church. It suggests the way in which the Eucharist differs and complements the other sacraments, and opens up the wider question as to what are their material and spiritual benefits.

4. Tertullian's description of the Eucharist as a "figure" of Christ's passion and death has given rise to much debate. For some, the word has mere symbolic significance; others emphasize the close union between the "figure" and the "event" so that one cannot be separated from the other without doing damage to their intended relationship. Since Tertullian did not present his teaching in a systematic manner, and since his writing on the subject was, at best, occasional, we cannot expect a highly nuanced demonstration of the finer points of Eucharistic theology. It would be anachronistic to expect such precision from one of the founders of Latin theology (indeed, in this context he was the first Christian to use the word *sacramentum*, which originally meant an "oath" such as that sworn by Roman soldiers). It would be a much better approach to admit certain tensions in Tertullian's teaching on the Eucharist relating to the relationship between its sign value and the reality to which it points. Although these tensions are embodied in the notion of "prophetic prefiguring" mentioned earlier in this chapter, they would only be resolved (and never fully) much later in Latin theology. In any case, Tertullian's teaching raises questions about whether there are any tensions in our own Eucharistic understanding and its relation to the Church's teaching. Some tensions we can live with, and they may even nourish our faith, while others may be more of a hindrance.

5. Tertullian looked upon the Eucharist as a spiritual sacrifice, one that was uniquely tied to Jesus' sacrifice on Calvary. He does not go into the nature of that sacrifice in any great depth. He looks upon it as the fulfilment of the bloody sacrifices of the Old Testament and the one and only sacrifice of the New. In drawing out this continuity between the Old and New Testaments, he affirms the unity of God's

salvific action through history and combats the outright rejection of the Old Testament by Marcion and his followers. By emphasizing the continuity between the Eucharistic sacrifice and the sacrifice of Calvary, moreover, he provides a way for the faithful to participate in Jesus' offering of self to the Father: "There is no greater love than this: to lay down one's life for one's friends" (Jn 15:13). Because they are basic teachings of the faith, we can easily forget the tense theological battles that preceded them. These teachings of Tertullian ask us to consider what we think of the unity of God's salvific action in the Old and New Testaments, especially with regard to our Eucharistic faith. The Eucharist can be seen as the fulfillment of the bloody sacrifices of the Old Covenant, especially as there is an intrinsic link between the Eucharistic sacrifice and the sacrifice of Calvary. This leads us to consider how the Eucharist puts us in touch with Jesus' self-emptying on the cross, especially in the light of the hymn in Philippians 2:5-11, where Paul encourages us to have the same mind in us as was in Christ Jesus. This "mind," which took him to the cross, was one of extreme service leading him to "empty himself" even of his equality with God.

6. As stated earlier, Tertullian expresses a strong dose of Eucharistic realism in his teaching. He emphasizes the importance of receiving Jesus' body and blood often, even on a daily basis if possible. The connection he draws between the Eucharist and the request for daily bread in the Lord's Prayer is a case in point. Tertullian offered practical ways for the faithful to do so. Since many of them were not able to receive communion at the celebration of Eucharist because of their being unable to keep the required fast, he encouraged them to take the consecrated bread and wine home so that they could receive at a later time. Implied here in this very practical solution to a concrete pastoral problem is the supposition of the Lord's continuing presence in the consecrated bread and wine (and thus the necessity of preserving it in a dignified fashion). Tertullian had no difficulties allowing members of the faithful to take the consecrated bread and wine to their own homes so that they could receive later. Although the reasons are different, we too could one day find ourselves in a position where the Eucharist is much less available than previous usage. Tertullian's example

urges us to look at the concrete, practical pastoral problems of the faithful and offer appropriate solutions. If, like Tertullian, we see the importance of making the Eucharist available to as many people as possible, we too will seek creative pastoral responses suited to our own day and age.

7. Finally, Tertullian gives us some insight into the structure of Christian worship in the early third century. He tells us of the reading of Scriptures, the singing of psalms, the giving of sermons, and the offering up of prayers.[11] While it is not clear if this description refers to a Eucharistic celebration or simple gathering of Christians for an agape-like meal, the emphasis on the Word of God comes through very strongly. As a lawyer, Tertullian was skilled in rhetoric and the art of persuasion. He appreciated the power of words to build up and to do harm. He used words to defend the Christian faith against those who would undermine it. He also wrote to explain the faith to those interested in becoming Christians or in deepening their faith in the God of Jesus Christ. Tertullian's emphasis on the Word of God sits well with our present approach to Eucharistic worship. Since the Second Vatican Council, in the West many have grown accustomed to viewing the Mass in terms of a single action of Christ expressed through the diptych structure of the "Liturgy of the Word" and the "Liturgy of the Eucharist." These two integral parts of the Mass are like the hands of Christ whose action makes our Christian worship possible. Tertullian's emphasis on the Word of God reminds us of its important role in Christian worship and asks us whether we appreciate the Liturgy of the Word as much as we should. It would be helpful to ready ourselves for it so that we can try to get as much as we possibly can out of it. This obviously means listening intently to the readings, psalms, and homily, but it also means having an attitude of expectation, so that we look forward to the nourishment we will receive. The Word will then be sown in willing hearts.

---

11. See *On the Soul*, 9 (*ANF*, 3:188).

Conclusion

Although he does not devote a tract specifically dedicated to the Eucharist or offer a systematic presentation of it, Tertullian makes a considerable contribution to the Eucharistic theology of the early Latin Church. He developed his teaching on "the banquet of the Lord" as a way of defending the faith against the inroads of Gnostic and Docetist heterodoxy. He developed a Latin vocabulary for the Eucharist and looked upon it in relation to the other sacraments of initiation. He saw the sacrament as a prophetic prefiguring of Jesus' passion and death, a true spiritual sacrifice, and a manifestation of the real presence. He brought to the surface tensions within the developing Latin approach to the sacrament that would eventually be reflected upon in depth by others and resolutely settled. He offered pastoral solutions to the concrete problems faced by the people he served.

Tertullian's teaching on the Eucharist reminds us of the importance of creative thinking and pastoral sensitivity at a time when some of the most basic tenets of the Christian faith were being undermined by contrary internal and external forces. It challenges us to examine our most basic presuppositions about the sacrament and reminds us of our own responsibility to defend the faith and carry it forward through time. Even during his Montanist period, Tertullian treasured the Eucharist as "the supper of God" and "the prayer of sacrifice." He recognized the central role it played in the Christian life and never lost sight of it. His teaching reminds us of the importance of focusing our lives on the basics of the faith—and never letting go.

Reflection Questions

1. Tertullian considers the Eucharist a prophetic prefiguring of the Christ's passion and death. Do you agree? In what way can the Eucharist be considered prophetic? How does it prefigure Christ's passion and death? Does it prefigure anything else?
2. Tertullian used the Eucharist as a way of emphasizing the importance of the Christian doctrine of the incarnation. Why did Tertullian draw such a connection? Does his reason for doing so

hold true today? Besides the incarnation, what other important Christian doctrine could the Eucharist be used to highlight?

3. Tertullian stresses the Eucharist's relationship to Baptism and Confirmation. How does he describe its relationship to these other rites of Christian initiation? Do you agree with him? Does he leave anything out? Are there any other elements you would stress?

4. Tertullian looks upon the Eucharist as a spiritual sacrifice, one uniquely tied to the events of Jesus' passion and death. Is this connection of essential importance to him? Is it of essential importance to you? Why does he call the Eucharist a "spiritual sacrifice"? Would you use this phrase when trying to talk about the sacrificial dimension of the sacrament today?

5. Tertullian has a strong sense of Eucharistic realism. Why does he emphasize this aspect of the Eucharist so much? What are the strengths and weaknesses of his approach? What are its pastoral implications? Do you yourself have a strong sense of Eucharistic realism? If so, how does it express itself in your life and service of others? in the way you participate in liturgy? in the way you face concrete pastoral concerns?

Voice Nine

The Apostolic Tradition
A Eucharistic Prayer

Wherefore remembering His death and Resurrection, we offer to you the bread and the cup, giving thanks to you because
you have accounted us worthy to stand in your presence and
serve you.

The Apostolic Tradition

H ave you ever wondered where the various prayers of the Eucharistic liturgy come from? Those who have done their homework
know that some of the oldest of these prayers have been associated
with Hippolytus (c. 170–c. 235), a presbyter of unknown origin for
the Church of Rome who died while in exile in Sardinia during the
persecution of the emperor Maximin of Thrace.[1] Hippolytus was
influenced by the writings of Irenaeus of Lyons and may even have
studied under him. He wrote in Greek and was an outspoken op-
ponent of the Gnostics and Modalists, that is, those who taught that
the Father, the Word and the Spirit are merely modes or ways in
which God presents himself. While in Rome, he set himself up as
an antipope from the pontificates of Callistus to Pontian because he
thought the ecclesiastical establishment was too friendly to the proponents of various forms of heresy, initially Modalism and then the
error of seeing Jesus as no more than a man on whom divine power
rested. He wrote various kinds of theological works: apologetics,
exegesis, dogmatics, liturgical texts — to name but a few. For the
liturgy, his name is often associated with *The Apostolic Tradition*

---

1. Biographical information concerning Hippolytus comes from *CH*, 1:189–91; *Eucharist*, 354.

(c. 215), a text containing the oldest extant Eucharistic prayer and which offers unique theological insights into the ancient Roman liturgy. In this chapter, we will examine each of the major parts of this prayer and make appropriate comments about its significance for today's Eucharistic worship.

An Early Eucharistic Prayer

Written in Greek, but surviving only in oriental and Latin versions, *The Apostolic Tradition* was attributed to Hippolytus only in 1916 by the Benedictine scholar R. H. Connolly, O.S.B.[2] Recent scholarship, however, disputes this claim and views the work as the product of two redactors, one who gathered traditional material, and another who expanded upon the material left by the first.[3] Regardless of its authorship, scholars generally agree that the work is probably the most influential liturgical document of the early Church. The Eucharistic Prayer, or "*anaphora*," which comes in chapter four, is complete, and follows a description of the rubrics for the consecration of a bishop. Its opening lines come in the form of an instruction and an invitation to pray:

> Let all offer the kiss of peace to him who has been made a bishop, saluting him because he has been made worthy. Let the deacons present the oblation to him, and, after placing his hands upon it, along with the entire presbytery, let him say, giving thanks:

> > The Lord be with you.
> > And let all say: And with your spirit.
> > Lift up your hearts.
> > We have them [lifted] to the Lord
> > Let us give thanks to the Lord.
> > It is fitting and right.[4]

The context of this opening passage indicates that consecration of the bishop occurred between the Liturgy of the Word and the Liturgy

---

2. See *CH*, 1:191.
3. See, for example, Alistair Stewart-Sykes, *On the Apostolic Tradition* (Crestwood, NY: St. Vladimir's Seminary Press, 2002), 22f.
4. *Eucharist*, 354–55.

of the Eucharist. Immediately after his consecration, a kiss of peace is exchanged, the gifts are then prepared by the deacons, and the newly consecrated bishop places his hands on them, followed by the body of presbyters. Once these preparatory prayers and rituals have been performed, the bishop invites the entire congregation to join him in prayer. This dialogue between the one who presides and the congregation opens all Eucharistic prayers in the formal worship of nearly all Christian churches to this very day.

After this invitation to prayer, a brief instruction tells the bishop to continue to pray in the following manner:

> We give thanks to you, O God, through your beloved servant Jesus Christ, whom you have sent to us in the last times as Savior and Redeemer and Angel of your Will. He is your inseparable Word, through whom you have created all things, and in Him you were well-pleased. You sent Him from heaven into the womb of the Virgin, and He, dwelling in the womb, was made flesh, and was manifested as your Son, born of the Holy Spirit and the Virgin.[5]

As in all Eucharistic prayers that follow the traditional pattern, the presider's words are addressed to God, the Father, in the form of thanksgiving. He thanks God for sending his Son, Jesus Christ, as savior of the world. Through Christ, God has both created and redeemed the world. Jesus is described as a Savior, a Redeemer, and an Angel, that is, a Messenger of God's will. He was sent from heaven into the womb of the virgin in order to become flesh by the power of the Spirit. This first paragraph of the prayer resonates with the themes of creation, redemption, and incarnation. It upholds the virgin birth and contains Trinitarian references to Father, Son, and Spirit. Through Christ, history has moved into the last times and is drawing to a close.

The presider continues with a special reference to Christ's passion and death on the cross: "When He had fulfilled your will, and obtained a holy people for you, He stretched forth His hands when he suffered, that He might free from suffering those who believed

5. Ibid., 355.

in you."[6] This part of the prayer continues the prayer of thanksgiving begun in the previous paragraph. On behalf of those gathered, the presider thanks God not only for sending his only Son into the womb of the Virgin, but also for asking him to stretch out his arms on the cross in order to set his people free. Jesus' suffering and death somehow relieves the suffering of those who believe in him. He stretches his arms out in place of theirs. As a result, those who believe in him not only participate in his suffering, but are also liberated from it. Such is the mystery of Christ's passion and death. He relieves others' suffering by embracing it, making it his own, and giving it new meaning.

After recalling the salvific significance of Jesus' passion and death, the presider then goes into the words of institution:

> When He was handed over to His voluntary suffering, that He might destroy death, and burst the bonds of the devil, and tread upon the nether world, and illumine the just, and fix the limit, and reveal the Resurrection, taking bread, He gave thanks to you, and said: Take, eat, this is my body, which will be broken for you.
>
> Similarly also the cup, saying: This is my blood which is shed for you. When you do this, you are making a remembrance of me.[7]

In this section of the Eucharistic prayer, the drama of the Redemption builds to its climax. The presider recalls not only what happened to Jesus (i.e., he was handed over), but also his interior mindset (i.e., he suffered voluntarily), and his main purpose for doing so (i.e., to destroy death). Jesus embraces death in order to destroy it. In destroying it, he breaks Satan's mortal hold over humanity and proclaims the power of divine love in the midst of the nether world. That power illumines the just, establishes the extent to which darkness can hold sway over the human heart, and reveals the Resurrection. Yet before any of this happened, he instituted the Eucharist for his followers to remember him by and through which they could proclaim all for which he lived and died. These words of institution link Jesus' Last Supper with his intimate circle of friends very closely to his passion, death, and resurrection. The Eucharist cannot be separated from

6. Ibid.
7. Ibid.

Jesus' Paschal mystery — and vice versa. The same Jesus who died on the cross and rose from the dead is present in the breaking of the bread and the sharing of the cup.

After the words of institution, the presider then asks God to send the Spirit upon the Church:

> Wherefore remembering His death and Resurrection, we offer to you the bread and the cup, giving thanks to you because you have accounted us worthy to stand in your presence and serve you. And we ask that you send your Holy Spirit upon the oblation of holy church, and that gathering it together into one, you grant to all who partake of the holy things a fullness of the Holy Spirit for the strengthening of faith in truth, that we may praise you and glorify you through your Servant Jesus Christ, through whom be glory and honor to you, to the Father and to the Son with the Holy Spirit in your holy church, both now, and unto the ages of ages. Amen.[8]

The prayer continues to render thanks to God as it recalls the death and resurrection by offering the bread and the cup in Jesus' memory. It also thanks God for deeming them worthy to offer this sacrifice of praise in the name of Jesus. In offering the bread and wine in Jesus' name, those gathered are incorporated in Jesus' sacrificial offering and become a living oblation, a "holy church." On behalf of those gathered, the presider then asks God to send his Holy Spirit upon them so that they might become one, be strengthened in their faith, and able to praise and glorify Father, Son, and Spirit both now and forever. At the conclusion of the prayer, the people affirm the presider's words with a simple "Amen," a Hebrew term meaning, "Let it be so."

Observations

As the oldest surviving example of a Eucharistic Prayer in the Christian tradition, chapter four of *The Apostolic Tradition* has much to tell us about the liturgical worship of the early third-century Church at Rome. The following remarks offer some insights into the

---

8. Ibid., 355–56.

purpose of this prayer and the role it played for the believing community gathering for worship.

1. In all likelihood, the prayer is not a required liturgical text, but a model or a set of guidelines upon which the presider could base his own.[9] Eucharistic worship in the Church of early third-century Rome was considerably more flexible than it was in later centuries. The presider was given a great deal of leeway to compose his own memorial prayers of thanksgiving. In doing so, he demonstrated his capacity to pray in the Spirit and to lead the congregation in giving glory, honor, and praise to God. Since some presiders, however, were more able to compose such prayers than others, certain guidelines developed over the years as an aid to those in need. When seen in this light, the *anaphora* of chapter four represents an intermediate stage between a self-composed, often spontaneous, prayer of an individual presider and a required liturgical text for all those leading the assembly in worship to follow.

2. The prayer demonstrates the tone with which the Eucharistic Prayer was celebrated at the time. Although succinct, adding force to the suggestion that it may have been more of an outline than a fully developed prayer, it presents Christ as the fulfillment of God's providential plan whose sacrifice effects humanity's redemption. It also asks God to bless those participating in the Eucharist, to strengthen them in faith and to make them one so that they might be able to give glory and honor to God both in the present and for ages to come. Directed to God the Father, but prayed through the Son and with the Holy Spirit, it has a marked Trinitarian emphasis that incorporates the important themes of creation, redemption, and sanctification. It is also prayed by a single person (the presider), but in the name of the entire believing community, a style which, by the time of Hippolytus, seems already to have become a fixed feature in the Church's liturgical worship.

3. Given the above, there are also a number of notable differences between this Eucharistic Prayer and those coming later in the tradition. The prayer, for example, is very restrained in its use of Old Testament texts to show how God worked in the history of the Jewish people

---

9. Ibid., 354. See also, Cyprian Vagaggini, *Theological Dimensions of the Liturgy*, trans. Leonard J. Doyle and W. A. Jurgens (Collegeville, Minn., 1976), 163.

to prepare the coming of Christ. The themes of creation and God's providence, moreover, while present, are not as highly developed as they are in later texts. The prevalence of such themes in the works of authors both before and contemporary to *The Apostolic Tradition* make it hard to explain such restraint in a text that was specifically designed for liturgical worship. These inconsistencies once again add strength to the argument that the *anaphora* is not a full-blown liturgical text, but merely a sketch or set of guidelines which others would simply use as a point of departure for their own more polished and fully developed reflections.[10]

4. Of particular interest in this prayer are the themes in places in close proximity to the words of institution. Later Eucharistic prayers usually introduce these words with a simple descriptive phrase such as, "before he was given up to death, a death he freely accepted...." The present prayer, however, emphasizes not only Jesus' voluntary suffering, but also the reasons for his doing so. According to *The Apostolic Tradition*, these reasons are: (1) to destroy death, (2) to burst the bonds of the devil, (3) to tread upon the nether world, (4) to illumine the just, (5) to fix the limit, and (6) to reveal the Resurrection. From a stylistic standpoint, the placement of so many reasons for Jesus' being handed over so close to the words of institution highlights the importance of these words and serves to unite them even more closely to the Christ-event, i.e., Jesus' passion, death, and resurrection.

5. The prayer makes good use of New Testament references at a time when the canon of the Christian Scriptures was still in a state of formation. Most of these occur in the prayer's opening paragraphs. There, *The Apostolic Tradition* alludes or makes reference to Paul (2 Tm 4:22; 2 Thes 1:3; Gal 4:4), the Gospels of Matthew (Mt 3:17) and John (Jn 1:3), the Acts of the Apostles (Acts 20:28), and the First Letter of Peter (1 Pt 2:9).[11] The use of these references in the most sacred part of the Eucharistic celebration demonstrates the great respect these writings enjoyed in the early Christian community even before the canon of the New Testament was finally set. Their occurrence near the beginning of the prayer, moreover, offers a smooth transition from the Liturgy of the Word that normally came immediately before it.

---

10. See Vagaggini, *Theological Dimensions of the Liturgy*, 162–63.
11. See *Eucharist*, 355.

6. The prayer orients the community to God in a number of different ways. It is a prayer of thanksgiving to God for sending Jesus his Son to bring about the work of humanity's redemption. It is a recollection of what Jesus did to effect this act of redemption, one that ties the institution of the Eucharist closely to his passion, death, and resurrection. It is a prayer of petition, asking God to send his Spirit to unify his people and strengthen them in faith. It is an act of hope that orients the body of believers toward the future so that they can glorify God and offer him praise, honor, and glory both now and for ages to come. It is a celebration of love for all God has done for humanity through the person of his Son. By orienting those present to God in so many ways, the prayer manifests the richness and depth of the relationship that God has with his people.

7. Toward the end of the prayer, *The Apostolic Tradition* makes specific reference to the "holy church."[12] Coming at the end of the prayer as it does, this reference to the Church's holiness can be understood only in terms of what has come before it. The Church can call itself holy, not on account of anything it has done, but because of the suffering and death of Jesus Christ. His offering on the cross brings about the sanctity of God's people. Because the Eucharist is intimately related to Jesus' sacrificial offering, it becomes the sacrament par excellence of the Church's holiness. The Church becomes holy by participating in Christ's paschal mystery. It does so most clearly when the body of believers gathers to break bread and to share the cup. By nourishing itself on Christ's body and blood in this way, this body of believers becomes the body of Christ. The Church is holy because Christ is holy. It seeks to do the Father's will, because Jesus has done so and continues to do so through the members of his body.

8. Finally, the words of institution occur at a decisive point in the prayer. Before they are said, the presider thanks God on behalf of the people and recalls the great event of Redemption that occurred through Jesus' passion, death, and resurrection. Once they are said, however, he changes his tone by offering prayers of petition for the holy Church, asking the Lord to bless it, to make it one, and to strengthen its faith by the power of the Spirit. Once these petitions

---

12. Ibid., 355–56.

are made, he then embarks on a prayer of glory, praise, and honor to God through the Son and with the Spirit. The reason for this shift in emphasis seems plain. At this important point in the liturgy, words of thanksgiving are no longer necessary. After the words of institution, the Eucharist, a word which itself means "thanksgiving," becomes present in a new way. The Word, who was once made flesh, now assumes the form of bread and wine for the believing community. Their only appropriate response is to offer glory, praise and honor to God for the offering Christ has made on their behalf.

While in no way exhaustive, these insights into chapter four of *The Apostolic Tradition* highlight the basic elements of the Eucharistic prayer as it was understood by the Church of Rome in the early part of the third century. They remind today's readers of the important role of the *anaphora* in the Church's liturgy and of the various elements that constitute it. If nothing else, they should encourage today's believing community to pay attention to the theological message behind the prayers that the presider offers to God on their behalf.

Conclusion

Hippolytus of Rome is an enigmatic figure in the early Church. He lived in Rome but wrote in Greek, which was the language of the common people of Rome at this time and for a century or so longer. He was a prolific author, but many of his works have not survived. He also was one of the first antipopes known to Christian history. *The Apostolic Tradition* was both associated with his name and then judiciously separated from it. Regardless of its authorship, this early liturgical text offers its readers a close-up look at the Eucharistic worship of early third-century Rome, showing the earliest extant *anaphora* on record.

Although this prayer is more a model or set of guidelines for presiders to follow than a fully developed liturgical text, it contains a number of elements that later Eucharistic prayers would emulate and develop further. It is difficult to determine the originality of this prayer, since it contains elements that, by the early third century, were probably already firmly rooted in Church practice. The prayer, one might say, is one author's attempt to set down in writing elements of this common practice that could be set forth as worthy of imitation.

As a model for liturgical worship, the prayer is cautious in its style and choice of themes. It also possesses a refreshing simplicity for a prayer specifically written for one of the most dramatic moments of the Eucharistic celebration. It has great importance for those wishing to understand the origins of the Eucharistic prayer and its role in the liturgical worship of the early Church at Rome. Because of its historical origins, its sound theology, and its simplicity of style, the Church has come to revere it as an invaluable liturgical resource. It served in that capacity during the reform of the liturgy at the time of the Second Vatican Council and, as a result, has left its mark on the celebration of the Eucharist in the present day.

Reflection Questions

1. The Eucharistic prayer of *The Apostolic Tradition* is probably not a required liturgical text, but a model or flexible set of guidelines upon which the presider could base his own. Do you think presiders should be allowed a similar amount of flexibility when celebrating the Eucharist? Should they be required instead to stick to preestablished liturgical formats? Is there any way of permitting a more flexible use of such formats?

2. The Eucharistic prayer of *The Apostolic Tradition* has a marked Trinitarian emphasis. Have you noticed this emphasis in the Church's approved liturgical texts? Why does the Church think it important for the believing community to pray to the Father, through the Son, and in the Spirit? Are there other ways that such Trinitarian prayer can be formulated? Should it?

3. *The Apostolic Tradition* offers six specific reasons for Jesus' voluntary suffering and death. Are any in his list more important than others? Can you think of any others? Which would you emphasize today? Which, if any, would you de-emphasize? Why?

4. The Eucharistic prayer of *The Apostolic Tradition* orients the community to God in a number of different ways. When you attend the Eucharistic liturgy, do you sense the community offering God prayers of thanksgiving? Of recollection? Of petition? Of hope? Of love? Are some prayers emphasized more than others?

Are some left out? How are these prayers offered? What part does the presider play in the prayer of the community? Should his role be increased or lessened?

5. The Eucharistic prayer of *The Apostolic Tradition* makes a specific reference to "holy church." In what sense is the Church holy? In what sense is it not? Is it possible for the Church to be holy and sinful at the same time? Is the Church always in need of reform? If so, what role does the Eucharist play in it?

Origen of Alexandria
Spiritual Meanings

And Jesus always taking bread from the Father for those who keep the festival along with Him, gives thanks, breaks it, and gives it to His disciples according as each of them is capable of receiving, and He gives it to them saying, "Take and eat," and He shows, when He feeds them with this bread, that it is His body, since He Himself is the word which is needful for us, both now, and when it will have been completed in the Kingdom of God.

Origen of Alexandria

Have you ever thought that there might be different levels of meaning to the Eucharist? Origen of Alexandria (c. 185–c. 254), our next voice from the past, approached this important ritual of Christian worship in precisely this way. A pupil of Clement of Alexandria at the city's renowned Catechetical School, Origen took charge of the institute when Clement was forced to flee in 202/3 and remained its head until 231.[1] A highly creative and prolific author, he developed a thoroughly Christian approach to interpreting the Scriptures and was the first Christian theologian to comment on them in a careful and systematic way. With the help of this method, he sought to probe the deeper meaning of the Christian mysteries in a way that would nourish and sustain believers in their life of faith. His teaching on the Eucharist is a case in point.

---

1. All biographical information on Origen comes from *Origen: Homilies on Genesis and Exodus*, trans. Ronald E. Heine in *FC*, 71:1–24.

Origen's Way of Interpretation

Before turning to this teaching, it would first be helpful to take a careful look at Origen's exegetical approach to Scripture. Origen develops this approach in Book Four of his *De Principiis* (*On First Principles*), which he wrote just before he left Alexandria for Caesarea in Palestine in 231 C.E. For him, the meaning of the Scriptures — in both the New and Old Testaments — revolves entirely around Jesus Christ, so much so that something pertaining to his life and message can be found in every verse of Scripture, regardless of however far removed from him in time, place, and context its literal meaning might seem.

Origen was able to do so by attributing three different levels of meaning to the text of Scripture: the literal, the moral, and the mystical.[2] These levels corresponded to his understanding of human existence as comprised of body, soul, and spirit, a claim he substantiated with the words of none other than the Apostle Paul himself, "May the God of peace make you perfect in holiness. May he preserve you whole and entire, spirit, soul, and body, irreproachable at the coming of our Lord Jesus Christ" (1 Th 5:23–24). Origen's way of interpreting the Scriptures was thus at once both allegorical and anthropological. To discover the full meaning of the Scriptures, he believed it was necessary to delve beneath the literal surface of the text and to find relevant patterns of meaning that related to Jesus who, as the Gospel of John attests, is "the Way, the Truth, and the Life" (Jn 14:6). At any one time, a passage from Scripture could reveal one or two or all three of these various levels of meaning.

For Origen, these patterns conveyed the very substance and shape of divine revelation. They had great significance for the spiritual well-being of the human person and existed in the very mind of God himself. For Origen, the whole purpose of reading the Scriptures was to nourish the human person on every level of his or her existence. Although he respected the literal meaning of the text as the revealed Word of God, he emphasized the importance of delving beneath it in order to discover its deeper moral and spiritual treasures. To this end,

---

2. This presentation of Origen's ideas about the structure of meaning in Scripture is based on *Origen: Homilies on Leviticus 1–16*, trans. Gary Wayne Barklev (FC, 83:14–20).

he wrote innumerable commentaries on the books of the Bible, the majority of which have not survived.

The Meaning of the Eucharist

Origen's allegorical approach to Scripture offers a fitting background against which to view his teaching on the Eucharist. Whenever he discusses the breaking of the bread and the sharing of the cup, he presents it as a mystery with various levels of meaning, each an essential part of its sacramental makeup.

On the literal level, Origen is a sacramental realist and has no doubt whatsoever that the bread and wine in the Eucharist are the body and blood of Christ. He affirms this very clearly in homily nineteen on the Book of Jeremiah: "If you go up with him [the Lord] to celebrate the Passover, he gives you the cup of the new covenant, he also gives you the bread of blessing. In short, he gives you the gift of his own body and his own blood."[3] Rather than denying that the bread and wine become the body and blood of Christ, Origen adamantly affirms it. Although he did not have the theological terminology to draw the fine distinctions about the doctrine that would be made in later centuries, he firmly holds to the literal meaning of Jesus' words of institution: "This is my body … this is my blood" (Mt 26:26,28). In this regard, his teaching on the Eucharist is fully in line with the teaching of the Apostolic Fathers before him.

In his teaching, however, Origen also delves beneath the surface of the Eucharistic mystery to uncover its deeper spiritual meanings. On the moral level, he emphasizes the intention of those who participate in the Eucharistic banquet: "We give thanks to the Creator of all, and, along with thanksgiving and prayer for the blessings we have received, we also eat the bread presented to us, and this bread becomes by prayer a sacred body, *which sanctifies those who sincerely partake of it.*"[4] Sincerity, for Origen, is essential for the pursuit of holiness. Those who partake of the Eucharist must do so with purity of heart and the sincere desire to build up the body of Christ, the Church. To receive communion presupposes

---

3. Origen, *Homily on Jeremiah* (*Homiliae in Jeremiam*), 19.13. Cited in Patrick Jacquemont. "Origen" in *EEC*, 184.
4. Origen, *Against Celsus*, 8.33 (*ANF*, 4:651–52).

a genuine desire to live in communion with one's brothers and sisters in the Lord. One should not approach the altar of God, if one does not intend to live in peace with the body of believers.

On the mystical level, Origen applies his Eucharistic realism to the mystery of the Word of God: "What else can the body or the blood of God the Logos be but the word which nourishes and the word which gives joy to the heart?"[5] In his mind, the same Logos, who became flesh in Jesus Christ and whose body and blood come to the believing community at the Eucharistic banquet, reveals himself in the Scriptures: "… we are said to drink the blood of Christ, not only in the rite of the mysteries, but also when we receive his words in which life consists."[6] Holy Writ, for Origen, deserves the very same reverence and respect given the Eucharist. Because of the nourishment it brings to the human heart, it too comprises the body and blood of Christ.

Origen, here, is not spiritualizing the meaning of the Eucharist, but simply offering his readers a deeper appreciation of the parameters and extension of Christ's body and blood. Christ's body and blood becomes the Eucharistic species, but also extends beyond it to include the body of believers and the Word of God that nourishes it: "What else can the body or the blood of God the Logos be but the word which nourishes and the word which gives joy to the heart?" This "sacramentalizing of Scripture"[7] does not denigrate what takes place at the Eucharist, but deepens one's appreciation of Christ's presence and action in the universe:

> When we speak mystic, dogmatic words filled with Trinitarian faith, when we speak substantial words and push aside the "veil of the letter" to manifest the mysteries of the coming age that are hidden in the spiritual law, when we carry the soul's hopes far from the earth and set them on the blessings which "eye has not seen nor ear heard nor the heart of man imagined": then we communicate the flesh of the Word of God.[8]

5. Origen, *Mat. Ser.* 86. Cited in Jacquemont, "Origen," in *EEC*, 188.
6. Origen, *Homily on Numbers*, 16.9. Cited in *Eucharist*, 180.
7. See *EUC*, 177.
8. Origen, *Homily on Numbers*, 23.6. Cited in Jacquemoni, "Origen," in *EEC*, 189.

Origen sees the Word of God in the Eucharist and the Eucharist in the Word of God. He wants the body of believers, the Church, to see this intimate communion of the Word that is Sacrament and of Sacrament that is the Word.

Observations

Brief as it is, the above presentation of Origen's teaching on the Eucharist conveys the major elements of his thought without doing damage to the complexity of his overall theological vision. The following observations seek to draw out some of the implications of his teaching and demonstrate their relevance for today's believers.

1. Origen applies his allegorical method not only to the Scriptures, but also to the Eucharist. This method was considered the higher criticism of its day. It worked especially well for the educated Christians of the time because it helped them to explain how the crude common Greek of the evangelists could be the revealed Word of God. By challenging Christians to discover deeper, more hidden meanings beneath the text, it helped them to overcome their initial discomfort with the awkward language of the Gospel texts. Similarly, by applying this method to the Eucharist, Origen is able to offer a variety of levels of meaning to the various social strata of the Christian assembly. While Origen always identified the bread and wine of the Eucharistic banquet with the body and blood of Christ, those with more sophisticated tastes are invited to uncover these deeper truths.

2. At the same time, Origen also applies the principle of sacramental realism to the Church and the Word of God. For him, the body of Christ is not merely the consecrated bread and wine of the Eucharistic banquet, but a much wider reality that embraces the communion of believers and Sacred Scripture. In making this claim, he is not merely employing an appropriate liturgical metaphor or even making a statement about the various other presences of Christ in the liturgical assembly. For Origen, both the Church and the Scriptures are the body of Christ, albeit deeper and more real expressions of it.[9] For Origen, the Logos of God is the body of Christ par excellence.

---

9. See Jacquemont, "Origen," in *EEC*, 187.

All other representations of it, while real in themselves, point to it and anticipate the fullness of its coming at the end of time.

3. In his approach to the Eucharist, Origen thus juxtaposes sacramental realism with allegorical symbolism. On the literal level, he recognizes the bread and wine as the body and blood of the Lord. This reality, however, is only the surface of a much deeper mystery of the presence of the Logos in the Church and in the revealed Word of God. If Origen uses his threefold allegorical approach to Scripture as a way of understanding the various levels of meaning concealed in the Eucharistic mystery, he also applies the principle of sacramental realism to his understanding of the Church and Word. This relationship of circularity enables him to preserve an underlying unity in theology, one that he seeks to sustain in his entire literary corpus.

4. To appreciate Origen's teaching on the Eucharist fully, it is important to recognize that all three levels of interpretation (i.e., the literal, the moral, and the mystical) are closely related. In attributing other levels of meaning to the Eucharist, he does not intend to downplay the literal meaning in favor of the spiritual senses, but merely indicates the deeper riches that the mystery of this sacrament contains for the believing community. By identifying the literal, the moral, and the mystical sense respectively with the presence of the body and blood of Christ in the Eucharistic species, in the Church, and in the Scriptures, Origen finds a way of binding these diverse mysteries of the faith into a close theological unity.

5. Origen's teaching on the Eucharist must be viewed in relationship to the whole of his theology. His allegorical method enables him to unify his diverse insights into the revealed Word of God and to root them in the dramatic movement of the sacred narrative. He considers that method not as an end in itself, but as a divinely inspired means of drawing out as much divine truth as possible from the holy texts. Jesus, the Word made flesh, is the central focus of Origen's theology. He uses his allegorical method to uncover whatever truths he can about the mystery of his life and message. When applying his method to the Eucharist, his intentions remain resolutely and steadfastly the same.

6. Coupled with his Logos theology, Origen's teaching on the Eucharist must be understood against the backdrop of his various

philosophical assumptions. Origen was strongly influenced by the tenets of Middle Platonism, a mystical systematization of Plato's thought that was prevalent in the early centuries of the early Christian writers. As in all forms of Platonism, it recognized the existence of a world of Forms as the patterns in which the various objects of the visible world participated and derived their being. When seen in this light, the immaterial forms possess a greater degree of being than their visible counterparts. For Origen, this holds true for the various levels of meaning in the Scripture, as well as for his teaching on the Eucharist.

7. By making these claims, Origen is not "spiritualizing" his teaching on the Eucharist, but affirming that the material world, real as it is, is only the visible surface of still yet deeper and deeper realities. The body of the resurrected Lord manifests these deeper realities and the Eucharistic species anticipate them in the form of a sign of the end times.

8. Origen's emphasis on Christ's body and blood in the Eucharistic species, in the body of believers, and in the Scriptures should help today's believers to appreciate better the many presences of Christ in their common liturgical worship. He reveals a deep awareness on his part that the mystery of Christ's presence to his people takes on many shapes and uses many different mediums. Origen's emphasis on approaching the Eucharist with the right intention, moreover, points to the important contribution the faithful must make as they participate in the sacrament and sincerely live out their faith. This participation, for Origen, is not something peripheral, but touches the very heart of the community's Eucharistic worship.

9. Finally, Origen's teaching on the Eucharist emphasizes the close link between the reception of the sacrament and a sincere dedication to the life of fraternal charity. To receive the body of Christ without dedicating oneself to living in communion with one's brothers and sisters in the Lord is to receive the sacrament unworthily. In doing so, a person commits a sin against both God and neighbor. For Origen, participating in the Eucharist presupposes a firm desire to dedicate oneself to a life of service in the body of Christ, the Church. Love of God, while not identical to it, is intimately bound up in the love of neighbor. Those who say they love God, but do not express this through

their love of neighbor should not approach the altar of the Lord and receive communion. Purity of intention, for Origen, means a firm desire to demonstrate one's love for God in the Christian community. To desecrate one body of Christ (i.e., the Church) is to desecrate the other.

These observations in no way exhaust the deep spiritual riches of Origen's teaching on the Eucharist. They seek only to point out the depth of his insights and even to demonstrate their relevance for today's believing community. If his teaching has sometimes suffered from caricature and misrepresentation, the above presentation seeks to affirm his contribution to the Christian theology of the Eucharist and secure his rightful place as one of the theological geniuses of the Christian tradition.

Conclusion

It is unfortunate that history remembers Origen more for the exaggerated asceticism of his youth (i.e., his self-inflicted castration) and for one or more of his untimely and quite obvious doctrinal lapses (i.e., his belief in the transmigration of souls and his doctrine of universal salvation) than for his original contributions to the development of Christian theological reflection. As one of the great creative minds of the early Church, he discovered and explored new ways of understanding the faith and presenting it to the Hellenistic world. His teaching on the Eucharist is one such example.

Although he was not equipped with the concepts and terminology to expound the doctrine of the real presence as it would develop later in the tradition, Origen had an intuitive grasp of the multifaceted nature of the mystery with which he was dealing and communicated that sense to his readers. By applying his allegorical method to the sacrament, he was able to draw close bonds between the Eucharistic banquet, the holiness of the body of believers, and the centrality of the Word in the community's journey to God. His emphasis on purity of intention for those participating in the Eucharist, moreover, accentuates the role of the faithful in building up the kingdom by manifesting their love for God through their love for their neighbor.

He also recognized that the mystery of the Eucharist had to offer nourishment to people with varying degrees of sophistication and educational backgrounds.

Origen's teaching on the Eucharist should encourage theologians to explore new ways of understanding the sacrament and explaining it today. His intense loyalty to the Church never stopped him from developing instruments of theological reflection that would at once crystallize the tradition he had received and move it in new directions. While his theological mindset and the philosophical assumptions supporting it may seem strange to many of today's readers, the spirit and dedication that motivated it gives witness to the nature and scope of a rigorous theological program that few Christian thinkers, if any, have surpassed.

Reflection Questions

1. Origen applies the allegorical method not only to the Scriptures, but also to the Eucharist. Do you think this approach is valid today? What are its various strengths and weaknesses?

2. Origen applies the principle of sacramental realism not only to the Eucharist, but also to the Scriptures and the Church. What can we learn from this approach? In what sense are the Eucharist, the Scriptures, and the Church all the Body of Christ? Are they the Body of Christ in exactly the same way? Are there any important distinctions to make? Does one have priority over the others?

3. In his presentation of the Eucharist, Origen juxtaposes sacramental realism with allegorical symbolism. This approach allows him to recognize the Eucharist as the body and blood of Christ, while at the same time finding deeper spiritual meanings in it. Do you find this approach helpful? If so, what deeper spiritual meanings do you find in the Eucharist? How relevant are they to you personally? How relevant are they to the life of the Church?

4. Origen's approach to the Eucharist is intimately related to his teaching on the Logos, the unifying principle of his entire theological outlook. What is the unifying principle of your theologi-

cal outlook? How would you formulate it? How does it relate
to the Eucharist? The Scriptures? The Church? Does it differ in
any way from official Catholic teaching?

5. Origen's presentation of the Eucharist helps us to appreciate the
    many presences of Christ in the Church's common liturgical
    worship (e.g., in the community, in the presider, in the Word, in
    the Eucharistic species). In your approach to the Eucharist, do
    you emphasize one of these presences over another? Are there
    any you overlook completely? How strong in your understand-
    ing of the Eucharist is the connection between the reception of
    the sacrament and the life of fraternal charity?

Voice Eleven

Cyprian of Carthage
Mingling Water with Wine

For if anyone offer wine only, the blood of Christ is dissociated from us; but if the water be alone, the people are dissociated from Christ; but when both are mingled, and are joined with one another by a close union, there is completed a spiritual and heavenly sacrament.

Cyprian of Carthage

A woman once asked me why the priest always pours a little water into the chalice full of wine during the preparation of the gifts at Mass. Having never thought about it at length, I responded by reciting the words the priest says when performing the action: "By the mystery of this water and wine may we come to share in the divinity of Christ, who humbled himself to share in our humanity."[1] I explained that this mixing of water and wine points to the mystery of God becoming human in the Incarnation and that the action symbolizes our hope of somehow participating in the life of Christ himself. This response was a pretty good one, at least for starters. The trouble with it is that the action symbolizes so very much more. Cyprian of Carthage, our next voice from the past, tells us as much in his *Epistle 62*, a letter dedicated entirely to the celebration of the Eucharist.[2]

---

1. See *The Roman Missal, The Sacramentary* (New York: Catholic Book Publishing, Co., 1974), 371.
2. The English text of this letter comes from Cyprian, *Letter* 62 (*ANF*, 5:358–64). This edition follows the order and arrangement followed by Migne's *Patrologia Latina*.

Cyprian and the Eucharist

Cyprian stands with Tertullian and Augustine as one of the three great Latin theologians of the Church in North Africa. Born around 200 C.E., he was trained in rhetoric and converted to Christianity in 246 through the influence of an elder Carthaginian presbyter named Caecilius. After immersing himself in the truths of the faith, he was consecrated a presbyter and then a bishop around 248. For the next ten years he guided the Church at Carthage through a time of persecution and inner turmoil. He was martyred in 258 during the persecution of the Emperor Valerian.

Near the beginning of his episcopacy, Cyprian went into hiding for a period of time to escape execution during the Decian persecution of 250. He did so because he thought he could be of more help to his struggling flock alive than dead. Upon his return, he was criticized by some for not publicly holding his ground before the Roman authorities. His decision, however, proved to be beneficial, since he was able from his place of hiding to encourage those entrusted to his care and to provide the Christian community at Carthage with the leadership it so desperately needed.

A pastor at heart, and deeply aware of the heart's propensity for evil, Cyprian dealt with the problems at hand prudently, patiently, and with compassion. His fair and balanced treatment of the *lapsi* (those who had recanted their faith in Christ) when the time of persecution was over gives evidence of his keen pastoral sense. His valiant defense of orthodox Christianity during the Novatian schism in Rome demonstrates his deep suspicion of divisive opinion and his strong belief in Church unity. His writings on Church unity during a time of mounting divisions root him firmly in the soil of orthodoxy. Cyprian was a staunch defender of the faith at a time when it was being challenged from both within and without. His writings had and still do have a great influence on the Church's self-identity and understanding of its mission in the world. To verify this claim, we need only look to his teaching on the Eucharist.

The Eucharist was central to Cyprian's understanding and presentation of the Christian faith. He considered it a memorial sacrifice of Christ's passion and death, a commemorative meal that was intimately tied to Jesus' passage from life through death on a cross. He did not believe that the Eucharist could be separated from the cross — or vice versa. The two actions were intimately related, like two sides of the same coin. Each embodies the one mystery of redemption, but in different ways.

In addition to it being a memorial sacrifice, Cyprian also firmly believed that the Eucharist was the "sacrament of unity." For him, a person can have access to the Eucharist only if he or she lives in Christ and in communion with his body, the Church. When we eat and drink the body and blood of the Lord we proclaim our union with him and with each other. For Cyprian, the Church is one because the Eucharist is one. There can be no discord within the Church because there can be no fragmentation or division in the Eucharist. Unity is one of the essential marks of the Church; the Eucharist reflects that unity and constitutes the Church both locally and universally.

Finally, Cyprian looked upon the Eucharist as a source of spiritual food and nourishment. When we partake of it, we ourselves become Eucharist for ourselves and one another. Through it we receive the strength to give ourselves to others through lives of service. We are empowered to lay down our lives for others through acts of charity and, if need be, even to make the ultimate sacrifice of dying a martyr's death. Cyprian believed that sharing in the Eucharist strengthened us and prepared us for the difficult and arduous task of Christian living and Christian dying. Without it, we would not have the wherewithal to carry through.[3]

Epistle 62

Written in 253, *Epistle 62* is the only work of Cyprian entirely dedicated to the celebration of the Eucharist. Addressed to Caecilius, a neighboring bishop and brother in the Lord, it refutes the Aquarian heresy, a teaching that encouraged celebrating the Lord's Supper using bread and water instead of bread and wine. Cyprian does not give details about the origins of this practice. Some scholars sug-

---

3. For an expanded presentation of these themes in Cyprian's Eucharistic theology, see Raymond Johanny, "Cyprian of Carthage" (*EEC*, 156–78, esp. 165–78).

gest that it might stem from a certain Judaizing influence upon early Christianity through such sects as the Encratites and Ebionites.[4] Cyprian himself admits that he does not know where such a practice came from and he is careful not to accuse or find fault with any of his fellow bishops. It is possible that the practice was tied to a fear some had of being accused of practicing the Christian faith before the Roman authorities. How so?

In mid-third century Carthage, the Eucharist, Cyprian tells us, was often celebrated in the morning. It was done so to commemorate the resurrection of the Lord in the morning. If wine were used at this hour, however, those partaking in it could be detected by merely smelling their breath.[5] Cyprian encourages the morning Eucharist, but condemns such a practice of omitting wine as cowardly: "… how can we shed our blood for Christ, who blush to drink the blood of Christ?"[6] He provides sound reasons for using wine during the Eucharistic celebration and for mixing it with a little bit of water. He offers numerous examples from the Scriptures showing wine as a figure of blood.[7] He invokes the instructions of the Lord himself at the Last Supper and insists on being faithful to the tradition.[8] He also mentions that water is used by the Gospel writers as a symbol of Baptism, while bread and wine are used to depict the sacramental action of the Eucharist.[9]

Cyprian's most convincing argument comes from the way he explains the symbolic meaning of the mixing of water and wine at the table of the Lord:

> For because Christ bore us all, in that He also bore our sins, we see that in the water is understood the people, but in the wine is showed the blood of Christ. But when the water is mingled in the cup with wine, the people are made one with Christ, and the assembly of be-

---

4. See Ibid., 160.
5. See Cyprian, *Letter* 62, nos. 11, 16 (*ANF*, 5:361, 363).
6. Ibid., no. 15 (*ANF*, 5:362–63).
7. Ibid., nos. 3–8 (*ANF*, 5:359–60).
8. Ibid., nos. 2,9 (*ANF*, 5:359, 360). Although there is no mention of Jesus mixing water with wine in the Gospels, it is referred to in the Church fathers (e.g., Justin's *First Apology*, chap. 65) and is simply presumed by Cyprian to be part of an unbroken tradition dating back to Jesus.
9. Ibid., no. 9 (*ANF*, 5:360–61).

lievers is associated and conjoined with Him on whom it believes; which association and conjunction of water and wine is so mingled in the Lord's cup, that mixture cannot anymore be separated. Whence, moreover, nothing can separate the Church — that is, the people established in the Church, faithfully and firmly persevering in that which they have believed — from Christ, in such a way as to prevent their undivided love from always abiding and adhering.[10]

According to these words, the mingling of water and wine at the table of the Lord points to the process of divinization that takes place in the people of God by virtue of Christ's paschal mystery. It refers to the redemptive action that takes place in humanity by virtue of Christ's Incarnation, passion, death, and glorious resurrection. To use water alone at the table of the Lord distorts the mystery of the Christ event and drives a wedge between Jesus' last meal with his disciples and his sacrifice on Calvary. Water must be mixed with wine at the celebration of the Eucharist because blood and water flowed from his side on Good Friday. That blood and water represents not only Christ's divinity and humanity, but our own humanity and the divinity we hope to share with Christ by virtue of his paschal mystery. Nearly a century later, Athanasius of Alexandria would formulate this basic soteriological principle of the Christian faith in this way: "Christ became human so that we might become divine."[11] Cyprian of Carthage would concur wholeheartedly.

The Eucharist, for Cyprian, unites us to the body and blood of Christ. Not to mix water with wine during its celebration or, worse yet, simply to use water alone, misconstrues the entire meaning of the sacrament. He continues:

> Thus, therefore, in consecrating the cup of the Lord, water alone cannot be offered, even as wine alone cannot be offered. For if anyone offer wine only, the blood of Christ is dissociated from us; but if the water be alone, the people are dissociated from Christ; but when both are mingled, and are joined with one another by a close union, there is completed a spiritual and heavenly sacrament. Thus

---

10. Ibid., no. 13 (*ANF*, 5:362).
11. See *On the Incarnation of the Word*, 54.3 (NPNF, 4:65).

the cup of the Lord is not indeed water alone, nor wine alone, unless each be mingled with the other; just as, on the other hand, the
body of the Lord cannot be flour alone or water alone, unless both
should be united and joined together and compacted in the mass
of one bread; in which very sacrament our people are shown to be
made one, so that in like manner as many grains, collected, and
ground, and mixed together into one mass, make one bread; so in
Christ, who is the heavenly bread, we may know that there is one
body, with which our number is joined and united.[12]

The end of this passage contains marked similarities with a well-
known passage from *The Didache* (c. 200): "As this piece [of bread]
was scattered over the hills and then was brought together and made
one, so let your Church be brought together from the ends of the earth
into your Kingdom."[13] Cyprian's teaching on the Eucharist evokes the
very same sentiments of the intimate union between Christ and his
body, the Church. It resonates with the past and, as we have seen
with the saying of Athanasius, also points to the future. For Cyprian,
the mingling of the water and wine was an essential element of the
Eucharistic action. Without it, we have no concrete, visible way of
allowing Christ's redemptive action to touch our daily lives. If we
are not mingled with the blood of Christ as the water is mixed with
wine during the preparation of the gifts, we have no hope "… to
share in the divinity of Christ, who humbled himself to share in our
humanity."

Observations

Cyprian's explanation of the mixing of water with wine at the
Eucharistic celebration sheds important light on the meaning of the
sacrament.

1. To begin with, mixing water with the wine at the Eucharist
highlights the intimate union between the Last Supper and the events
of Good Friday. Cyprian maintains that the Eucharist and Jesus' death
on the cross are two dimensions of a single mystery. His explanation

---

12. Cyprian, *Letter* 62, no. 13 (*ANF*, 5:362).
13. This text of *The Didache* comes from *ECF*, 175.

of the mingling of water and wine at the Eucharist show why they are so intimately connected. If there were no Last Supper, then we would have no concrete sign of our union with Jesus' sacrificial death. With the mingling of the water and wine at the Last Supper, we come to see that our humanity was mingled with his and that, in some way, our story of sin, death, and redemption is an important part of his own.

2. Jesus himself, we must remember, ate and drank of the Eucharistic bread and wine at the Last Supper. The significance of this action cannot be emphasized enough. The imagery of mixture with water used by Cyprian to describe both the loaf of bread and the cup of wine reminds us that, even before his death, Jesus embraced our sinful humanity and made it a part of himself. When Christ dies on the cross on Good Friday, therefore, the whole of Christ's body (i.e., the community of believers) suffers and dies with him. The same must be said for his resurrection from the dead three days later.

3. If the body of Christ (in the sense of the community of believers) was already fully constituted at the Last Supper, then we see that the Church's mission was from the very beginning intimately involved in the full scope of Christ's redemptive action. When seen in this light, the Church's mission on earth is not only to proclaim the Gospel message to the ends of the earth, but also to make Christ's redemptive action everywhere present. It does so primarily through its sacramental ministry that accompanies and is closely related to its ministry of the Word. The intimate relationship between these two dimensions of the Good News is present at every sacrament celebrated, especially at Eucharist.

4. Cyprian's explanation highlights the significance of the mingling of the water with wine during the preparation of the gifts. What has often seemed a mere perfunctory ritual can now be looked upon with new meaning and explained to the community of believers in a way that highlights their intimate union with Christ's redemptive action. The mingling of the water and wine signifies not only that Christ unites himself to our humanity (in the Incarnation), but also that we willingly unite ours to his (in his sacrificial death on the cross). We participate in that offering whenever we break bread together at the table of the Lord and drink from the one cup. Jesus'

body and blood, in other words, gives us the strength to follow the path of discipleship by taking up the way of the cross, and allowing Christ's paschal mystery to unfold and take shape in our lives.

5. The close connection of the Last Supper with Jesus' sacrificial death on the cross thus highlights our participation in the paschal mystery. Cyprian's explanation of the mingling of water with wine helps us to see how we — as individuals and as a community of believers — participate in Christ's dying and rising. Cyprian saw Christian martyrdom, the giving of one's life for the sake of Christ, as the fullest expression of that participation. He also closely aligned actions of service and Christian charity with an intimate involvement in Christ's redemptive action. The Eucharist gives us the strength and courage to follow the way of the Lord Jesus. Whether through martyrdom or a life of dedicated service to others, the power unleashed in our lives through the sacrament comes through, with, and in the Spirit of Christ.

6. Cyprian's teaching stems from his deep desire to preserve the integrity of the Christian tradition. To support his claim, he uses arguments from Scripture and the example of Jesus himself. He insists that Christians must not change the composition of a ritual that the Lord himself instituted with such care and forethought. The Eucharist is so central to the Christian faith that it should not be tampered with. His motivation in all of this is to ensure that the Eucharist remain what Jesus intended it to be, a commemorative sacrifice that maintains the intimate communion between him and the members of his body.

7. Finally, Cyprian thought of the Eucharist as the "sacrament of unity." Through it, the communion of believers is made one with Christ and one another. Because the Eucharist lies at the very heart of the Church, Cyprian does not see any reason for changing an essential element in its makeup. He considers the mixture of water and wine an important part of the celebration because of the deep symbolic significance it has for the believing community's union with Christ. To do away with the practice (as the Aquarians were doing) would disrupt the community's relationship with Christ and ultimately with each other. If this were to happen, the Eucharist would no longer be a sacrament of unity and the Church itself could no longer exist.

Conclusion

Cyprian devotes all of *Letter 62* to the celebration of the Eucharist. In it, he goes to great pains to defend a simple practice of mingling water with wine during the preparation of the gifts. Basing himself on Scripture and invoking both the example and the authority of Jesus, he upholds the traditional practice and criticizes those who would do otherwise simply to accommodate their fears of possible detection following morning celebrations.

Throughout this letter, we are also given a close look at some of the key issues and controversies going on in the Church of mid-third century Carthage. We see Cyprian's pastoral sensitivity in action and his strong desire to preserve the "sacrament of unity" for the good and well-being of the community of believers. The Church, for Cyprian, derives its identity, strength, and moral fiber from its celebration of the Eucharist. For him the mixture of water and wine during the preparation of the gifts is an important part of that celebration and cannot be omitted.

Cyprian's teaching on the admixture of water and wine sheds light on the meaning of a simple ritual which has its roots in the very foundations of the Church. It offers us a concrete, visible sign of how our union with Christ is brought about and effectively maintained. It also enables us to look upon Jesus' death on the cross as something in which we are intimately involved. Through this mixture of water and wine, our humanity is symbolically united with Christ's, thus allowing his offering of self to become our own and ours his. This intimate union lies at the very heart of the Church's life and mission. Without it, the community of believers would lose its inner cohesiveness and lose sight of the very reason for its existence.

Reflection Questions

1. For Cyprian, mixing water with wine at Eucharist highlights the intimate union between the Last Supper and the events of Good Friday. How have you interpreted the significance of the priest

mixing water with wine at Eucharist in the past? Did you draw a connection between the Last Supper and Jesus' passion and death? Are there any other ways of interpreting this action?

2. The mingling of the water and wine during the Offertory signifies not only that Christ unites himself to our humanity (in the Incarnation), but also that we unite ours to his (in his sacrificial death on the cross). Do you think this brief ritualistic action deserves more attention during the celebration of the Eucharist? How could this be done? What concrete steps could be taken to emphasize this ritual within the larger ritual?

3. For Cyprian, the Church as the body of Christ was already fully constituted at the Last Supper. Do you agree that the Church was involved in Jesus' redemptive action from the very beginning? What ramifications does that have for the Church's mission today? What does it mean for you today as a member of Christ's body?

4. Cyprian saw martyrdom as the fullest expression of one's participation in Jesus' suffering and death. What is the meaning of Christian martyrdom? What are its purpose and prerequisites? Can you see yourself in the position of giving up your life because of your faith in Christ? In what way would you say this offering of self is prefigured in the mingling of water and wine during the Offertory? In what way is the Church itself a martyr for Christ?

5. Cyprian thought of the Eucharist as the "sacrament of unity." Do you believe that the Eucharist lies at the very heart of the Church? Do you believe that it constitutes the Church as the Body of Christ? Do you believe this only in the abstract or does it have any practical effect for the life of your local community? What kind of unity does the Eucharist bring about? What does the Eucharist as the "sacrament of unity" mean in an ecumenical context? What does it not mean?

Voice Twelve

Athanasius of Alexandria
Countering the Arian Threat

We do not worship a creature. Inconceivable! For such an error belongs to heathens and Arians. Rather, we worship the Lord of creation, the Incarnate Word of God. For if the flesh, too, is in itself a part of the created world, still, it had become God's body. Nor, indeed, the body being such, do we divide it from the Word and adore it by itself; neither, when we wish to worship the Word, do we separate Him from the flesh.

Athanasius of Alexandria

Was Jesus God or merely the greatest of all creatures? Should we worship him as the Son of God or merely show him deep respect for all that he accomplished for us? Athanasius of Alexandria (295–373), our next voice from the past, was one of the great defenders of the Nicene faith, formulated during his lifetime, and did more than anyone else to secure for the Church a solemn definition of Christ's divinity. Exiled no less than five times during his tenure as bishop of the patriarchal see of Alexandria in Egypt, he struggled relentlessly to counter the threat posed to orthodox Christianity by the teachings of Arianism. This form of Christianity took its name from Arius, an eminent priest of Alexandria, who taught that Christ was not God in the same way as the Father is God, but a divine being created by the Father and thus the highest of all creatures. This teaching was condemned at the Council of Nicea (325), when Christ's fully divine status was solemnly declared and made a dogmatic truth of the faith. Arianism found favor in the imperial court, however, and, by means of that connection, proved extremely resilient. In 359, at the synods of Seleucia and Rimini, of the bishops in the East and in the West respectively, the emperor used imperial threats and intrigue to pressure the bishops into making sweeping concessions in favor of Arianism. This led St. Jerome to remark that one morning "... the whole world groaned and marvelled to find itself Arian."[1] Despite this and other alarming setbacks, Athanasius remained steadfast in his defense of the Nicene faith and worked tirelessly to promote its legitimacy and theological agenda. His teachings on the Eucharist flow from and closely relate to his attempts to counteract the Arian threat.

The Theology of Athanasius

Athanasius' teaching on the Eucharist developed against the backdrop of his overall theological vision. A staunch defender of Nicene orthodoxy, a position he helped both to formulate and to disseminate, he refused to compromise on issues he believed were essential to and constituent of the faith. By all counts, he was an architect, leading spokesman, and chief protagonist of the Nicene position. He suffered exile and derision for this position and refused to back down when it was later brought into question. Such courage in the face of adversity lent authority to his words and raised his stature as the leading theological voice of his day. No less a figure than the Cappadocian bishop-theologian, Gregory of Nazianzus (329/30–c. 390), considered him "the pillar of the Church."[2] Such testimony adds even more weight to the widely held position that no other figure of fourth-century Christianity had greater impact on the future of the Church than he.

Athanasius' contribution to Christian theology comes in his presentation of the doctrines of the Trinity and the Logos (i.e., Word). Although he was neither systematic in approach nor sophisticated in questions of literary style, he went to great lengths to ensure that he was clear in meaning and precise in his usage of terms. The fact that many of his writings were composed while in exile and written under pressure to combat specific Arian claims helps to explain why he favored substance over form and dialectic conciseness over rhetorical flourish.

---

1. Cited in *CH*, 1:255.
2. Ibid., 1:381.

In marked contrast to Arius, who claimed that the Logos was a created intermediary between the Godhead and creation, Athanasius affirmed that the Son was one in being (*homoousios*) with the Father. This language indicated that the Son was not a creation of the Father's will, but generated from the Father. The Father and the Son, in other words, shared the same divine nature and were distinct from one another only by virtue of their mutual relationship. The Father is the generator; the Son, the generated; the Father is the origin; the Son is derived from that origin, but still sharing in the same divine nature. In part through Athanasius' influence, this language found its way into the Nicene Creed and became the rallying point for the orthodox position. As bishop of Alexandria, Athanasius would later affirm that Christ was one Person in both his humanity and divinity and that Mary was Theotokos (i.e., Mother of God), a position solemnly defined years later at the Council of Ephesus (431).

A proper assessment of Athanasius' Trinitarian and Christological teachings requires the backdrop of his innovative contribution to the theology of redemption. His soteriological principle that God became human so that humanity might become divine presupposes the juxtaposition of the divine and human in Christ. Jesus, for Athanasius, was both God *and* man. He could not be God, however, if the Logos did not possess the same divine nature as the Father. Nor could he be truly human, if his humanity was a mere cosmetic overlay. Although he did not possess the theological terminology that would enable later generations of Christians to articulate a comprehensive and highly nuanced response, his intuition into the purpose and scope of God's redemptive plan was very much on target. Athanasius' teaching on the Eucharist is an outgrowth of his understanding of God's redemptive plan for humanity.[3]

Athanasius' Eucharistic Teaching

Two specific passages from Athanasius' writings provide a good glimpse into his theological understanding of the Eucharist. The first comes from his fourth letter to Serapion, where he discusses the mean-

---

3. For more on Athanasius' theology, see *NPNF*, 4: lxviii–lxxx.

ing of the sin against the Holy Spirit. Commenting on the distinction between "spirit" and "flesh" found in John 6:62–64 ("… the spirit gives life; the flesh is useless. The words I spoke to you are spirit and life"), he describes the Eucharist as a kind of "spiritual meat":

> For here also He has used both terms of Himself, flesh and spirit; and He distinguished the spirit from what is of the flesh in order that they might believe not only in what was visible in Him, but in what was invisible, and so understand that what He says is not fleshly, but spiritual. For how many would the body suffice as food, for it to become meat even for the whole world? But this is why He mentioned the ascending of the Son of Man into heaven; namely, to draw them off from their corporeal idea, and that from thenceforth they might understand that the aforesaid flesh was heavenly from above, and *spiritual meat*, to be given at His hands. For "what I have said unto you," says He, "is spirit and life"; as much as to say, "what is manifested, and to be given for the salvation of the world, is the flesh which I wear. But this, and the blood from it, shall be given to you spiritually at My hands as meat, so as to be imparted spiritually in each one, and to become for all a preservative to resurrection of life eternal."[4]

"Spirit" here stands for the divine personality of Christ. Elsewhere in the letter, Athanasius identifies those who blaspheme against the Spirit as people, like the Pharisees, who refused to recognize Jesus' miracles as signs of his divinity, but attributed them instead to the works of Beelzebub. Jesus, he maintains, was not a mere prophet through whom the Spirit worked wonders, but God himself who worked miracles through the power of the Spirit. To blaspheme against the Spirit is thus to refuse to recognize Christ's divinity and his miracles as works of God.[5]

In this passage, Athanasius highlights two dimensions of the Incarnate Word: Jesus' humanity (i.e., the Son of man in the flesh) and his divinity (i.e., his divine personhood). Through the Eucharist, he offers believers his real body and blood, but as spiritual food through the instrumentality of his Spirit. In this sense, the sacrament is one

---

4. *To Serapion*, iv. 19 (*NPNF*, 4:lxxix).
5. See Ibid.

of the great manifestations of the Lord's power, since it allows God to nourish believers on his Son's body and blood throughout history. By feeding on this "spiritual meat," people nourish themselves on the divinity and undergo a complete transformation in Christ. Through this process of divinization, Athanasius' soteriological principle reverberates through time. If God became human so that humanity might become divine, then through the Eucharist, God's divinizing love becomes concretely available to believers. Redemption is not some abstract, cosmic phenomenon, but a process involving the transformation of the whole person.[6]

The second passage comes from a sermon to the newly baptized and lays to rest any doubts from the preceding text that Athanasius may have over-spiritualized the Eucharist or assigned to it a mere symbolic value. The following text comes from a fragment of the sermon (now lost) preserved by Eutyches. It reads:

> You shall see the Levites bringing loaves and a cup of wine, and placing them on the table. So long as the prayers of supplication and entreaties have not been made, there is only bread and wine. But after the great and wonderful prayers have been completed, then the bread has become the Body, and the wine the Blood, of our Lord Jesus.... Let us approach the celebration of the mysteries. This bread and this wine, so long as the prayers and supplications have not taken place, remain simply what they are. But after the great prayers and holy supplications have been sent forth, the Word comes down into the bread and wine — and thus is His Body confected.[7]

Athanasius obviously does not discuss the Eucharist in terms and concepts developed only at a much later date. One cannot read this passage, however, without seeing that, for him, the bread and wine undergo a profound change during the Eucharistic celebration. After the prayers and supplications, they are no longer bread and wine, but the body and blood of the Lord. Although Athanasius does not discuss how the outward appearances of bread and wine relate to the inner reality of

---

6. See HD, 2:147–50, 171–72.
7. *Fragment Kept by Eutyches* (*Fragmentum Apud Eutychium*). Greek and Latin versions cited in M.J. Rouët de Journel, *Enchiridion Patristicum*, 25th ed., no. 802 (Barcelona/Rome: Herder, 1981), 294.

the Lord's presence, it is clear that he does not consider the Eucharist a mere symbolic ritual. On the contrary, it is a place where bread and wine are actually transformed into the body and blood of Christ.

Elsewhere, Athanasius provides a few other insights into the nature of the Eucharistic celebration in the fourth century Church of Alexandria. The service, he indicates, usually takes place on Sundays and is reserved for the bishop or an appointed presbyter. The altar, moreover, is made of wood and placed in a special place of the church. He says little regarding the sacrificial nature of the celebration, although he proposes nothing that directly contradicts or opposes it. Although Athanasius says little else directly pertaining to the sacrament, his important contribution to the understanding of Christ's nature and Trinitarian theology during the time of the Arian crisis provides a firm foundation for later developments in Eucharistic theology.[8]

Observations

Athanasius' teaching on the Eucharist invites analysis and commentary from a variety of perspectives. The following remarks, while in no way exhaustive, consider its relevance for his day as well as our own.

1. To begin with, a proper understanding of Athanasius' teaching on the Eucharist requires a knowledge of his larger theological vision. That vision embraces the divine love shared by the Father and the Son (Logos), present in the redemptive mystery of the Word becoming flesh (i.e., the Incarnation), and spread to others throughout time by the celebration of the Christian mysteries (especially Baptism and Eucharist). The Eucharist, for Athanasius, is a primary point of contact between the human and the divine. It offers Christians the concrete means through which God's love touches and transforms them.

2. Athanasius sees the Eucharist as a facet of God's redemptive plan for humanity. That plan flows from the divine mystery and transcends intelligible concepts constructed by human reason. He considers the Eucharist a mystery and resists attempts to rationalize

----

8. The above details appear in *NPNF*, 4:lxxix.

it or explain it away with abstract or reductive terminology. Even a purely symbolic interpretation of the Eucharist would, in his mind, deprive the sacrament of it true meaning. That is not to say that Athanasius sees no symbolic value whatsoever in the Eucharist, but only that such an interpretation does not exhaust its significance for the believing community.

3. The Eucharist concretizes the soteriological principle that God became human so that humanity might become divine. The Incarnation stands in the forefront of Athanasius' redemptive theology, but needs a way of extending its divinizing effects through time to all believers. The Eucharist, for Athanasius, assumes this all-important task. God so loved the world that he not only became man, but also turned bread and wine into his very flesh and blood so that we could become members of his body and benefit from the fruits of his redemptive action. The Eucharist is the sacrament through which God extends his divinizing love to every dimension of space and time.

4. For this reason, the Eucharist also possesses a strong Trinitarian dimension. The soteriological principle requires Jesus to be God *and* man. It cannot allow him to be merely the highest of all creatures or some other created intermediary. For Jesus to be God, however, it is necessary to identify the Son of the Father with the Logos and to assign a divine status to him. In direct opposition to Arius, Athanasius identifies the Logos as "one in being" (*homoousios*) with the Father. This strong theological affirmation opens up Christian reflection on the nature of the Godhead and lays the foundation for the further developments in Trinitarian theology.

5. For similar reasons, the Eucharist also possesses a strong Christological dimension. Because the Incarnation lies at the center of God's redemptive plan, Athanasius has to find a way of bringing both divinity and humanity together in Christ without compromising the integrity of either. He preserves this mysterious balance by juxtaposing the divine and human in the earthly Jesus and by giving each an important role in the redemptive mission. In doing so, he provides an alternative to the general rationalizing tendencies of Arian teaching and creates a key condition for the action of salvation.

6. Although Athanasius speaks of certain prayers and supplications that are essential for changing the bread and wine into the body and blood of Christ, he does not specify a specific moment when that transformation takes place or a time in the celebration when such prayers must be recited. Rather, by speaking of them in the plural (i.e., prayers and supplications), he implies that the transformation takes place during an extended period of prayer within the celebration. Representing the Alexandrian Church as he does, Athanasius is not so much concerned with the chronological time of the transformation or with the precise rubrics and phraseology needed for that change as he is with the drama of the messianic banquet in which those gathered for Eucharist are taking part.

7. The image of "spiritual meat" used by Athanasius to describe the Eucharist embodies the same kind of juxtaposition of extremes at work in his understanding of Christ. Just as Jesus is both God and man, so is the Eucharist both spiritual and material. Through this union of opposites, Athanasius refuses to reduce the Eucharist to either realm and thus preserves its mystery for the community of believers. The image also highlights the transformative effect of the Eucharist on the spiritual and moral life of those receiving it. Receiving the "spiritual meat" of the Eucharist deepens a person's encounter with Christ's divine personality and enables him or her to respond more readily to the promptings of the Spirit.

8. Finally, it would not be fair to expect Athanasius to have a knowledge of theological distinctions, terms, and nuances that would come to light only much later and as a result of much debate and heated controversy. His own input was crucial to the development of the tradition and is a part of a continuous and ongoing stream of insights that eventually made their way into the core of orthodox Catholic teaching. It matters little that Athanasius was not very precise in describing the relationship between the visible signs and the invisible presence of Christ's body and blood in the Eucharist species. What *does* matter, however, is that he stood firmly within the orthodox Catholic tradition that would one day bring such distinctions to light.

Conclusion

Throughout history, Athanasius has been revered as one of the great champions of the Nicene faith. He earned this reputation through his steadfast leadership, his theological writings, and his willingness to suffer for his convictions. His theological contribution to the Christian faith arose from his struggle against Arianism.

Although he was not a systematic theologian, Athanasius went to great pains to counter the Arian threat with doctrinal clarity and terminological precision. He did so, because he saw the great danger a triumph of Arianism would bring to the Gospel message. He reasoned that if Christians considered the Logos not divine but merely the highest of all creatures, then the Word-made-flesh could not be an authentic instrument of humanity's divinization. This firm conviction led him to help forge the language that would form the groundwork of the Church's developing Trinitarian and Christological theology, as well as the important soteriological principle that what is not assumed cannot be redeemed.

Athanasius' teaching on the Eucharist flows from this larger theological vision and offers the means by which God's divinizing grace touches people throughout history. When present at the Eucharist, believers nourish themselves on the "spiritual meat" of Christ's body and blood. By coming into contact with Christ in this way, they receive God into their lives and allow the process of the divinization to take shape within them.

Reflection Questions

1. Do you believe in the divinity of Jesus? Do you believe it with all your heart, mind, and soul? Do you have any doubts about it? If so, do you know anyone who shares the same doubts? How can such doubts be resolved? Does your belief in Jesus' divinity make any difference in the way you live your life?
2. Why does Athanasius say that God became human so that humanity might become divine? How should such a statement be interpreted? In what ways could it be misunderstood? What does it mean to say that humanity can be divinized? What does it not

mean? What practical effects would this process of divinization have on a person's life?

3. How is Athanasius' teaching on the Eucharist an extension of his view of the nature of Christ? Does his teaching on the Eucharist add anything to his understanding of the relationship between the human and divine in Christ? Does it add anything to his understanding of the nature of Christ's redemptive work? Does it make this teaching more abstract or more concrete?

4. Do you believe that it is through the Eucharist that God's divinizing love becomes available to believers? If so, then what does such a belief say about the nature of the celebration of the Eucharist? What does it say about the nature of the consecrated elements? Is it possible to become divinized without the benefit of this sacrament? What would Athanasius say?

5. Do you like Athanasius' description of the Eucharist as "spiritual meat"? Why does he use such vivid imagery? What is he trying to say through it? Can you think of another way of expressing the same ideas? What are its positive and negative aspects? Can you see yourself describing the Eucharist in this way to one of your contemporaries?

Voice Thirteen

Cyril of Jerusalem
Sharing the Fullness of Life

Wherefore with full assurance let us partake as of the Body and Blood of Christ: for in this figure of Bread is given to you His body, and in this figure of Wine His blood; that you by partaking of the Body and Blood of Christ may be made of the same body and the same blood with Him. For thus we come to bear Christ in us, because His Body and Blood are distributed through our members; thus it is that, according to the blessed Peter, *we become partakers of the divine nature.*

Cyril of Jerusalem

How do we share fully in the life of the Church? What does it mean to be full-fledged members of the Body of Christ? What must we do to partake of the divine nature? Our next voice from the past looks to the sacraments for an answer to these questions. Cyril of Jerusalem (c. 313–87) is most remembered for his twenty-four *Catecheses*, which he delivered in the Church of the Holy Sepulchre between 348–49, while still a presbyter. Besides an introductory address, these include eighteen Lenten instructions for catechumens and five instructions for the newly baptized given during Easter Week. Although some scholars have questioned his authorship of the Easter catecheses, many find the arguments unconvincing and continue to assign them to Cyril. The fourth and fifth Easter Week instructions deal specifically with the Eucharist.[1]

---

1. See *Eucharist*, 64. See also *NPNF*, 7:lxii–lxiii, xlix–li.

Cyril's Twenty-Four Catecheses

Cyril's life spans the time when the Christian Church, both
East and West, was mired in the Arian controversy. He did not
particularly like the term adopted by the proponents of Nicene
orthodoxy to define the consubstantiality of the Father and the
Son (i.e., *homoousios*) and avoided using it because he thought it
promoted a type of modalism. His writings nevertheless display
a staunch anti-Arian position and clearly affirm the divine status
of the Logos. His major work reflects this orthodox position and
offers important insights into the nature of liturgical worship in the
fourth-century Church at Jerusalem.[2]

As Cyril uses the term, a "catechesis" is an instruction to believers
on the mysteries of the faith. They were given during Lent to those
preparing for baptism at the Easter Vigil and continued for the newly
baptized at set times during Easter Week. Cyril's twenty-four *Catecheses* fall into three categories. The opening instruction, known as a
Procatechesis, prepares the catechumens for what lies ahead and
encourages them to pay close attention to the various instructions. The following eighteen instructions are Lenten *Catecheses*
dealing with such themes as sin, penance and faith (nos. 1–5),
and the meaning of the baptismal creed (nos. 6–18). The final five
instructions are known as the *Mystagogical Catecheses* and are for the
newly baptized. These dealt with such themes as Baptism (nos. 1–2),
Confirmation (no. 3), and the Eucharist (nos. 4–5).[3]

Taken as a whole, Cyril's *Catecheses* demonstrate the great care
taken at the fourth-century Church of Jerusalem in the preparation
of catechumens. These people were converts from paganism or
Judaism, or possibly the sons and daughters of Christians, whose
baptism had been put off. Throughout his instructions, Cyril demonstrates a deep concern for communicating the foundations of the
faith. His aim is to foster a sense of repentance and faith in the lives
of believers and to impart a basic knowledge of the creed and the
mysteries of initiation (i.e., Baptism, Confirmation, and Eucharist).

---

2. See *P*, 362.
3. Ibid., 361.

Through these instructions, he readies his listeners for full participation in the life of the believing community.[4]

Cyril on the Real Presence

As mentioned above, Cyril's teaching on the Eucharist appears
in the fourth and fifth *Mystagogical Catecheses* for the newly baptized. In the first of these instructions, Cyril deals specifically with
his teaching on the real presence of Christ in the Eucharist. In the
second, he describes the ritual of the Eucharistic liturgy in detail.

Cyril's words leave little doubt that he believes in the real presence. In his fourth *Mystagogical Catechesis*, he writes:

> When the Master Himself has declared and said, "This is my body,"
> who will dare to doubt? When He is himself our warranty, saying,
> "This is my blood," who will ever waver and say it is not His blood?
> … With perfect confidence, then, let us partake as of the body and
> blood of Christ. For in the type of bread His body is given to you,
> and in the type of wine His blood, that by partaking of the body and
> blood of Christ you may become one body and one blood with Him.
> Thus, when His body and blood are imparted to our bodies, we be-
> come Christbearers…. Do not then think of the elements as mere
> bread and wine. They are, according to the Lord's declaration, body
> and blood. Though the perception suggests the contrary, let faith be
> your stay. Instead of judging the matter by taste, let faith give you
> an unwavering confidence that you have been privileged to receive
> the body and blood of Christ…. You have learned and become quite
> convinced that the perceptible bread is not bread, though it is bread
> to the taste, but the body of Christ, and that the perceptible wine is
> not wine, though taste will have it so, but the blood of Christ.[5]

In Cyril's mind, the invocation of the Holy Spirit effects a clear
change in the bread and wine. Unlike the oil of chrism, which receives the Holy Spirit during the sacrament of confirmation but does
not cease to exist, the Eucharistic elements actually cease to be bread

---

4. See *NPNF*, 7:xxi–xxii.
5. Cyril of Jerusalem, *Mystagogical Catechesis* 4, nos. 1–9 (*Eucharist*, 64–67). The
selection of the texts comes from *HD*, 2:174–75.

and wine and are transformed into the body and blood of Christ. Although Cyril here uses the term "type" to convey his meaning, a word that could possibly introduce a symbolic as opposed to realist sense of Jesus presence in the Eucharist, the combined effect of the passage leaves little doubt that Cyril believes the bread and wine are no longer mere bread and wine.[6]

Cyril is a thorough realist when it comes to Christ's presence in the Eucharist. He uses such terms as "type" (and elsewhere, "figure," "antitype," "image," and "symbol"), because he believes that the Eucharistic elements — the bread and wine — are in themselves already a symbolic foreshadowing of Christ's body and blood . The bread and wine, in other words, are "figures" or "types" of the body and blood of Christ that will soon be made present. To put it another way, Cyril views the Eucharist as having inner and outer dimensions. Before the consecration, the bread and wine correspond to the outer dimension of the sacrament and are "types" or "figures" of the inner reality that is to come. After the consecration, the inner and outer dimensions become the one sacramental mystery of Christ's body and blood. A sign of Cyril's deep belief in the real presence of Christ's body and blood is his caution about not losing any particles of the consecrated species and his insistence that communicants receive the Eucharist with great reverence and devotion.[7]

Cyril and the Eucharistic Liturgy

In his fifth *Mystagogical Catechesis*, Cyril reminds his hearers of what they had witnessed at their first Communion on Easter Sunday and thus provides a valuable testimony to the prescribed form of administering the Holy Eucharist in the Eastern Church in the middle of the fourth century.

In this description, Cyril passes over the opening prayers of the Liturgy and the Liturgy of the Word, but describes the washing of the hands, the kiss of peace, the preface, the Sanctus, the *epiclesis*, and the prayers for the dead, and the great Amen. He also provides an

---

6. See *HD*, 2:175.
7. See *HD*, 2:175–76.

extended commentary on the meaning of the Our Father and offers a detailed description of the proper way of receiving the body of Christ in one's hands and of drinking the blood of Christ from the cup. The latter description is well worth mentioning:

> Coming up to receive, then, do not have your wrists extended or your fingers spread, but making your left hand a throne for the right, for it is about to receive a King, and cupping your palm, receive the body of Christ, and answer "Amen." Carefully hallow your eyes by the touch of the sacred body, and then partake, taking care to lose no part of it. Tell me, if someone gave you gold-dust, would you not take the greatest care to hold it fast, so as not to lose any of it and endure its loss? How much more carefully, then, will you guard against losing so much as a crumb of that which is more precious than gold or precious stones?
>
> After partaking of the body of Christ, approach also the cup of His blood. Do not stretch out your hands, but, bowing low in a posture of worship and reverence as you say, "Amen," sanctify yourself by partaking of the blood of Christ. While it is still moist on your lips, touch it with your fingers, and so sanctify your eyes, your forehead, and other senses. Then wait for the prayer, and give thanks to God who has counted you worthy of such mysteries.[8]

From the above description, Cyril clearly wants his communicants to receive the Eucharist as if they were welcoming a king. The "posture of worship" to which he refers is clear evidence that Jesus is divine and that his body and blood are worthy of the glory, honor, and praise that one reserves for God alone.

It is interesting to note that Cyril overlooks the Liturgy of the Word in this instruction and says nothing about the words of Institution. One possible explanation for omitting the Liturgy of the Word is that he is speaking to the newly baptized about aspects of the Eucharistic celebration not very familiar to them. When they were still catechumens, Cyril's listeners would have attended the Liturgy of the Word on a regular basis, leaving the assembly of the faithful only at the outset of the Liturgy of the Eucharist. According to

---

8. Cyril of Jerusalem, *Mystagogical Catechesis* 5, nos. 21–22 (*Eucharist*, 72–73).

this way of thinking, he focuses on the Liturgy of the Eucharist in this final catechetical instruction because, as newly baptized, they would not have been as familiar with this part of the celebration and needed instruction on the meaning of the rituals in which they were participating. As far as Cyril's omission of the words of institution is concerned, it may very well be that he did so because he had already treated them in some detail in the previous instruction.[9]

Also in this instruction, Cyril testifies to the use of the first person plural in many of the prayers recited by the presiding priest or bishop during the Eucharistic canon. In doing so, he shows how the Eucharistic prayers themselves sought to reflect a close bond between the priest and the rest of the believing community. The priest, in other words, prays to God not apart from but as a representative member on behalf of the believing community.[10]

Observations

Cyril's teaching on the Eucharist in his fourth and fifth *Mystagogical Catecheses* offers a number of insights into the theology of the real presence and the nature of the Eucharistic liturgy.

1. To begin with, Cyril upholds the basic tenets of Nicene orthodoxy without using the term *homoousios*, which does not appear in Scripture and which, in his mind, runs the danger of falling into the pitfalls of Sabellian modalism. In this sense, he appears even more orthodox than the proponents of the Nicene faith. He is well aware of how language can be misused and misinterpreted and therefore believes that the explanation of the faith should be rooted in terms and concepts found in the Scriptures. With regard to the Logos doctrine, he believes it sufficient to say that the Son is "truly God" and "God from God."[11]

2. Cyril's teaching on the Eucharist must be understood in the context of the medium of catechetical instruction through which he presents it. He designed these instructions to prepare converts for baptism and full participation in the life of the Church. Coming at the

---

9. See Cyril of Jerusalem, *Mystagogical Catechesis* 4, no. 1 (*Eucharist*, 64–65; *NPNF*, 7:xxxv).
10. See *NPNF*, 7:xxxv.
11. See *NPNF*, 7:68–69; *P*, 362.

end of a series of twenty-four instructions, his Eucharistic teaching represents the culmination of his teaching to those who listened to his words and are now newly baptized. In this sense, Cyril presents the Eucharist as the final sacrament of initiation and the source and summit of the Christian life.

3. Because of the above, Cyril's presentation of the Eucharist in the fourth and fifth *Mystagogical Catecheses* should not be treated in isolation from one another, but as one flowing from the other and related to the larger whole. In the fourth *Mystagogical Catechesis*, he focuses on the real presence, one of the fundamental truths of the Eucharistic celebration. After having accomplished that task, he goes on to explain to the recently baptized those aspects of the Eucharistic celebration that are new to them. Neither instruction offers a sufficient explanation of the Eucharist in and of itself. Each presupposes the other, as well as the larger catechetical context in which they appear.

4. Cyril states that the bread and wine cease to exist during the Eucharistic celebration and become Jesus' body and blood. From such an affirmation, it is clear that he not only believes in the real presence, but also seeks to explain it through a notion of conversion or trans-formation. He does so, moreover, not by referring to philosophical concepts, but by referring to the Scriptures and the longstanding tradi-tion of Christian belief and practice. The Eucharist, for Cyril, enables believers to become "Christbearers" and to become "partakers of the divine nature."[12]

5. Cyril gears his teaching on the Eucharist toward the newly baptized. He presents the Eucharist in his fourth *Mystagogical Catechesis* as the last of the sacraments of initiation, after having ex-plained Baptism and Confirmation in the previous three instructions. In explaining the Eucharist to his listeners, his first priority is to make sure they realize the immensity of what is taking place before them. To this end, he uses traditional language such as "type" and "figure" to explain the transformation of the bread and wine into the body and blood of Christ. For him, the bread and wine are symbolic foreshadowings of the inner conversion soon to take place.

---

12. Cf. 1Pt 1:4; Cyril of Jerusalem, *Mystagogical Catechesis* 4, no. 3 (*Eucharist*, 65).

6. At one point in his fifth *Mystagogical Catechesis*, Cyril describes the Eucharist as a "spiritual sacrifice," a "bloodless worship," and a "sacrifice of propitiation."[13] In doing so, he clearly intends to associate the Eucharistic celebration with the notion of sacrifice. Elsewhere in the instruction he refers to the Eucharist as "the mystical and spiritual table which God has prepared for us."[14] When taken in conjunction with all that he says regarding Jesus' real presence in the Eucharist, Cyril's writings contain the main three elements of Catholic belief concerning the Eucharist: true presence, bloodless sacrifice, and spiritual banquet.

7. In his fifth *Mystagogical Catechesis*, Cyril devotes a great deal of time providing a commentary on the Lord's Prayer, which the believing community recites together. He does so because those gathered for Eucharist have an active role to play in the recitation of this prayer, and he wishes to make sure that they understand the full significance of what they are saying. As a good catechist, Cyril places himself in the shoes of his listeners and goes out of his way to explain in detail those parts of the ritual in which the newly baptized must assume an active participatory role. In effect, he is providing them with a step-by-step explanation of what is new to them and also expected of them.

8. Finally, Cyril provides a moving description of the piety and devotion with which one should receive the Eucharist. Although it differs in some ways from present Roman Catholic liturgical practice (which has the right hand going under the left, instead of vice versa), other Churches retain it, for it evokes images that even today continue to capture the imagination. Cyril's description gives rise to a deep sense of reverence for the Eucharistic presence. His emphasis on the precious value of the Eucharist and on its sanctification of the mind and bodily senses offers a reminder of how it should permeate every aspect of a person's life.

---

13. Cyril of Jerusalem, *Mystagogical Catechesis 5*, no. 8 (*Eucharist*, 69).
14. Ibid., 4, no. 7 (*Eucharist*, 66).

Conclusion

Cyril of Jerusalem's teaching on the Eucharist in his fourth and fifth *Mystagogical Catecheses* flows from his strong anti-Arian convictions and his staunch defence of Nicene orthodoxy. He presents the Eucharist as the last of the sacraments of initiation, whereby believers gain full participation into the life of the Church and become "Christbearers" and "partakers of the divine nature."

Cyril is a Eucharistic realist, who firmly believes in the real presence of Jesus' body and blood in the Eucharist. For him, the bread and wine are "types" and "figures" of the inward transformation that takes place after the invocation of the Holy Spirit and the words of institution. Once consecrated, these elements cease being mere bread and wine and are, in a spiritual form, one and the same as the body and blood of Christ. This underlying change lies at the very heart of the Eucharistic liturgy and supplies the primary reason for his describing the celebration in terms of bloodless worship and spiritual sacrifice.

Cyril roots his teaching on the Eucharist in the Scriptures and the traditions of liturgical practice that had been handed down at the Church of Jerusalem from one generation to the next. He goes out of his way to explain the meaning of the liturgy to the newly baptized and to encourage them to take part in the celebration with heartfelt reverence and devotion. His explanation of the liturgy seeks to lead his listeners into a deeper appreciation of the mysteries unfolding before them at the table of the Lord. In doing so, he hopes to inspire them to participate fully in the life of the believing community.

Reflection Questions

1. Cyril speaks of the Eucharist at the end of his catechetical instructions to stress its importance for the life of the believer. What are the advantages of waiting to the end of his instructions to explain the Eucharist? Does it generate expectations and highlight the mystery of the sacrament? Can you think of any disadvantages?
2. Along with Baptism and Confirmation, Cyril presents the Eucharist as one of the sacraments of initiation. What does it mean to be fully initiated into the Church? Are there differ-

ent degrees of membership? Is the Eucharist important for full participation in the life of the Church?

3. Do you agree with Cyril's notion of the Eucharist as having both inner and outer dimensions? Of what does the inner dimension consist? Of what does the outer dimension consist? How are these dimensions united? Do you find this approach helpful in coming to understand the mystery of the Real Presence?

4. What have you learned from Cyril's description of the Eucharist as a "spiritual sacrifice," a "bloodless worship," and a "sacrifice of propitiation"? Do you find any of these phrases difficult to accept? Do you find any of these phrases difficult to grasp? Do these phrases have any relevance for your daily life?

5. Do you like the way Cyril describes the way a person should receive the Eucharist? Are his suggestions applicable today? Can you think of any other suggestions that would get across the same sense of deep devotion and piety?

Voice Fourteen

Hilary of Poitiers
Defending the Faith

When we speak of the reality of Christ's nature being in us, we would be speaking foolishly and impiously — had we not learned it from Him. For He Himself says: "My Flesh is truly Food, and My Blood truly Drink. He that eats My Flesh and drinks My Blood will remain in Me and I in him." As to the reality of His Flesh and Blood, there is no room left for doubt, because, now, both by the declaration of the Lord Himself and by our own faith, it is truly Flesh and it is truly Blood. And these Elements bring it about, when taken and consumed, that we are in Christ and Christ is in us.

Hilary of Poitiers

How do we defend our faith against those who fail to appreciate it or who seek to undermine it? What concrete steps can we take to secure the integrity of our faith for those who come after us? Our next voice from the past was known for a spirited and comprehensive defense of the Nicene faith that earned him the title, "the Athanasius of the West."[1] Hilary of Poitiers (c. 315–67) was born of wealthy pagan parentage in the town of Poitiers in east central Gaul; he received a classical education in philosophy and rhetoric and converted to Christianity at a mature age. After his baptism, he dedicated himself to a study of the Scriptures and gained a reputation for sanctity. In 350, the clergy and people of Poitiers elected him bishop. He assumed his pastoral responsibilities at the very time when Arianism was in its ascendancy. He devoted the rest of his life to countering this

---

1. Cited in *CH*, 1:397.

dangerous threat to the orthodox faith. Because of his refusal to cave in to the threats of the Arian emperor Constantius, he was exiled to Phrygia (in modern-day Turkey) from 356–59 and sent back to Gaul only when he had gained a reputation of being "the mischief-maker of the East."[2] Hilary used his time in exile to familiarize himself with orthodox Eastern theology and to write his *On the Trinity*. His main teaching on the Eucharist appears there.

Hilary's Theological Outlook

Hilary produced a wide range of literary works (i.e., Scripture commentaries, theological treatises, polemical tracts, letters, and hymns). Most of these served to counteract the growing influence of Arianism. He wrote the twelve books of *On the Trinity* specifically with the Arians in mind, arguing in favor of the true divinity and consubstantiality of the Logos with the Father. A look at some of the primary arguments of this work will provide a good sense of the breadth and scope of Hilary's theological outlook.

Hilary develops his approach from the theology of Athanasius. He affirms the distinction of the Persons between Father and Son. Each of them is perfect in himself and, except for what makes them either Father or Son, they share all the same divine attributes, such as wisdom, power, and glory. The Son is not a mere creation, but eternally begotten by the Father. Although they are two distinct Persons, the Father and Son both possess the fullness of divinity. They are one God because they have the same substance. Hilary uses the Nicene term *homoousios*, meaning "of one substance," to express this oneness of being. Although he is open to other terms that demonstrate the relationship between the Father and the Son, he singles out the Nicene formula, because it represents the clearest expression of the unity of the Father and the Son. Although Hilary does not specifically attribute divine status to the Holy Spirit, he affirms that he is not a creature and not foreign to the divine nature.[3]

---

2. *P*, 424.
3. See *HD*, 2:259–60, 268.

As far as the doctrine of the two natures in Christ is concerned, Hilary understands the eternal Word to exist with God before all things were made, who empties himself (*kenosis*) in taking on flesh at the Incarnation, and who is glorified after the humiliation of the cross. In other words, he adopts a theology of pre-existence, kenosis, and exaltation. This approach to Christology takes into account not only the relationship between the divine and human natures of Christ, but also the relationship between the various states of the Logos both in and out of time. He identifies three states of Christ who is: (1) only divine in his pre-existent state, (2) both human and divine in the kenosis of the Incarnation, and (3) fully human and fully divine in the exaltation of Christ's resurrection and ascension. This approach to Christology provides a wider framework for understanding the various nuances involved in Christological controversies of the day. In doing so, it enables Hilary to incorporate the theology of the hypostatic union, that is, the union of the divine and human natures in the one Person, Jesus Christ, while also being sensitive to the insights of the opposing theology of the indwelling Logos. As such, it became a compromise formula for opposing positions and became the touchstone for future development.[4]

Hilary's Teaching on the Eucharist

Throughout his writings, Hilary affirms the reality of the body and blood of Jesus Christ in the Eucharist. While this is typical of most 4th-century Latin theology, he provides some innovative ways of expressing and arguing in favor of this important doctrinal truth of the orthodox faith.

Although Hilary confesses his belief in the real presence at various times in his writings, his main ideas on the subject appear in Book VIII of his *On the Trinity*. At this point in his treatise, he argues for a union between the Father and the Son that is natural (i.e., at the level of being) rather than moral (i.e., a matter of the will) and uses the mysteries of the Incarnation and the Eucharist as an analogy to demonstrate his point:

---

4. See *CT*, 1:256–57.

All of us are one in this manner because the Father is in Christ and Christ is in us. Therefore, whoever will deny that the Father is not in Christ by His nature, let him first deny that he is not in Christ by his nature, or that Christ is not present within him, because the Father in Christ and Christ in us cause us to be one in them. If, therefore, Christ has truly taken the flesh of our body, and that man who was born of Mary is truly Christ, and we truly receive the flesh of His body in the mystery (and we are one, therefore, because the Father is in Him and He is in us), how can you assert that there is a unity of will, since the attribute of the nature in the sacrament is the mystery of the perfect unity?[5]

For Hilary, the union between the Father and Son must be one of nature rather than will. Otherwise, the validity of both the Incarnation *and* the mystery of the Eucharist could be brought into question, and adherents of the orthodox Christian faith are not willing to let that happen. He follows an analogical line of reasoning. If the Divine Logos dwells in human flesh by virtue of its nature, as Christ also dwells in the Eucharistic elements in their very being, why should the Son not be similarly united to the Father? To put it in diagram form: Jesus/Eucharistic elements = Logos/human nature = Father/Son. Although the equations are not meant to be precise, Hilary makes it clear that each relationship depends on the others and cannot be denied without seriously undermining the validity of the other two.[6]

In drawing this analogy, Hilary creates a strong line of continuity between his Trinitarian theology, his Christology, and his teaching on the Eucharist. In his mind, the Father relates to the Son in much the same way that the Logos enters into union with human nature in the Incarnation and Jesus becomes truly present in the mystery of the Eucharist. The integrity of these relationships must be maintained for the good of the faith. If they are in any way compromised, then God's plan for humanity's redemption and sanctification can itself be brought into question.

---

5. Hilary of Poitiers, *On the Trinity*, 8.13 (*FC*, 25:285).
6. See *HD*, 2:313–14.

Hilary uses this extended analogy in an interesting way. His aim is to provide a theological foundation for a natural (that is, at the level of being) rather than moral unity of the Father and Son. In doing so, he takes the real indwelling of Jesus in the Eucharistic elements as a fundamental premise of the faith with no need of proof. The presence of Jesus' body and blood in the Eucharist are simple "givens" that cannot be questioned. Hilary puts it this way:

> He Himself declares: "For my flesh is food indeed, and my blood is drink indeed. He who eats my flesh and drinks my blood abides in me and I in him." It is no longer permitted us to raise doubts about the true nature of the body and the blood, for, according to the statement of the Lord Himself as well as our faith, this is indeed flesh and blood. And these things that we receive bring it about that we are in Christ and Christ is in us. Is this not the truth? Those who deny that Jesus Christ is the true God are welcome to regard these words as false. He Himself, therefore, is in us through His flesh, and we are in Him, while that which we are with Him is in God.[7]

From this theological starting point, Hilary draws similar conclusions about the Incarnate Word and the Father/Son relationship. Jesus' indwelling in the Eucharistic elements presupposes the Divine Word's indwelling of human nature which, in turn, presupposes the Son sharing the same divine nature as the Father:

> ... if we live through Him by His nature according to the flesh, that is, have received the nature of His flesh, why should He not possess the Father in Himself by His nature according to the Spirit, since He Himself lives through the Father? But He lives through the Father while His birth has not brought Him an alien and a distinct nature, while that which He is, is from Him and yet is not removed from Him by any hampering dissimilarity of nature, while through His birth he possesses the Father in Himself in the power of the nature.[8]

---

7. Hilary of Poitiers, *On the Trinity*, 8.14 (*FC*, 25:286).
8. Ibid., 8.16 (*FC*, 287).

The point of his argument is to reiterate that the consubstantial relationship between the Father and the Son is a theological prerequisite for the relationship between the divine and human in the Incarnate Word and between Jesus and the bread and wine transformed at the Eucharistic celebration. To question the divine status of the Logos is to undermine God's plan of humanity's redemption and sanctification. The consecrated Eucharistic elements, in other words, cannot be Christ's real flesh and blood, if a real natural union does not exist between the humanity and divinity of the Incarnate Word, and if the Word existing before all time does not share the same substance as the Father. Hilary considered Arianism a threat to the orthodox faith precisely because it denied the full divinity of the pre-existent Word. In doing so, he believed that it denigrated the true meaning of the Incarnation and cast doubt upon the unique access believers are given to God through their celebration of the Eucharist.[9]

Hilary's Eucharistic realism is beyond question. The consecrated bread and wine are not mere "types" or "figures" of Jesus' body and blood, but his *real* body and blood. This emphasis on the real presence permeates his writings and, as stated earlier, typifies most Eucharistic writing of fourth-century Latin theological writing. It bears underlining, moreover, that Hilary's Christological framework of "pre-existence, kenosis, and exaltation" has a direct bearing on his Eucharistic theology, for it offers a conceptual framework for arriving at a deeper understanding of the nature of this presence. For Hilary, Jesus' exaltation comes to the fore in this sacrament. He is present in the Eucharistic elements through his exalted state, i.e., by virtue of his glorified humanity and divinity. When believers receive the Eucharist, they come into contact with Jesus' glorified humanity and, as members of his body, are more deeply incorporated into it. By receiving Jesus in this way, they allow the process of divinization begun in them at baptism to take root more deeply in their lives. As Hilary himself puts it: "… He lives through the Father, and, as He lives through the Father, we live in the same manner through His flesh."[10]

---

9. See *HD*, 2:313–14.
10. Hilary of Poitiers, *On the Trinity*, 8.16 (*FC*, 287).

Observations

Hilary's teaching on the Eucharist offers a number of probing and relevant insights. The following remarks, while in no way exhaustive, seek to summarize his contributions and draw out their implications for today.

1. For Hilary, faith in the divinity of Christ forms the foundation of Christian belief. His strong anti-Arian sentiments stem from this conviction and strongly influence his teaching on the Eucharist. For Hilary, to receive the body and blood of Christ in the Eucharist is to proclaim both the humanity *and* the divinity of the Incarnate Word. The Eucharist, for him, is a proclamation of the mystery of God becoming man in order to make humanity whole. As such, he considers it a powerful statement against the reductive rationalizing tendencies of the Arian threat.

2. Hilary integrates his teaching on the Eucharist with his entire theological vision. In his mind, the theology of the Eucharist is intimately related to Christology and the theology of the Trinity. Affirmations about the Eucharist have implications about one's belief in the Trinity and the identity of Christ — and vice versa. With this in mind, he uses the Church's firm belief in the real presence of Jesus' body and blood in the Eucharistic elements to argue for a similar relationship between the humanity and divinity in the Incarnate Word and between the Father and the Son.

3. By centering his Christology on the notions of pre-existence, kenosis, and exaltation, Hilary offers a broad framework within which opposing opinions can come together and find common ground. In his teaching on the Eucharist, Hilary uses this framework to affirm the real presence of Jesus' exalted humanity and divinity in the consecrated elements. In doing so, he makes the Eucharist the sacrament of human fulfillment. Those who partake of Jesus' body and blood encounter the fullness of humanity that promises to transform them and make them whole.

4. Hilary believes that God became man in the mystery of the Incarnation. Uncorrupted by sin, Jesus' earthly body actually anticipates the benefits of heavenly glory even before the resurrection,

when it will be fully exalted and complete.[11] The Eucharist, for him, puts believers in direct contact with this glorified humanity and provides them with the means by which their own humanity undergoes a process of transformation. When seen in this light, the Eucharist is the sacrament of humanity's glorification and exaltation.

5. Hilary's most extensive treatment of the Eucharist appears in *On the Trinity*, a work of systematic theology dedicated to the refutation of Arianism. In a dogmatic and polemical work of this kind, his main objective is to elucidate the truths of Nicene orthodoxy so that the opposing Arian doctrine will not be seriously entertained and gain acceptance. Hilary uses the Eucharist as a part of his overall strategy for demonstrating the theological soundness of the Nicene faith. For him, the real presence of Jesus' body and blood in the consecrated Eucharist is the means by which God divinizes his people and presupposes the divinity of the pre-existent Logos and the Incarnate Word.

6. From a literary perspective, Hilary writes in an attractive, dignified style that adds weight to theological arguments against the underlying fallacies of the Arian position. His concern for the presentation of his arguments stems from his training in classical rhetoric and his belief that discussion of the sacred requires a serious, dignified form.[12] His teaching on the Eucharist reflects this appreciation for eloquence in style and form. In it, he creates a unique blend of rational argument, metaphor, Scriptural testimony, and rhetorical flourish to convey his deepest convictions about the sacrament.

7. Hilary uses Jesus' testimony in the Scriptures (especially Jn 6:56–57) to argue for the real presence in the consecrated Eucharistic elements. From that base, he argues further for a union of the Logos with human nature in the Incarnation and the mutual indwelling of the Father and Son. On any of these levels, the nature of the union in question is not a moral union of wills, but something much deeper — what he calls a "natural" union.[13] Hilary does not draw out the particulars of these relationships or discuss the various nuances that later generations would put in place regarding the nature of the hypostatic union between Jesus' human and divine natures or the relationship

11. See *P*, 427–28.
12. Ibid., 424.
13. See Hilary of Poitiers, *On the Trinity*, 8.13 (*FC*, 285).

between outward appearance and inner reality in the Eucharist. His main concern is to argue against the Arian position and affirm that the Father and the Son have the same substance.

8. Finally, Hilary took advantage of his four-year exile to Phrygia by immersing himself in the theology of the East, specifically authors, like Athanasius, who were staunch defenders of the Nicene faith. This acquaintance with Eastern Christian thought led him to bring its sensitivities and concerns to the Latin West and to incorporate them into his own theological reflection. In doing so, he gave the patristic era an important bridge for Eastern and Western Christian thought, showing how certain terms translated from one context to another. As an important Christian sacrament in both East and West, the Eucharist gave Hilary an excellent means of bringing these varying perspectives together.

Conclusion

Hilary of Poitiers was called "the Athanasius of the West" with good reason. He staunchly defended the tenets of the Nicene faith against the Arian threat and was willing to suffer exile for his convictions. As bishop of Poitiers, he wrote important treatises in support of the orthodox position and through his letters and polemical writings was instrumental in preventing the spread of Arianism in the Latin West.

The Eucharist, for Hilary, was central to the Nicene faith and practice. As with most other 4th-century Latin writers, he believed the body and blood of Jesus was truly present in the Eucharist and that, through it, the community of believers encountered the glorified humanity of the Risen Lord. Jesus' physical, glorified presence in the Eucharist formed one of the bases from which he argued for the nature of relationship of the divine and human natures and for the consubstantiality of the Father and Son. As such, it proved to be a powerful tool for him in his efforts to curb the growing Arian influence in Poitiers and its environs.

Hilary's teaching on the Eucharist represents just a small part of his larger pastoral and theological strategy to stem the tide of Arianism. By his death in 367, Arianism was losing its hold over Christianity in both Eastern and Western parts of the Roman Empire. Hilary played no small part in the demise of this threat to the orthodox faith and would later receive the title "doctor of the Church" for his tireless efforts to preserve the faith in his own time and for future generations.

Reflection Questions

1. In what sense did Hilary serve in his day as a bridge between the Christian East and the Christian West? Are such bridges still necessary today? Can you identify any people or institutions that are fulfilling this role today? Besides the bridge between Christian East and the Christian West, does the Church need other bridges to carry out its mission? In your opinion, what other areas need to be bridged? Do you have any idea about how to go about doing so?

2. To what extent does Hilary use the Eucharist as a means of promoting the tenets of the Nicene faith? How effective is he? In what ways can today's believers use the Eucharist as a means of promoting Catholic orthodoxy? How effective an instrument would this be? What would the advantages be in using such an approach? Can you see any drawbacks?

3. What does it mean to say that the union between the Father and Son must be one of nature rather than will? Which type of union is more fundamental? To what extent do the doctrines of the Incarnation and the Eucharist rest on the assertion that the Father and Son share the same divine nature? Why is this substantial union between the Father and the Son so important?

4. Do you agree with Hilary's basic analogy that Jesus/Eucharistic elements = Logos/human nature = Father /Son? Does Hilary mean this analogy to hold on every point? What are the strengths and weakness of such a depiction? How does this analogy preserve the continuity between Trinitarian theology, the understanding of the nature of Christ, and the doctrine of the Eucharist?

5. What does Hilary mean when he says that Jesus is present in the Eucharist through his exalted state? What does such an affirmation say about the nature of one's encounter with Christ in the Eucharist? Is the resulting union substantial or moral in nature? Is it a union of natures or of wills? Why are such distinctions important?

Voice Fifteen

Ambrose of Milan
Food for the Journey

Before it be consecrated it is bread, but where the words of
Christ come in, it is the Body of Christ. Finally, hear Him
saying: "All of you take and eat of this, for this is My Body."
And before the words of Christ the chalice is full of wine
and water, but where the words of Christ have been operative it is made the Blood of Christ, which redeems people.

Ambrose of Milan

What kind of leaders did the early Church need? How were
these leaders selected? How did they develop their teaching on the
Eucharist? Our next voice from the past was one of the most influential Latin bishops of the fourth century. Ambrose of Milan (339–97)
was born in Trier of an aristocratic Roman family. He trained in law
and rhetoric, and eventually became the Roman Prefect of northern
Italy with his residence in Milan. In 374, the clergy and people of
Milan elected him their bishop. Since he was only a catechumen at
the time, it was necessary for him to be ordained deacon, presbyter,
and bishop within the short space of a week. After his episcopal consecration, and as an important prelude to the proper administration
of his pastoral duties, he immersed himself in theological studies
and eventually became an expert pastor, theologian, and Church
administrator. In keeping with his Roman education and upbring-
ing, Ambrose was eminently practical in his theological and pastoral
outlook. His teaching on the Eucharist reflects the deep concerns of
a shepherd for nourishing his flock during a time of great social and
spiritual unrest within the empire.[1]

---

1. See *P*, 443–45; *CH*, 1:398–400.

Ambrose's Theological Outlook

As bishop of Milan, Ambrose fought to uphold the rights and practice of orthodox Christian belief against paganism, Arianism, and Roman imperial power. While he relied on the Greek fathers for his dogmatic works, his moral and ascetical writings contain many original insights. His primary concern in his sermons and catechetical writings was to convey to his listeners the proper course of upright Christian action. Although he had received a sound classical education, he had neither the time nor the interest to engage in needless abstract speculation on the mysteries of faith.[2]

In keeping with his Roman propensities for order, Ambrose set to organize the doctrinal truths of the Christian faith into a well-balanced whole, trying his best to harmonize the best insights of both East and West. He carried out his theological endeavors with true discernment, careful to distinguish sound from unsound doctrine. With regard to the Trinity, he was a defender of Nicene orthodoxy, upholding the divinity of the Logos and attributing divine status to the Holy Spirit. In his understanding of Christ, he affirmed the relation between Christ's humanity and divinity as being One in two natures. In his theology of Redemption, he affirmed the need for infant baptism because of the universal guilt inherited through the sin of Adam. For Ambrose, even Mary was not free from this universal inherited guilt, although she was free from all personal sin.[3]

Ambrose produced a large literary corpus. His exegetical works include the *Hexaemeron* (*The Six Days of Creation*) and commentaries on Luke's Gospel and a variety of Old Testament books. In these works, he displays certain allegorizing tendencies, but is primarily interested in elucidating the text's moral message. His dogmatic works include *On Faith, On the Holy Spirit, On the Mysteries, On Repentance*, and *On the Sacraments*. In these treatises, he exposes the erroneous claims of the Arians and Novatianists (extreme moral rigorists), and develops Church doctrine in the areas of Trinitarian theology, Christology, and the sacraments. His *On the Offices of Ministers* is a moral-ascetical treatise offering a comprehensive treatment

---

2. See *P*, 445.
3. For appropriate references to these doctrinal positions of Ambrose, see *P*, 452–53.

of the Christian moral life. He also wrote five books on virginity and is widely considered the father of Western liturgical hymnody. He accomplished all of this while maintaining a rigorous schedule of pastoral and administrative duties for the church of Milan.[4]

Ambrose's Teaching on the Eucharist

Ambrose treats the Eucharist in a number of places in his writings. He is the first to use the word *missa* (i.e., "Mass") in connection with the celebration of the Eucharist.[5] He also strongly affirms the relationship between the sacrament and Christ's sacrifice on Calvary.[6] He treats the Eucharist at length in his *On the Mysteries* (c. 390) and *On the Sacraments* (c. 380–90), two very important sources for the history of the liturgy. Although some have questioned the authenticity of the second work, it is still generally attributed to Ambrose.[7]

Ambrose is a sacramental realist, believing that Christ's body and blood are truly present in the Eucharist. In his treatise *On Faith*, for example, he says that elements "by the mysterious efficacy of holy prayer are transformed [*transfigurantur*] into the Flesh and the Blood."[8] Elsewhere, he asserts that the words of institution bring about this sacramental conversion of the bread and wine into Jesus' body and blood.[9] This Eucharistic change takes place through God's infinite power. It is not necessary to ask how the change occurs, but only to affirm that God is capable of effecting such a fundamental change: "... the power of the blessing is greater than that of nature, because by the blessing even nature itself is changed."[10] To support this claim, he cites a number of miraculous transformations from the Old Testament (e.g., Moses' rod changing into a serpent, of the water of the Nile turning to blood).[11] From there, he asserts that Christ could give a new nature to the Eucharistic elements through the words of consecration:

---

4. See *CH*, 1:399.
5. See Ambrose of Milan, *Epistle 20*, no. 4 (*NPNF*, 10:423; *P*, 454).
6. Ibid., and *On the Offices of Ministers*, bk. 1, chap. 48, no. 248 (*NPNF*, 10:40,423; *P*, 454).
7. See EUC, 74.
8. Ambrose of Milan, *On Faith*, bk, 4, no. 125 (*NPNF*, 10:278, 280).
9. Ambrose of Milan, *On the Mysteries*, nos. 52, 54 (*NPNF* 10:324–25).
10. Ibid., no. 50 (*NPNF*, 10:324).
11. Ibid., no. 51 (*NPNF*, 10:324).

Shall not the word of Christ, which was able to make out of nothing that which was not, be able to change things which already are into what they were not? For it is not less to give a new nature to things than to change them…. The Lord Jesus Himself proclaims: "This is My Body." Before the blessing of the heavenly words another nature is spoken of, after the consecration the Body is signified. He Himself speaks of His Blood. Before the consecration it has another name, after it is called Blood. And you say, Amen, that is, It is true. Let the heart within confess what the mouth utters, let the soul feel what the voice speaks.[12]

In these and other texts, he emphasizes the power of Christ's word to change the nature of things into something else. He even goes so far as to say that Christ's Eucharistic body is continuous with his historical body: "Why do you seek the order of nature in the Body of Christ, seeing that the Lord Jesus Himself was born of a Virgin, not according to nature? It is the true Flesh of Christ which, crucified and buried, this is then truly the Sacrament of His Body."[13]

Such statements indicate that Ambrose has a very clear understanding of the transformation of the bread and wine into the body and blood of Christ and saw a strict continuity between the real presence and Jesus' historical existence. Because of this continuity, he believes that the Eucharist is true spiritual food for it possesses the power and efficacy to sanctify human souls. For this very reason, he recommends frequent, even daily, communion and that the faithful prepare to receive it in appropriate ways. Believers must eat from the banquet table of the Lord to receive nourishment for their spiritual journey to God:

How often have you heard Psalm 22 and have not understood it! See how applicable it is to the heavenly sacraments: "The Lord feeds me and nothing will be lacking to me. He has set me in a place of pasture. He has brought me upon the water of refreshment. He has converted my soul."[14]

12. Ibid., nos. 52–54 (*NPNF*, 10:324–25).
13. Ibid., no. 53 (*NPNF*, 10:324).
14. Ambrose of Milan, *On the Sacraments,* bk. 5, no. 12 (*Eucharist*, 83). Psalm 22 is Psalm 23 in today's numbering.

In addition to the real presence and the notion of the Eucharist as spiritual food, Ambrose also draws out the sacrificial dimensions of the sacrament. He makes this very clear in *On the Sacraments*:

> Next, realize how great a sacrament it is. See what He says: "As often as you shall do this, so often will you make a remembrance of me, until I come again." And the priest says: "Therefore, mindful of His most glorious Passion and Resurrection from the dead and Ascension into heaven, we offer to you this immaculate victim, a spiritual victim, an unbloody victim, this holy bread and the chalice of eternal life. And we ask and pray that you receive this offering upon your altar on high through the hands of your angels, just as you deigned to receive the gifts of your servant, Abel the Just, and the sacrifice of our priest, Abraham, and what the high priest Melchizedech offered to you."[15]

Here, Ambrose draws a close relationship between the Eucharist and the sacrifice of Calvary by incorporating into his treatise a portion of the Latin canon directly dealing with the sacrificial dimensions of the sacrament. Elsewhere he indicates that priests consecrate this sacrifice daily and that Jesus offers it through their hands. Perhaps his clearest reference to the sacrificial nature of the Eucharist appears in his *On the Offices of Ministers*:

> In old times a lamb, a calf was offered; now Christ is offered. But He is offered as man and as enduring suffering.[16]

Ambrose's teaching on the Eucharist flows out of his preaching and pastoral care. In it, he emphasizes three primary themes: the real presence, a spiritual banquet, and an unbloody sacrifice for the forgiveness of sins, three themes that would eventually become the mainstay of Catholic teaching. He mentions these themes in many of his works, but especially in *On the Mysteries* and *On the Sacraments,* where he treats the Eucharist in detail. His teaching is solidly orthodox and does not veer off into needless speculations. He is concerned with presenting a clear teaching on the Eucharist, one rooted in the liturgical

---

15. Ibid., bk. 4, nos. 26–27 (*Eucharist*, 80).
16. Ambrose of Milan, *On the Offices of Ministers*, bk. 1, chap. 48, no. 248 (*NPNF*, 10:40).

celebration itself and with clear moral and spiritual implications. For Ambrose, the mystery of the Eucharist has practical consequences for the life of the believer. To partake of the Eucharist is to profess one's belief in Jesus Christ, who is both true man and God from God. By eating the Lord's body and blood, the believer shares in Christ's sacrificial offering and receives spiritual nourishment leading to life everlasting. The Eucharist, for Ambrose, is the last of the sacraments of initiation and the center of Christian life and worship. Through it, one becomes a full member of Christ's body and gains full access to the life of the believing community. For him, it is what binds the believing community together and gives believers spiritual food for the journey ahead of them.[17]

Observations

Ambrose's teaching on the Eucharist invites comment from a number of perspectives. The following remarks seek to enter more fully into his presentation and to draw out relevant points of contact with the tradition.

1. To begin with, Ambrose develops his teaching on the Eucharist out of a strong anti-Arian stance. Auxentius, Ambrose's predecessor at Milan, was a strong supporter of Arianism. As the administrative governor of the region, Ambrose sought to alleviate tensions between Catholics and Arians after the bishop's death. The clergy and people of Milan elected him bishop so that he could use his considerable talents to resolve these tensions.[18] Ambrose used the Eucharist as a pastoral tool for imparting to the faithful the fundamental tenets of Nicene orthodoxy. Since only God could forgive sins, Christ's divinity had to be firmly upheld if the Eucharist was to mediate God's healing and forgiveness.

2. Ambrose's teaching on the Eucharist is characterized by his deep pastoral sensitivities. He develops this teaching primarily in the context of his catechetical sermons and instructions to the newly baptized. In presenting the Eucharist to this group of listeners, he roots the sacrament

---

17. For a summary of Ambrose's teaching on the Eucharist, see *HD* 2:315–18.
18. See *P*. 443–444.

in the Sacred Scriptures and presents it as the central act of worship of the New Covenant. This act of worship is a spiritual sacrifice offered by Jesus Christ through the hands of the presiding bishop or priest. Celebrating the Eucharist on behalf of the people is, for Ambrose, one of the primary pastoral responsibilities of the local clergy.

3. Ambrose is quick to point out, however, that Christians are all members of "a chosen race, a royal priesthood, a holy nation."[19] He has a deep sense of the holiness of the Church, the body of Christ and recognizes that the entire believing community is engaged in Christ's sacrificial offering to the Father. For him, the Eucharist is a participatory event, with clearly assigned roles and functions. Each role is important for the proper celebration of the sacrament and should not be underestimated. It is only when all the members perform the proper function in the body that the spiritual offering of those gathered becomes pleasing and acceptable to the Father.

4. Ambrose was a firm realist in his Eucharistic teaching. He not only believed that Jesus Christ was truly present in the consecrated species, but also that the elements themselves were converted from one nature to another. Although he does not use terms such as "transubstantiation" that would later become the primary means of expressing Jesus' Eucharistic presence in the Catholic tradition, his writings make it quite clear that the bread and wine cease being bread and wine, and are instead changed or converted into the body and blood of Christ. For this reason, Ambrose is an important fourth-century witness in the Church's developing understanding of the mystery of Christ's presence in the Eucharist.

5. Ambrose also looks upon the Eucharist as providing spiritual food to the believing community. This food comes in the form of Christ's body and blood, which was offered to the Father in the sacrifice of Calvary on Good Friday, but which was also made in anticipation the night before when Jesus broke bread with his closest disciples at the Last Supper. The Eucharist as spiritual banquet is never far from Ambrose's thoughts. The food it supplies enables believers to enter into close contact with the Risen Lord and to receive the gift of eternal life: "What is greater, manna from heaven or the body of Christ?

19. Ambrose of Milan, *On the Sacraments,* bk. 4. no. 1 (*Eucharist,* 74–75).

The body of Christ, of course, for He is the Creator of heaven. In addition, he who ate the manna died but he who has eaten this body, it will become for him the forgiveness of sins and he 'shall not die forever.' "[20]

6. Ambrose also emphasizes the sacrificial dimensions of the Eucharistic celebration. He does so by drawing typological connections with sacrificial offerings from the Old Testament (e.g., Abel, Abraham, Melchizedech).[21] He goes on to draw a close connection between Jesus' spilling of blood on Calvary, the forgiveness of sins, and frequent reception of the Eucharist as a remedy for sin: "In His death, then, we proclaim the forgiveness of sins.... I ought to receive Him, that He may always forgive my sins. I, who sin always, should have a medicine always."[22] The Eucharist, for Ambrose, is a "medicine" of healing for the forgiveness of sins.

7. Part of the reason why Ambrose associates the Eucharist with forgiveness is because sacramental confession in his day was public and administered only once for serious sins. Ambrose criticizes those who wish frequent access to this canonical rite, and instructs them instead to perform private penance for their lesser sins (*delicta leviora*).[23] When combined with this private penance, the Eucharist became a concrete sign of forgiveness to the penitent. While serious sins were always reserved to the mediation of the Church through public canonical penance, the Eucharist became the sacrament of conversion in the daily life of the believing community.

8. Finally, Ambrose views the Eucharist as a divine miracle. It is an expression of God's power to enter the world of nature and transform it into something completely different. Because God has the power to change nature itself, he also has the power to transform and change the human heart. The Eucharist is a sacrament of forgiveness precisely in this sense. It has the capacity to turn hardened hearts into hearts of compassion. When seen in this light, the change of bread and wine into the body and blood of Christ is also a sign of the transformation that takes place in the lives of believers.

---

20. Ibid., bk. 4. no. 24 (*Eucharist*, 80).
21. See Ibid., bk. 4. no. 27 (*Eucharist*, 80).
22. Ibid., bk. 4, no. 28 (*Eucharist*, 81).
23. See Ambrose of Milan, *On Repentance*, bk. 2. chap. 10. no. 95 (*NPNF*, 10:357).

Conclusion

As bishop of Milan, Ambrose put his pastoral responsibilities before all else. He went to great lengths to ensure that his flock received sound teaching to help them in practical ways in their walk of faith. He wrote in order to instruct his people in the mysteries of the faith and to capture their hearts for the Lord. His teaching on the Eucharist reflects his deep pastoral concerns for those he served.

Ambrose is a sacramental realist, who believes that through God's action the priestly words of consecration change the bread and wine into the body and blood of Christ. He considers the Eucharist a true spiritual sacrifice, an act of bloodless worship that brings Christ's Paschal mystery into the midst of the believing community. In this sacrifice, Christ offers himself to the Father on humanity's behalf and bridges the infinite abyss between the human and the divine. By eating and drinking Christ's body and blood, believers receive forgiveness and the fruits of divine grace. The Eucharist, from this perspective, is a spiritual banquet at which believers receive spiritual food to help them on their journey of faith. This food nourishes their souls and gives them strength to live the life of discipleship.

Ambrose's teaching on the Eucharist rests firmly within the mainstream of fourth-century Christianity. His sermons and catechetical instructions on the sacrament affirm the fundamental tenets of Nicene orthodoxy and lead believers along sure, practical ways of faithful Christian service. Although he treats the Eucharist in many of his writings, his primary teaching appears in his works devoted to the catechetical instructions to the newly baptized. In these writings, he wishes to impress upon his listeners from the very outset the importance of the sacrament as a source of forgiveness and spiritual nourishment. For this reason, he exhorts his listeners to approach the altar frequently and confess in their hearts the words their lips profess.

Reflection Questions

1. Do you believe in the power of Christ's word to change the nature of things into something else? If so, is this power limited in any way? Is it confined only to the Eucharist? Only to the sacraments?

Can the power of Christ's word change the ways of nature itself? Does it have the power to change the human heart?

2. Do you see a close relationship between the Eucharist and the sacrifice of Calvary? If so, what is the nature of this relationship? What connects the two events? What makes them one? Does the Eucharist foreshadow what takes place on Calvary? In what sense can the Eucharist be considered a sacrifice?

3. Do you believe that the Eucharist is the central act of worship of the New Covenant? If so, what are the essential components of this act of worship? Is the Eucharist a sacred meal? A participation in the sacrifice of Calvary? A sacrament of the real presence? A combination of all three? With which of these dimensions of the sacrament do you identify the most?

4. Do you consider the Eucharist a "medicine" of healing for the forgiveness of sins? If so, how does it perform such healing? Have you ever experienced such healing from the sacrament in your life? Does the Eucharist do more than heal spiritually? Does it heal physically and mentally as well? Does the Eucharist elevate and transform as well as heal?

5. In what sense is the celebration of the Eucharist an event people shared in? Does everyone participate in the Eucharist in the same way? What are the various roles that the faithful are called upon to assume? What role do you yourself feel called to assume? When you attend the Eucharist do you feel as though you are actually participating in what is taking place or instead are a detached and passive onlooker? What would you do to make the participatory roles of the Eucharistic celebration more pronounced?

Basil the Great
Loving Service of God and Others

> Little given, much gained; by the gift of food, original sin
> was let loose in the world. Just as Adam passed on this ter-
> rible sin through his evil consumption, so we destroy this
> corrupt food whenever we genuinely satisfy the needs and
> hungers of others.
>
> *Basil the Great*

What relationship does the Eucharist have to the rest of
theology? What institutions support it and are supported by it?
What does this sacrament tell us about how we should live our
lives in loving service of God and others? Our next voice from
the past was known for his proficient administrative abilities, his
polished rhetoric, and his profound theological writings. In addition to carrying out his episcopal duties, Basil the Great (d. 379),
Archbishop of Caesarea in Cappadocia, wrote two monastic rules
that brought institutional stability to Eastern monasticism, and
founded the "Basilias," one of the great charitable centers of the
ancient Church. A brother to Gregory of Nyssa, his fellow bishop
and mystical theologian, and a close friend to the other great Cappadocian bishop, Gregory of Nazianzus, he wrote treatises, sermons,
and letters on a wide variety of topics. His most noteworthy works
include his *Against Eunomius, On the Holy Spirit* and the nine sermons in the *Hexaemeron*. His numerous letters paint a vivid picture
of the political, ecclesiastical, and cultural climate of his time. He
also did much in the area of liturgical renewal, although substantial
changes over time have made it impossible to determine his original
contribution to the Eastern Liturgy that bears his name. Mention of

the Eucharist comes in a number of his writings and flows from his overall theological vision.[1]

Basil's Theological Outlook

Basil benefited from a strong classical education, but was essentially a monk and ascetic at heart. Deeply influenced by Neoplatonic thought and the writings of Origen, the great third-century theologian of Alexandria, his theological vision sprang from the ongoing tension between the opposing worlds of spirit and flesh. According to Hans von Campenhaussen, "his thinking was based on the antithesis between flesh and spirit, earth and heaven, time and eternity, and the eschatological point of view always played a very vital part in his theological thinking."[2] Basil did not think the visible, material world inherently evil, but only a constant incitement to it. To counteract the temptations of the flesh, a person must be rooted in the spirit, in God, and in eternity. One effects this by liberating the self through training and discipline, which enables one to love God and neighbor more fully. For Basil, the monastic life provides the communal context that enables a person to grow with others to full Christian maturity.[3]

Although Basil devoted much of his time to Church administration and ecclesiastical politics, he never shirked his duties as a pastor and theologian. According to Quasten, he "is certainly one of the most brilliant ecclesiastical orators of antiquity, who combines rhetorical display with simplicity of thought and clarity of expression."[4] His sermons are carefully crafted rhetorical pieces rooted in biblical texts and focusing on theological and moral themes reflecting the contemporary needs of the Church. In the tradition of Athanasius, he was a loyal son of Nicea, who stood firm against unorthodox theological speculation and opted instead to mediate to conflicting factions the "simplicity of sound belief."[5] Amidst grow-

---

1. The above information comes from *P*, 335–45; *CH*, 1:382–83; *Pat.*, 3:204–36; *FGC*, 84–100.
2. *FGC*, 88.
3. *FGC*, 87–88.
4. *Pat.*, 3:216.
5. *FGC*, 94.

ing theological conflicts in the Eastern Church, he sought to bolster the universal teaching voice of episcopal authority with the aim of promoting Nicene orthodoxy, while retaining as far as possible the unique theological voice of the Eastern Church.

For Basil, all sound theology must pass the test of Nicene orthodoxy: "... it is impossible for me to make even the slightest addition to the Nicene Creed, except the ascription of Glory to the Holy Ghost, because our Fathers treated this point cursorily, no question having at that time arisen concerning the Spirit."[6] Against the Arian Eunomius, he maintained that human beings, even in eternity, could know God only through his "energies," that is his operations in which he reveals himself, and not in his essence. With regard to the Trinity, he clarified the thought of Nicea, by insisting upon the difference in meaning between *ousia* and *hypostasis*. In his mind, the former referred to the substance of God's being and the latter to the reality of each of the Persons. He was the first to insist on the phrase "one *ousia* and three *hypostases* in God" as the only correct formula.[7] In doing so, he provided the language and conceptual framework for later theological developments.

In his doctrine of the Holy Spirit, Basil formulated a position that anticipated the definition of Constantinople in 381. He taught that the Holy Spirit was divine, although he did not say in so many words that the Spirit was "one in being with the Father." Nonetheless in *On the Holy Spirit* he was at pains to show that the Spirit was equal to and undivided from the Father and the Son. As with most Greek fathers, he maintained that the Holy Spirit proceeds "from the Father through the Son," and disagreed with the Arian Eunomius that the Son is his only source. Since the Son holds everything in common with the Father, he maintained that it was correct to speak of the Spirit of the Father as well as the Spirit of the Son.[8]

A few other doctrinal points are worth noting. Basil distinguishes four types of public penitents in the Church and exhorts monks to confess all their sins to an experienced spiritual guide, either the religious superior or a chosen delegate. Nowhere does he say anything

---

6. Basil the Great, *Epistle*, 258, no. 2 (*NPNF*, 8:295). See also *Pat.*, 3:228.
7. See *P*, 342; *Pat.*, 3:228–31.
8. *P*, 343; *Pat.*, 3:231–33.

about absolution or insist that the confessor specifically be a priest. With regard to Roman primacy, he asserts that the bishop of Rome has an authoritative position in dogmatic questions but says nothing about being the jurisdictional head of the universal church. In the spirit of Pachomius, the father of cenobitic monasticism, he rejects the anchoritic notion of monastic life and espouses a communal ideal based on ascetical ideals and the service of God and neighbor.[9]

Basil's Eucharistic Teaching

Basil's teaching on the Eucharist flows from his overall theological outlook and is shaped by the *disciplina arcana* (the discipline of secrecy), an early Church practice that limited information given to catechumens about the mysteries of the faith to the Creed, the Lord's Prayer, and certain aspects of the rites of initiation. To preserve the secret mysteries, non-Christians and catechumens typically left the liturgical assembly at the conclusion of the Liturgy of the Word.[10]

In line with this practice, Basil speaks of an unwritten apostolic tradition with the same authoritative standing as the written. From this unwritten tradition comes the invocation of the Holy Spirit (i.e., *epiclesis*) which, along with other prayers, he maintains is necessary for the validity of the Eucharistic celebration. "Which of the saints," he states, "has left us in writing the words of the invocation at the displaying of the bread of the Eucharist and the cup of blessing? For we are not, as is well known, content with what the apostle or the Gospel has recorded, but both in preface and conclusion we add other words as being of great importance to the validity of the ministry, and these we derive from unwritten teaching."[11]

For Basil, unwritten teaching has preserved many important insights regarding the sacred mysteries, the invocation of the Holy Spirit at the Eucharistic liturgy being just one of many examples.

Basil clearly states his belief in the real presence. One receives Christ himself at communion: "Do you not know ... that it is he

---

9. See *P*, 343–45.
10. See *Eucharist*, 51.
11. Basil the Great, *On the Holy Spirit*, no. 66 (*NPNF*, 8:41–42). See also *HD*, 2:182.

whom you must receive? It is he who said: 'My Father and I will come and make our home in him.'"[12] He teaches that one must approach the altar with faith, hope, and love. One must share the same disposition and readiness to give one's life in service to others as Christ himself:

> And thus is the soul able to obey the Apostle who establishes a good conscience as a sort of benchmark for those who are sound in these matters by saying: "For the love of Christ presses us on, for we judge that if One died for all, then all died. And He died for all, that living they should no longer live for themselves, but for Him who died and rose for their sakes" (2 Cor 5:14–15). He who partakes of the bread and the cup should have such a disposition and such readiness.[13]

To receive the Eucharist unworthily is to eat and drink judgment upon oneself. Because one receives Christ himself in the Eucharist, one must be ready and willing to share in his paschal mystery. Basil looks to the Lord's words themselves for certainty in faith: "Assurance is created in us by belief in the words of the Lord: 'This is my body which is given up for you. Do this in remembrance of me'" (Lk 22:19).[14] His point here is that one must not doubt the word of the Lord, but instead be ready to believe that everything he said is possible and true, even when nature thinks otherwise. Among the words to accept are: "If you do not eat the flesh of the Son of man and drink his blood, you will not have life in you" (Jn 6:52).[15] Although this realistic language does not disallow allegorical interpretations that would identify eating the flesh of Christ and drinking his blood with participating in the wisdom of the Word, Basil does not want such interpretations of Scripture to displace the literal sense of these passages.[16]

Basil's Eucharistic teaching also emphasizes the importance of frequent communion. In a letter to the noble woman, Caesaria, he encourages the practice of daily communion and even offers details about his own approach to the sacrament:

---

12. Basil the Great, *Homily on Fasting* (*De ieiunio, homil.*) , 1.11 (*Eucharistie*, col. 1147 [my translation]).
13. Basil the Great, *Lesser Rules* (*Regulae brevius tractatae*), no. 172 (*Eucharist*, 287).
14. Ibid. (*Eucharist*, 286).
15. Basil the Great, *Moralia*, 8, reg. 1 (*Eucharistie*, cols. 1147–48 [my translation]).
16. See *Eucharistie*, col. 1148.

To communicate every day, to be a sharer in the holy body and blood of Christ is, indeed, a good and beneficial practice, for He says plainly: "He who eats my flesh and drinks my blood has eternal life" (Jn 6:55). Who doubts but that to share continually in life is nothing other than to live in manifold ways. We, for our part, communicate four times in each week: on the Lord's day, on the fourth day [Wednesday], on the day of preparation [Friday], and on the Sabbath [Saturday], also on other days if there is a commemoration of a saint.[17]

Basil says it is beneficial to receive daily communion. By sharing in the body and blood of Jesus Christ in this way, a person participates more deeply in the divine life. Later in the letter, he refers to the Alexandrian practice of monks and laity reserving communion at home so that they could receive communion daily by administering it to themselves by hand. "Daily communion," in this context, does not necessarily mean within the context of a Eucharistic liturgy, although Basil's own practice of receiving communion four times a week most likely took place within the liturgy.[18]

Observations

Basil's teaching on the Eucharist invites comment and critical inquiry. The following remarks examine it in more detail and looks specifically to its contribution to the Church's understanding of the sacrament.

1. Basil is suspicious of needless theological speculation and uses his rhetorical acumen to expound the "simplicity of sound belief." When applied to the Eucharist, he is critical of those who try to explain away Jesus' words of institution at the Last Supper. While Basil is careful not to adopt the overly realistic concept of the Eucharist as a "bloody meal," he avoids the other extreme of merely attributing to the words symbolic meaning. The Eucharist, for Basil, is real food and drink. It is Jesus' glorified body and blood present in a spiritual form in the consecrated species. Basil encourages the faithful to give Jesus' words the presumption that they are both true and possible.

17. Basil the Great, *Epistle*, 93 (*Eucharist*, 304–5).
18. See *HD*, 2:173–74; *Eucharist*, 304.

2. For Basil, the goal of human life is to participate in the life of God by liberating the self from the temptations of the flesh through training and self-discipline. Because of humanity's fallen nature, however, no one can do this without the aid of God's grace made available through Christ's redemptive death on the cross. The Eucharist, for Basil, is one of the primary ways in which God makes this grace available. When they receive communion, believers are nourished by Christ's own body and blood. The Eucharist enables believers to be rooted in God and in eternity. It helps them to conquer the desires of the flesh and to live in the Spirit.

3. Basil is especially remembered for his theology of the Holy Spirit, being among the first to draw out the implications of his relationship to the Father and Son and to attribute to him divine status. It should not be surprising, therefore, to find in his Eucharist teaching a special emphasis on the *epiclesis* or invocation of the Holy Spirit. The Eucharist celebration is an act of worship to God the Father through Christ the Son, and in the Holy Spirit. By emphasizing the importance of the *epiclesis* for the sacrament, Basil heightens the Spirit's role for the valid exercise of the ministry and makes it easier for the faithful to see that the Spirit is one of the three *hypostases* of the one God.

4. Basil asserts that Jesus died and rose for humanity and that the Eucharist gives the faithful a real participation in Jesus' paschal mystery. When they receive communion, they proclaim their belief in the Risen Lord and their desire to live not for themselves, but for him. To live for Jesus, however, means to live for God and others. For Basil, to partake in the Eucharist is to make a statement about one's belief in the Church, the body of Christ, and its mission of loving service to the world. To receive communion requires a desire and readiness to participate in that life of loving service.

5. Basil saw the Eucharist as the means by which God's love for humanity entered into the midst of the Church community and inspired similar acts of love and service for God and neighbor in the hearts of the faithful. Such love has an intrinsic communal dimension oriented toward general welfare of society. As a bishop concerned with the administrative care of his diocese, he saw the need for charitable services for the poor and needy. The charitable Church institutions that he established in his diocese (e.g., hospitals, homes for the poor) were,

in his mind, concrete manifestations of this Eucharistic love for God and neighbor flowing from the heart of the believing community.

6. Basil was archbishop of the Church at Caesarea in Cappadocia, as well as the author of two monastic rules. His service both to the local Church and to monastic communities he founded is permeated by the notion of community. At the heart of the community is the Eucharistic liturgy. The centrality of the Eucharist to the life of the Christian community explains why Basil spent so much effort on liturgical reforms. Although it is difficult to distinguish his original contribution to the Liturgy which bears his name, his concern for a well-ordered and theologically sound Eucharistic celebration is well known and widely acclaimed.

7. Basil teaches that the faithful must properly prepare themselves before receiving communion. They must fear the Lord, be pure of heart, filled with faith, and rooted in love. They must have the same dispositions as Jesus and be ready to offer themselves as he himself offered his life for others. By making sure that they have the proper dispositions when receiving the body and blood of Christ, they manifest their desire to receive their Lord into their lives and to participate fully in his passion, death, and resurrection. When they are not properly prepared, they do not reap the benefits of Christ's redemptive self-offering, but eat and drink judgment upon themselves.

8. Basil encourages the frequent reception of communion, although not necessarily in the context of a Eucharistic liturgy. The practice of reserving communion in the home gives the faithful greater access to the spiritual nourishment afforded by the consecrated elements. Allowing the faithful to administer communion to themselves and others in this way also emphasizes the important connection between the liturgical worship and daily life. Communion, for Basil, is the food of eternal life and can be received outside the Eucharistic celebration. By its very nature, the Eucharistic celebration overflows into the rest of life. Although abuses could arise and must be avoided with care, his teaching reveals the great trust he places in his flock to treat the consecrated species with reverence and respect.

Conclusion

Designated "the Great" during his own lifetime, Basil led the Church of Caesarea through a period of great political, ecclesiastical, and theological unrest. He was an ascetic, a theologian, preacher, a liturgist, a letter writer, an excellent pastoral administrator — and much more. A staunch defender of Nicene orthodoxy, he drew out many of the implications of the faith and laid the theological and linguistic foundations for later definitions. This holds true especially for his teaching on the Holy Spirit and the expression that there was "one *ousia* and three *hypostases* in God."

As the archbishop of Caesarea, Basil's reputation extended beyond the Christian communities of Cappadocia to many other Churches in the empire. Concerned primarily with the unity of the Church, he mediated between opposing parties, laid the groundwork for the Council of Constantinople (381), contributed to the collapse of Arianism, and was largely responsible for bringing the semi-Arians back to the fold of the Nicene faith. His theological heritage is no less impressive. His training in classical rhetoric enabled him to write works admired as much for their style and literary form as for their theological content. His sermons were especially noteworthy for their use of rhetoric to move the hearts and consciences of his hearers. In his treatises, he drew distinctions to deepen his readers' understanding of accepted teaching and to move the Church's theological tradition to still further clarity.[19]

Basil's teaching on the Eucharist flowed from his Neoplatonic outlook and his dedication to the ascetical ideal that the spirit needs liberation from the evil inclinations of the flesh. He emphasized the centrality of the Eucharistic celebration for the life of the Christian community and pointed to the underlying continuity that should exist between worship and life, liturgical celebration and action in the world. He exhorted the faithful to have the proper dispositions before approaching the table of the Lord and encouraged them to receive communion frequently. Taking Jesus' words of institution at face value, he believed in the real presence and saw in the Eucharist the

---

19. See *P*, 337; *Pat.*, 3:207–8, 216.

means by which Christians received the nourishment they needed to dedicate themselves entirely to the following of Christ in the loving service of God and others.

Reflection Questions

1. What was the reason for the practice of the *disciplina arcana* in the early Church? What were the advantages to such a practice? Do you see any disadvantages? Why did this practice fall out of use? Should the practice be adapted to today's Eucharistic celebration? If not, why not?

2. What does Basil mean by the "simplicity of sound belief"? What does it mean when applied to theology in general? What does it mean with regard to the Eucharist? What does such a phrase imply about the speculative nature of theology? How does one know when one is engaged in needless speculation?

3. Do you believe that to partake in the Eucharist is to make a statement about one's belief in the Church and its mission of loving service to the world? Do you see a connection between participating in the Eucharist and in the Church's mission of compassionate and loving service to the world? If so, how does the continuity between these two dimensions of the faith manifest itself in your life?

4. What are the proper dispositions one should have to receive Jesus worthily in the Eucharist? Are these dispositions fixed or do they change over time? What does it mean to say one must have the same dispositions as Jesus? What does it mean to say that one must be ready to offer one's life for others? How does one know when one has these dispositions? How does one deal with the uncomfortable reality of mixed motives and dispositions?

5. Basil encouraged the practice of reserving communion in the home to give the faithful greater access to the spiritual nourishment afforded by the consecrated elements. Do you agree with such a practice? Do you think it should be implemented in today's believing communities? What would be the advantages and disadvantages of such a change for the life of the Church?

Voice Seventeen

Gregory of Nazianzus
Receiving Divine Medicine

Resting her head with another cry upon the altar, and with a
wealth of tears, as she who once bedewed the feet of Christ, and
declaring that she would not loose her hold until she was made
whole, she then applied her medicine to her whole body, viz.,
such a portion of *the antitypes of the Precious Body and Blood*
as she treasured in her hand, mingling therewith her tears, and,
O the wonder, she went away feeling at once that she was saved,
and with the lightness of health in body, soul, and mind, having
received, as the reward of her hope, that which she hoped for,
and having gained bodily by means of spiritual strength. (*From
Gregory's funeral oration for his sister*)

Gregory of Nazianzus

Who were the great Christian orators of old and how did they
communicate the Gospel message? Gregory of Nazianzus (329/30–c.
390), our next voice from the past, was one of the most renowned
orators of his time and used his skill to draw out the full implications
of the Nicene faith. Born in Arianzus in Cappadocia and educated
in classical Greek rhetoric at Caesarea, Alexandria, and Athens, he
often spoke of the medicinal properties of the Eucharist and of the
physical and spiritual cures that took place through it. A friend of
the two other great Cappadocian Fathers, Basil of Caesarea and
Gregory of Nyssa, he had a gentle, contemplative temperament, one
that leaned more toward study and worldly seclusion, than engaging
positions in Church leadership.

Gregory was a reluctant leader and Church administrator, who entered the clergy more in response to the demands of family and friends

179

than from his own personal inclinations. In 362, he became a priest for the Church at Nazianzus at the urging of his father Gregory, the local bishop. In 371, his friend Basil consecrated him bishop of the small village of Sasima in an attempt to retain his metropolitan control over the recently partitioned ecclesiastical province of Cappadocia. In 379, he accepted the see of Constantinople, but resigned from that post a couple of years later because of questions raised about the legitimacy of his appointment. Relieved of his ecclesiastical duties, Gregory lived the remaining years of his life in solitude and engaged in literary and theological pursuits at his family's estate in Arianzus.

One of the great orators of his day, religious or secular, Gregory was known in his own lifetime as "the Christian Demosthenes." Because of his ability to draw out the implications of Nicene orthodoxy and to provide sound theological formulations that contributed to its development, he was also known as, "The Theologian." Remembered especially for his 45 *Orations*, his literary corpus also includes some 245 *Letters* and a number of poems. His teaching on the Eucharist presupposes the fundamental tenets of Nicene orthodoxy and appears at various points in his writings.[1]

Gregory's Theological Outlook

Gregory derives much of his thought from his close friend Basil and acknowledges this dependence in one of his letters to him: "From the first I have taken you, and I take you still, for my guide of life and my teacher of dogma."[2] A careful analysis of Gregory's works supports this claim, but also shows that he often eclipses his close friend and teacher by refining the terminology of Christian orthodoxy and taking a more systematic approach to the theological questions before him. At various points in his writings, Gregory treats such topics as the nature and method of theology, its object and sources, the relationship between faith and reason, the teaching role of the Church, and the traits of a theologian.[3]

---

1. The above information comes from *P*, 345–47; *CH*, 1:383; *Pat.*, 3:236–49; *FGC*, 101–14.
2. Cited in *Pat.*, 3:248.
3. Ibid.

In his Trinitarian theology, Gregory was the first to give names to the various distinctions between the Persons of the Trinity: the eternal Father, the eternally generated Son, and the eternally proceeding Holy Spirit. Even more clearly than Basil, Gregory affirms the divinity of the Holy Spirit and confirms his consubstantial status with the Father and the Son: "For how long shall we hide the lamp under the bushel, and withhold from others the full knowledge of the Godhead, when it ought to be now put upon the lampstand and give light to all churches and souls and to the whole fullness of the world, no longer by means of metaphors, or intellectual sketches, but by distinct declaration?"[4] He differs from Basil because of his stronger emphasis on the unity of God and by having a much clearer understanding of the nature of the divine relations.[5]

In his understanding of Christ, Gregory affirms the complete humanity of Christ and lays the groundwork for solemn definitions of the Councils of Ephesus (431) and Chalcedon (451). His view of Christ affirms that the eternal Word (the *Logos*) is united with the complete human being of Jesus, as opposed to the view of Christ that sees the eternal Word united only with Jesus' fleshly part (his *sarx*), and so making no allowance for Jesus' human soul. Gregory, thus, can be said to adopt a *Logos-Man* over a *Logos-Sarx* Christology and teaches that Jesus assumed a human soul in the Incarnation. The mind, for him, is the image of the Logos and is the point of contact between the Godhead and human flesh: "Mind is mingled with mind, as nearer and more closely related, and through it with flesh, being a Mediator between God and carnality."[6] Gregory, moreover, is among the first of the Greek theologians to apply the Trinitarian terminology to the Christological formula. He states that in Christ "both natures are one by combination, the deity being made man, and the manhood deified or however one should express it."[7] Gregory clearly attests the unity of the Person in Christ: "For both are God, that which assumed, and that which was assumed; two Natures meeting in One, not two

---

4. Gregory of Nazianzus, *Orations*, 12.6 (*NPNF*, 7: 247). See also *P*, 350.
5. See *Pat.*, 3:249–50.
6. Gregory of Nazianzus, *Epistle*, 101.10 (*Pat.*, 3:252).
7. Ibid.

Sons"; "Christ is One out of two, two natures unite in him to One, there are not two Sons."[8]

Gregory's concern to protect the proper understanding of Christ also led him to examine the role of Mary's relationship to her son. He calls Mary "the Mother of God" (i.e., *Theotokos*) and coins a phrase that would greatly influence the Councils fathers at Ephesus: "If anyone does not believe that Saint Mary is the Mother of God, he is severed from the Godhead. If anyone should assert that he passed through the Virgin as through a channel, and was not at once divinely and humanly formed in her ... he is in like manner godless."[9] Gregory viewed Mary's motherhood of Christ as a key to understanding the mystery of Christ, the Church, and the whole of salvation history. He assigns a similar importance to the Eucharistic celebration.[10]

Gregory's Teaching on the Eucharist

Gregory uses words such as "type" or "antitype" when referring to the Eucharist. In his funeral oration for his sister, he speaks of the Eucharist as a medicine and says that to find a cure for her illness Gorgonia mingled her tears with the "antitype" of the body and blood of Jesus Christ:

> What then did this great soul, worthy offspring of the greatest, and what was the medicine for her disorder, for we have now come to the great secret? Despairing of all other aid, she betook herself to the Physician of all, and awaiting the silent hours of night, during a slight intermission of the disease, she approached the altar with faith, and, calling upon Him Who is honored thereon, with a mighty cry, and every kind of invocation, calling to mind all His former works of power, and well she knew those both of ancient and of later days, at last she ventured on an act of pious and splendid effrontery: she imitated the woman whose fountain of blood was dried up by the hem of Christ's garment. What did she do? Resting her head with another cry upon the altar, and with a wealth of tears, as she who once bedewed

---

8. Gregory of Nazianzus, *Orations*, 37.2 (*NPNF*, 7:339). See also *P*, 350; *Pat.*, 3:251–53.
9. Gregory of Nazianzus, *Epistle*, 101.10 (*Pat.*, 3:253).
10. See *Pat.*, 3:253.

the feet of Christ, and declaring that she would not loose her hold until she was made whole, she then applied her medicine to her whole body, viz., such a portion of *the antitypes of the Precious Body and Blood* as she treasured in her hand, mingling therewith her tears, and, O the wonder, she went away feeling at once that she was saved, and with the lightness of health in body, soul, and mind, having received, as the reward of her hope, that which she hoped for, and having gained bodily by means of spiritual strength. Great though these things be, they are not untrue. Believe them all of you, whether sick or sound, that ye may either keep or regain your health. And that my story is no mere boastfulness is plain from the silence in which she kept, while alive, what I have revealed. Nor should I now have published it, be well assured, had I not feared that so great a marvel would have been utterly hidden from the faithful and unbelieving of these and later days.[11]

Similarly, when making a request of a government official, he writes: "I place before your eyes this table where we receive communion together, and the images ('types') of my salvation, this sacrament that raises us to heaven, that I consecrate with the same mouth with which I make my request."[12] Gregory has a clear meaning in the use of such terms. While the bread and wine are natural or divinely ordained figures or symbols (i.e., "types") of Christ's body and blood, the words of consecration turn them into the sensible vessels (i.e., "antitypes") of Christ's bodily presence. Through the words of consecration, in other words, the bread and wine are more than mere symbols of Christ's body and blood, for they actually contain and make present the sacred mysteries they signify. In addition to Gregory, the language of "type" and "antitype" appears in a number of other Church fathers, but was eventually omitted or implicitly condemned because it was subject to misinterpretation. Proponents of the literalist (as opposed to allegorical) approach to Scriptural interpretation at Antioch were suspicious of such language and stressed time and again that the Eucharist is more than a mere symbol of Christ's body and blood.[13]

---

11. Gregory of Nazianzus, *Orations*, 8.18 (*NPNF*, 7:243).
12. Ibid., 17.12 (*Eucharistie*, col. 1148 [my translation]).
13. See *HD*, 2:173, 176.

In addition to the real presence, Gregory also believed in the sacrificial character of the Eucharist. He states this specifically in a letter to Amphilochius, the bishop of Iconium: "For the tongue of a priest meditating of the Lord raises the sick. Do then the greater thing in your priestly ministration, and loose the great mass of my sins when you lay hold of the Sacrifice of Resurrection."[14] In his *Apology on Fleeing*, he specifically refers to the Eucharist as a sacrifice:

> Since then I knew these things, and that no one is worthy of the mightiness of God, and the sacrifice, and priesthood, who has not first presented himself to God, a living, holy sacrifice, and set forth the reasonable, well-pleasing service, and sacrificed to God the sacrifice of praise and the contrite spirit, which is the only sacrifice required of us by the Giver of all; how could I dare to offer to Him the external sacrifice, the antitype of the great mysteries?[15]

In this passage, Gregory draws a contrast between internal and external sacrifice: the former is the offering of one's life to God through a contrite spirit and loving service; the latter, Christ's self-offering on Calvary made present at the Eucharistic celebration. For him the two belong together and should be an integral part of the life of a priest.

Gregory is not a mere symbolist in his approach to the Eucharist, for he encourages the faithful to receive the body and blood of Jesus Christ without hesitation and shame. He says in one of his Easter Sermons: "But without shame and without doubt you may eat the Flesh and drink the Blood, if you are desirous of true life, neither disbelieving His words about His Flesh, nor offended at those about His Passion."[16] To his friend bishop Amphilochius, he writes: "But, most reverend friend, cease not both to pray and to plead for me when you draw down the Word by your word, when with a bloodless cutting you sever the Body and Blood of the Lord, using your voice for the glaive."[17] Nowhere in his writings, however, does he attempt to explain the Eucharistic mystery or the mode of the real presence.

---

14. Gregory of Nazianzus, *Epistle*, 171 (*NPNF*, 7:469). See also *Pat.*, 3:254.
15. Gregory of Nazianzus, *Orations*, 2.95 (*NPNF*, 7:223). See also *Pat.*, 3:254.
16. Ibid., *Orations*, 45.19 (*NPNF*, 7:4309. See also *P*, 351.
17. Ibid., *Orations*, 2.95 (*NPNF*, 7:223). See also *Pat.*, 3:254.

He believes in the real presence on divine authority and merely affirms it without analyzing it.[18]

Observations

The following comments, while in no way exhaustive, look more closely at Gregory's teaching on the Eucharist and draw out its deeper significance for the life of the believing community.

1. Since Gregory nowhere offers an extended treatment of the Eucharist, his teaching on the sacrament must be drawn from a variety of sources, written in different literary genres, and addressing different audiences. In the midst of such diversity, one must be careful not to overstate his teaching and assign to it a degree of clarity and organization it does not possess. Simply because he does not write much about the Eucharist, however, does not mean that it was not important to him. On the contrary, although his teaching on the sacrament is occasional and sporadic, what he does say indicates that he believed it was central to his life in Christ and for the community of believers.

2. Given the above, Gregory's teaching on the Eucharist still flows from and is generally consistent with his overall theological outlook. A staunch defender of Nicene orthodoxy, he is remembered for his capacity to draw out the implications of the orthodox Catholic position and lay the groundwork for future developments (e.g., the divinity of the Holy Spirit, his Logos-Man Christology, the *Theotokos* doctrine). Given his theological acumen, one wonders why he did not explicitly connect some of the implications he drew out of the Nicene faith with their counterparts in the Eucharistic celebration. To cite but one example, he is clearly in line with Cappadocian thought on the Holy Spirit in fully recognizing the Spirit's divine status, yet unlike his friend Basil he does not say very much about the purpose of the invocation of the Spirit (i.e., the *epiclesis*) at the Eucharist.

3. Gregory's approach to the mystery of the Eucharist, however, is still remarkably close to Basil's. Gregory openly admits that he depends on his friend as "a guide for life and as a teacher of dogma."

---

18. See *Eucharistie*, col. 1148.

Like Basil, he does not try to explain the nature of Christ's presence in the consecrated elements, but is content with accepting it on the authority of Jesus' words of institution. He understands that there are some things which must simply be accepted on faith and that theological explanations sometimes obscure as much as they clarify.

4. Like Basil, Gregory affirms his belief in the real presence, but accepts it on the authority of Scripture rather than attempting to explain how it occurs. Given his reputation as a theologian, his appreciation for a systematic approach to theology, and his penchant for drawing out the full implications of Nicene orthodoxy, it seems unlikely that he did not at least think of analyzing the nature of the sacramental presence of Christ in more detail. Rather than doing so, however, he probably did not wish to intrude unnecessarily into the sphere of the sacred and show lack of respect for the divine mysteries. Instead of devising new terms to explain more clearly the manner or mode of Jesus' real presence in the Eucharist, he opts for traditional language such as "type" and "antitype" to convey his thoughts and preserve a sense of the sacramental mystery.

5. The Eucharist, for Gregory, also has the capacity to heal. His description of his sister's intercessions at the altar of the Lord demonstrates his deep belief that the sacrament confers not only spiritual benefits, but also physical and mental benefits on those who receive it with heartfelt faith. Gregory believes that the Eucharist can cure the whole person: body, mind, and spirit. Although he is not the first to speak of the Eucharist as a medicine, what is interesting in Gregory's presentation is the way passionate faith mingles with the consecrated elements to create a curative, healing balm that restores bodily health.

6. Far more important than restoring bodily health is the Eucharist's capacity to heal the soul of its sins. He is deeply conscious of the intercessory power of the priest to "loose the great mass of sins" when he takes hold of the "Sacrifice of the Resurrection." If the priest has the power to raise the sick simply by meditating on the Lord, how much more will he accomplish when he celebrates the liturgy and draws down the Word of God through his words. The words of consecration, for Gregory, are a display of divine power in

the midst of human limitations and weakness. As he says to Amphilochius, "... you draw down the Word by your word." Through the power of his words, God enters the world in the form of bread and wine to nourish the faithful and heal them of their wounds.

7. In line with the above, Gregory has a profound sense of the priestly mediation of divine power, especially during the Eucharistic celebration. The priest uses his voice to draw down the divine Word into the elements of bread and wine so that they become the body and blood of the Lord. His voice acts as a sword to cut open the body and blood of Christ in a bloodless sacrifice of praise and thanksgiving. Gregory is also conscious that the power to draw down the Word adds weight to his voice in the social and political arena. He reminds the political governor of the region that he is making his present request with the very same mouth that consecrates the bread and wine at the altar of the Lord.

8. Finally, Gregory's notion of internal and external sacrifice offers a way of understanding the objective status of the sacramental mystery, while relating it to the interior dispositions of the believer. Both are necessary if the grace of the sacrament is to have its full effect on the life of the individual and, by way of extension, on the community of faith. By calling the Eucharist an "external sacrifice," he roots the sacramental mystery outside the faith perceptions of the individual and in the death and resurrection of Jesus. The Eucharist is "external" to the Christian community insofar as it involves Jesus' passion, death, and resurrection. It becomes "internal" when communion is received with the dispositions of a humble and contrite heart.

Conclusion

Gregory of Nazianzus was one of the great orators, theologians, and poets of the fourth-century Church. He was not a great leader or administrator like his close friend Basil, nor was he as innovative and creative in theological matters as his other good friend and namesake, Basil's brother, Gregory of Nyssa. He is remembered mainly for his capacity to draw out the full implications of Basil's thought for Nicene orthodoxy, especially in the areas of Trinitarian theology and Christology.

Based on Basil, Gregory lays the groundwork for future developments in orthodox Christian theology. He fully draws out the divine nature of the Holy Spirit. He adopts a Logos-Man Christology which, against the Apollinarians, lays the groundwork for the soteriological principle that what is not assumed cannot be redeemed. He refers to Mary as *Theotokos*, the Mother of God, and offers expressions that will be often cited in events leading to the definition of the dogma. These contributions solidify his reputation as one of the great theologians of his day.

Gregory does not give a systematic presentation of the Eucharist teaching or break new ground in the Church's theological understanding of the sacrament. He uses figurative language and traditional "type/antitype" distinction to emphasize its centrality to the faith and its curative properties for the life of the Church. He believes in the real presence and in the sacrificial nature of the Eucharistic celebration, but does not delve as deeply as he does in other areas of theology.

Reflection Questions

1. Do you, like Gregory, believe that theological explanations sometimes obscure as much as they clarify and that there are some things that must simply be accepted on faith? If so, can you give any examples? Does this belief apply in any way to the Eucharist? If so, how?

2. To what extent does the Eucharist have the capacity to heal? Does Gregory's reference to the Eucharist as a "divine medicine" resonate with your experience or go contrary to it? How do the curative powers of the Eucharist manifest themselves in the life of the believing community? In what ways are they hidden or obscured? Is it possible to make too much of these curative powers?

3. How is the Eucharist the "Sacrifice of the Resurrection"? Is it valid to associate the term "sacrifice" with the empty tomb and not with Calvary? Does the Eucharist point more to the Cross

     or to the Resurrection? Which emphasis do you think would be more relevant and meaningful for today's believers?

4. Gregory has a profound sense of the priestly mediation of divine power, especially during the Eucharistic celebration. Is this same sense of priestly mediation alive in the Church today? Does it need to diminish or be rekindled? If so, what steps could be taken to deepen the believing community's perception of the role of priestly mediation in the sacraments?

5. Do you like Gregory's distinction between internal and external sacrifice in the Eucharist? Does it resonate with your experience? Do you find it an adequate explanation of the objective dimensions of the sacrament and the believer's internal dispositions when receiving the sacrament? Would you use it to help explain the mystery of the Eucharist to others?

Voice Eighteen

Gregory of Nyssa
Restoring the Divine Image

In the plan of His grace He spreads Himself to every believer
by means of that Flesh, the substance of which is from wine
and bread, blending Himself with the bodies of believers, so
that by this union with the Immortal, man, too, may become a
participant in incorruption. These things He bestows through
the power of the blessing which transforms the nature of the
visible things to that [of the Immortal].

Gregory of Nyssa

What do the great Christian mystics have to say about the
Eucharist? Gregory of Nyssa (c. 335–c. 395), our next voice from
the past and one of the great mystics of the early Church, often
presented it as God's way of restoring the divine image in man. The
third of the great Greek Cappadocian Fathers of the fourth century,
he was the younger brother of Basil the Great and a good friend of
Gregory of Nazianzus. Although Gregory was not a great leader and
monastic founder like his brother Basil or an eloquent preacher and
poet like their friend Gregory, he was extremely gifted in speculative theology and mysticism and is considered one of the fathers of
Christian mysticism.

Gregory married and began a career as a teacher of rhetoric, but
eventually decided to retire from the world and enter his brother's
monastery in Pontus. At Basil's bidding, he left the monastery in
371 to become bishop of Nyssa; nine years later, he was elected
archbishop of Sebaste and in 381 he played an important role at the
Council of Constantinople with his friend Gregory of Nazianzus. An
able and successful author, Gregory wrote many theological treatises,

exegetical works, ascetical writings, sermons, and letters. His most extensive teaching on the Eucharist appears in chapter 37 of his *Great Catechetical Oration.*[1]

Gregory's Theological Outlook

Gregory offers a systematic presentation of Christian doctrine. He makes extensive use of philosophy, and was especially influenced by Plato, Plotinus, and the Alexandrian Church father, Origen. In his doctrine on God, he proposes a natural knowledge of the divine that rises in hierarchical fashion from the visible, sensible world to the invisible, supra-sensible realities. The human mind, for Gregory, can be empowered to experience God in a mystical foretaste of the beatific vision. In his teaching on the divine names, he lays the groundwork for the development of a kind of theology that proceeds by way of saying what God is not (because God transcends all notions) that will greatly influence the negative (or *apophatic*) theology of Pseudo-Dionysius.[2]

Gregory adapts Plato's doctrine of universal ideas to his Trinitarian theology. He also affirms that the Father, Son, and Spirit are distinct only by virtue of their mutual relations and not through their creative, redemptive, and sanctifying actions. The Father is eternally unbegotten, the Son eternally begotten, and the Spirit eternally proceeding "from the Father through the Son." In his teaching on Christ, he distinguishes very clearly between the two natures of Christ, but proposes the "communication of properties" (sometimes called according to the Latin phrase *communication idiomatum*) which allows for the attributes of one of Christ's natures to be given to the other. Against Apollinaris, he adopts a Logos-Man Christology, which states that the Word of God assumed a full human nature. He also affirms Mary's Motherhood of God (*Theotokos*), a teaching that he uses to affirm the reality of the Incarnation and the union of divine and human natures in Christ. In his understanding of the end of time,

---

1. The above information comes from *P*, 351–55; CH, 1:383–84; *Pat.*, 3:254–83; *FGC*, 115–25.
2. See *Pat.*, 3:283–85; *P*, 355.

Gregory rejects the Origenist notion of the pre-existence of souls, but accepts the notion of *apokatastasis*, i.e., a belief in the ultimate salvation of all living creatures.[3]

Gregory's crowning intellectual achievement comes in his mystical theology. He believes that human beings are not just microcosms of the universe, but the very "image" of God. They reflect this divine image through the reason, freedom of will, and infused virtue present in the human soul. Created in God's image, human beings have the capacity to possess an intimate knowledge of God. This mystic vision takes place within the soul and, at its highest level, manifests itself as a "divine and sober inebriation."[4] To attain such knowledge, human beings must purify themselves by fighting temptation and freeing themselves from the passions and worldly desires. Only when someone reaches a state of holy indifference (*apatheia*) can he or she begin to rise by way of mystical ascent to this deep, intimate knowledge of the divine. The purpose of this ascent is to become God-like. Divinization or deification is the end-result of Gregory's mystical theology and is closely linked to his understanding of the sacrament of the Eucharist.[5]

Gregory's Teaching on the Eucharist

Gregory believes that during the Eucharist bread and wine are changed into the body and blood of Jesus Christ. In his *Oration on the Baptism of Christ*, he writes: "The bread again is at first common bread; but when the mystery sanctifies it, it is called and actually becomes the Body of Christ."[6] Elsewhere, he specifically identifies the Eucharist as a sacrificial meal with Christ as priest, victim, and sacrifice:

> He offered Himself for us, Victim and Sacrifice, and Priest as well, and "Lamb of God, who takes away the sin of the world." When did He do this? When He made His own Body food and His own Blood drink for His disciples; for this much is clear enough to anyone, that

---

3. See *Pat.*, 3:285–91; *P*, 355.56.
4. Gregory of Nyssa, *Accurate Exposition on the Canticle of Canticles*, 10 (*Pat.*, 3:295).
5. See *Pat.*, 3:292–96.
6. Gregory of Nyssa, *Oration on the Baptism of Christ*, no. 1062 (*FEF*, 2:58–59).

a sheep cannot be eaten by a man unless its being eaten be preceded by its being slaughtered. This giving of His own Body to His disciples for eating clearly indicates that the sacrifice of the Lamb has now been completed.[7]

This passage also shows that, for Gregory, the institution of the Eucharist at the Last Supper was an anticipation of Christ's sacrificial death on Golgotha and his resurrection on Easter morning. Jesus' paschal offering of his body and blood as food for his disciples anticipates his passion, death, and resurrection. All are intimately related and represent different aspects of the mystery of redemption.

As stated earlier, Gregory's most systematic presentation on the Eucharist comes in chapter 37 of his *The Great Catechetical Oration.* There, he deals with the question of how Jesus' body can be given to thousands of Christians the world over and yet remain intact. He explains this change by drawing an analogy between how Jesus received nourishment while on earth and how the Eucharist provides nourishment to the members of his body. When on earth, Jesus consumed food and drink like everyone else and turned that nourishment into his body and blood. According to Gregory, a similar process of turning food into flesh and blood takes place during the Eucharist. Rather than occurring over the space of a few hours, however, it takes place instantaneously at the words of institution:

> The manner, then, whereby the bread which was changed in that body was changed to divine power is the same which now brings about the like result. For in that case the grace of the Word sanctified the body which derived its subsistence from bread and, in a sense, was itself bread; whereas in this case, likewise, the bread, as the Apostle says, is sanctified by the word of God and prayer (1 Tm 4:5). Not by the process of being eaten does it go on to become the body of the word, but it is changed immediately into the body through the word, even as the Word has said: This is my body."[8]

---

7. Gregory of Nyssa, *Upon Holy Easter, namely, Upon Christ's Resurrection (I)*, no. 1063 (*FEF*, 2:59).
8. Gregory of Nyssa, *Great Catechetical Oration*, chap. 37 (*Eucharist*, 63).

What happens to the bread also happens to the wine. All creatures, Gregory maintains, require nourishment to sustain them and help them to live. The appropriate nourishment for human beings is bread and water which is often mixed with wine to provide heat for the human body: "For by passing into me, those elements become body and blood, seeing that the nourishment, by the power of assimilation, is changed in each case into the form of the body."[9]

In the Eucharist, Gregory explains, the power of assimilating bread and wine into Christ's body and blood takes place immediately. When Christians receive communion they come in contact with the body and blood of the Resurrected Lord. By partaking of this food, they enter into communion with the incorruptible body of Jesus the God-Man and thus become incorruptible and divinized themselves. By eating the body and blood of Christ, in other words, Christians feed on the "bread of heaven," which promises to transform them and make them whole. Gregory uses the example of an antidote to a poisonous drug: "For just as when a deadly drug is mingled with a healthy body, the whole of what it is mingled renders the drug worthless, so also that immortal body, passing into him who receives it, changes the entire body to its own nature."[10] When seen in this light, the Eucharist is the means by which humanity is healed of its mortal wounds and participates in the divinity:

> ... the God who manifested Himself mingled Himself with our perishable nature in order that by communion with his divinity humanity might at the same time be divinized, for this reason He plants himself, by the economy of His grace, in all believers by means of the flesh which derives its subsistence from both bread and wine, mingling Himself with the bodies of believers, in order that, by union with that which is immortal, man also might partake of incorruption. And this He bestows by the power of the eucharistic prayer, transforming the nature of the visible elements into that immortal thing.[11]

---

9. Ibid., 62.
10. Ibid., 60–61.
11. Ibid., 63.

Gregory affirms a real change in the bread and wine during the Eucharistic celebration. Even though, elsewhere in his writings, he sometimes uses words that hint of a mere moral or circumstantial change in the bread and wine, his analogy of the assimilation of food into one's body in chapter 37 of *The Great Catechetical Oration* clearly points to a real transformation of the bread and wine into the body and blood of Christ. Just as Jesus assimilated bread and wine into his body during his earthly life, so too bread and wine are immediately changed into his Resurrected flesh and blood at the Eucharistic prayer. Although Gregory does not speak of a change in "being" or "substance," and was unaware of the term "transubstantiation," which would later become the key term for Catholic dogma, he clearly states that the bread and wine takes on the form and nature of Christ's body and blood.[12]

Observations

Gregory's teaching on the Eucharist is highly original and numbers among the most extensive of the fourth-century Church fathers. The following comments seek to elaborate upon his understanding of the sacrament and offer appropriate insights into its significance for the rest of his thought.

1. To begin with, Gregory is a systematic thinker who outlines a close relationship between theology and spirituality, between doctrines about God and the actual experience of the divine. Much of his theology represents an attempt to draw out the doctrinal implications of his own experience of God in prayer. In his thought, he conveys a deep sense of the limitations of the human condition, but also a deep faith in the power of God to heal and elevate the human person to the dignity of divine adoption. The Eucharist, for Gregory, is a place where theology and spirituality, doctrine and spiritual experience converge in the lives of the faithful.

2. Gregory's teaching on the Eucharist is closely related to his mystical theology. For him, the whole purpose of human life is to calm one's passions, disentangle oneself from the worldly desires,

---

12. See *HD* 2:180–81; *Eucharistie*, cols. 1148–50.

and achieve the state of holy indifference (*apatheia*) so that one will be able to attain an intuitive, supra-sensual, mystical knowledge of the divine, which itself is an anticipation of the beatific vision. Gregory is quick to affirm that no human being can achieve this purpose apart from the assistance of divine grace. The Eucharist is one of the primary means by which human beings receive this important divinizing grace. Through it, those who receive it enter into close, personal communion with God.

3. Gregory's theology of mystical *ascent*, however, needs to be understood in the context of the divine *descent* in the mysteries of the Incarnation, Jesus' death and rising, and the Eucharist. Without God's decision to enter this world, to give of himself through his sacrificial self-offering, to become nourishment for humanity through the sacrament of the Eucharist, and a source of hope through the power of his resurrection, humanity would have no way whatsoever of ascending to the heights of a mystical knowledge of the divine. God's divine descent makes possible the mystical ascent of humanity and the action of divinization. For Gregory, the Eucharist is an essential element of this providential divine descent.

4. Gregory's most developed treatment of the Eucharist comes when he attempts to answer the question how "the one body of Christ gives life to all mankind, that is, to as many as have faith, being distributed to all and yet suffering no diminution itself."[13] His answer is that the same Word of God, who became a man and assimilated natural nutrients into his body and blood all during his earthly life, has the power to transform the same nutrients into his resurrected body and blood — and can do so in a single instant. Unlike his earthly body, Jesus' glorified body is divinized and cannot be diminished. By the power of God's Word spoken through the priestly words of consecration, bread and wine become Jesus' flesh and blood and have the power to divinize those who come in contact with it.

5. Gregory claims that the excellence of man rests "not upon his likeness to the created universe, but upon the fact that he has been made in the image of the nature of the Creator."[14] God's image is

---

13. Gregory of Nyssa, *Great Catechetical Oration*, chap. 37 (*Eucharist*, 62).
14. Gregory of Nyssa, *The Making of Man*, chap. 16 (*Pat.*, 3:292).

found in the reason, free will, and virtue of the human soul. Unfortunately, that image has become dulled and obscured through human sinfulness and needs help to regain its former luster. For Gregory, the Eucharist provides the proper nourishment that enables human beings to cast off their sinfulness and to be divinized by Christ's transforming grace. That grace is mediated to the soul both directly through faith and through the intimate communion that occurs when the faithful come in contact with Christ's body and blood.

6. In specifically associating the Eucharist with the process of divinization Gregory uses the analogy of a person's assimilation of nutrition. A person turns natural food and drink into flesh and blood through a process of assimilation. When he or she receives the body and blood of Christ, the reverse dynamic occurs. When believers partake of this food, they themselves are assimilated into Christ's glorified body and are able to participate palpably in the life of the divine. By partaking in this sacrificial meal, the faithful thus enter into intimate communion with Christ and embark on a journey that ultimately leads to becoming a perfect image of the divine.

7. Gregory's use of the analogy of a person's assimilation of nutrition also enables him to combine notions of real presence, sacrifice, and banquet in a single metaphor. Throughout his earthly life, Jesus had been assimilating bread and wine into his body and blood. For him to do so, however, this food and drink had first to be ingested and destroyed so that they could be appropriately digested for the nourishment they supply. In the Eucharist, all three of these processes converge in a sacrificial meal where Jesus is priest, sacrificial victim, and food offering. The bread and wine are changed immediately into his body and blood, which in turn are eaten and digested to provide divinizing nourishment that is a foretaste of the heavenly banquet.

8. Finally, Gregory presents the Eucharist as an antidote to sin and death. Christ's resurrected body has proven itself mightier than death. When his body and blood enter into a human person, it counteracts the poison of death and repels any harm it might inflict: "For just as a little leaven … makes the whole lump like itself, so the body which was made immortal by God, by passing into our body alters and

changes it to itself."[15] The person undergoes a transformation when it comes in touch with the leaven of the Eucharist. By eating Christ's body and drinking his blood, believers have access to the antidote that will break the hold of sin and death over their lives.

Conclusion

Because of their significance for the universal Church, the Cappadocian Church Fathers have been honored with specific titles of praise. For his role as a monastic legislator and highly influential Church leader, Basil has received the appellation, "the Great." For his theological acumen and skill in rhetoric, Gregory of Nazianzus (also called by some the "Christian Demosthenes") is known as "the Theologian." For his contributions to speculative theology and Christian mysticism, Gregory of Nyssa goes by the title of "the Mystic."[16]

Gregory's title is appropriate and well deserved. More than any other thinker of his day, he was able to probe the heights of Christian mystical experience and provide the Church with a systematic presentation of the human ascent into the mysteries of the divine. His use of Greek philosophy to articulate this experience has secured his reputation as one of the fathers of Christian mysticism.

Gregory's teaching on the Eucharist forms an integral part of his mystic vision. Through the Eucharist, the human person, created in God's image but tainted by sin and the ravages of death, enters in deep personal communion with the body and blood of Christ. Through that contact, believers receive the antidote to sin and death and undergo a process of divinization. This process, for Gregory, lies at the very heart of Christ's paschal mystery. It promises to purge them of worldly attachments, restore the divine image in them to its fullest splendor, and give them a foretaste of the beatific vision.

---

15. Gregory of Nyssa, *Great Catechetical Oration*, chap. 37 (*Eucharist*, 60–61).
16. See *CH*, 1:382–84.

Reflection Questions

1. Do you think of the Eucharist as a sacrificial meal with Christ as priest, victim, and sacrifice? Do you find it easy to do so? Is the notion of a sacrificial meal a difficult concept for people today to understand let alone espouse with deep conviction? Can you think of another way of getting the same fundamental values across?

2. Do you like Gregory's notion that, in the Eucharist, Jesus instantaneously assimilates the bread and wine into his body and blood? What are the strengths of such an explanation of the transformation of the Eucharistic elements into Jesus' body and blood? Do you see any weaknesses in it? Would you use it to explain to others what takes place in the Eucharist?

3. Are you inspired by Gregory's assertion that only God's divine descent makes possible the mystical ascent of humanity? Do you see the Eucharist as an essential element of God, in his providence, descending to us? Is it possible to experience intimacy with the divine apart from the Eucharist? Is it possible to participate in this sacrament in a subliminal, unconscious way?

4. Do you believe that when believers receive the Eucharist they are assimilated into Christ's glorified body and able to participate in a real and even felt way in the life of the divine? What is the nature of their union with the glorified Christ? Can they experience themselves as being mystically assumed into the glorified Christ, while still maintaining their own identities?

5. Do you think of the Eucharist as an antidote to sin and death? If so, then what dosage of it is necessary to root out these evil poisons from human experience? Is Gregory speaking literally or figuratively when he uses this phrase to describe the Eucharist? How does receiving the Eucharist help one to overcome sin and death?

Voice Nineteen

John Chrysostom
Real Presence and Real Sacrifice

When you see [the Body of Christ] lying on the altar, say to yourself, "Because of this body I am no longer earth and ash, no longer a prisoner, but free. Because of this Body I hope for heaven, and I hope to receive the good things that are in heaven, immortal life, the lot of the angels, familiar conversation with Christ. This body, scourged and crucified, has not been fetched by death.... This is that Body which was blood-stained, which was pierced by a lance, and from which gushed forth those saving fountains, one of blood and the other of water, for all the world." ... This is the Body which He gave us, both to hold in reserve and to eat, which was appropriate to intense love; for those whom we kiss with abandon we often even bite with our teeth.

John Chrysostom

Of all the Church fathers, who has the most to say about the Eucharist? Although all of them had a deep love for the sacrament, does anyone in particular stand out from the rest for the intensity, depth, and breadth of his teaching? With such a long and venerable list of names from which to choose, John Chrysostom (347–407), our next voice from the past, is our most likely candidate. John's sobriquet, "Chrysostom," means "Golden-mouthed" and was given to him more than a century after his death due to his great reputation for eloquence. Along with Basil the Great, Gregory of Nazianzus, and Gregory of Nyssa, he is one of the four great Fathers of the Eastern Church.

Chrysostom was born at Antioch in Syria of noble parentage. He grew up in that city and received a classical education there. He was baptized around 372, ordained a deacon in 381 and a priest in 386. He acquired a reputation for being a great preacher and in 398 was consecrated archbishop of Constantinople. He was sent into exile in 403 due to jealousy and ecclesiastical intrigue and, although he was briefly reinstated for a period of a couple of months, he would never again shepherd the flock he so dearly loved. He died in exile some four years later.

Chrysostom was a gifted preacher and a prolific writer. He was the foremost spokesman of the "literalist" (as opposed to "allegorical") method to interpret the Scriptures developed by the School of Antioch and was widely acclaimed for his exegetical skills. His writings treat a variety of themes and include sermons, treatises, and letters. He wrote a great deal on the Eucharist and is often referred to as the "Doctor of the Eucharist" (*Doctor Eucharistiae*).[1]

Chrysostom's Theological Outlook

Chrysostom was not interested in abstract speculation and did not take part in any of the theological controversies of his day. He was primarily a pastor, who used the pulpit to change the hearts of his hearers and reform the community of believers. His preaching displays a profound knowledge of Scripture and reflects the truths and piety of Nicene orthodoxy.

As in his approach to Scripture, Chrysostom reflects the teachings of the school of Antioch. Against the Arians, he emphasizes the full divinity of Christ, saying that the Son is of the same essence as the Father and using the Nicene formula "one in being" (*homoousios*) to describe their relationship. Against the Apollinarists, he teaches the full humanity of Christ, affirming a belief in two separate natures in Christ, one human and one divine, but avoiding extreme interpretations that would later develop into what was called Nestorianism. He does not refer to Mary as "Mother of God" (*Theotokos*), a term rejected by the Antiochenes, but avoids their preferred title of "Mother of Christ" (*Christotokos*). Although he affirms the two

---

1. The above information comes from *P*, 373–83; *CH*, 1:384–85; *Pat*, 3:424–82; *FGC*, 140–57.

natures in Christ, he is not interested in exploring how they relate to one another. He makes this very clear in an often-quoted sermon: "By a union and conjoining God the Word and the flesh are one, not by any confusion or obliteration of substances, but by a certain union ineffable and past understanding. Ask not how."[2]

On other theological matters, Chrysostom's large literary corpus provides a rich resource for historians and contributes to their understanding of beliefs and practices of the fourth-century Church. After his death, some of his opinions spawned a certain degree of controversy. In a homily to the newly baptized, for example, he states, "We baptize infants, though they do not have sins."[3] Years later, Julian of Eclanum would point to these words in support of the Pelagian position, insisting that Chrysostom denied the existence of original sin. Augustine responded to Julian by pointing out that Chrysostom's use of the plural, "sins," indicates that he was referring to personal sins not the one sin of human origins committed by humanity's first parents. As it turns out, neither was entirely correct. Although Chrysostom believed in inherited sin, was not a Pelagian, and certainly did not exclude the guilt of original sin, he also did not possess the developed theological concepts pertaining to the doctrine of original sin that arose later in the West and provided an important backdrop for the Pelagian controversy.[4]

Chrysostom's writings also open a window to the penitential practices of his day and make it clear that the frequent practice of private auricular confession was still unknown. In *On Priesthood*, he does not even list hearing confessions as one of the tasks priests are commonly asked to perform. Similarly, he says that priests have the power to forgive sins only twice: at baptism (the sacrament of regeneration) and again when administering extreme unction (the sacrament of the sick). At other times, one gains forgiveness for sins by bearing one's heart directly to God: "Unfold your consciences to God alone, show Him your wounds, and ask help from him. Show yourself to Him who will not reproach you, but who will heal you.

---

2. John Chrysostom, *Homily 11 on John*, 2 (*Pat*, 3:475–76).
3. John Chrysostom, *Homily to Neophytos* (*P*, 384).
4. See *P*, 383–84; *Pat.*, 3:478.

Even though you be silent, He knows all."[5] Chrysostom's frequent call for the confession of sins refers either to public confession in the presence of others or the outpouring of one's heart to God alone. Nowhere in his writings does he call for individual auricular confession to a priest.[6]

Chrysostom's Teaching on the Eucharist

The title *Doctor Eucharistiae* has no official ecclesiastical status. Its frequent use in connection with Chrysostom indicates that he has a close connection with this important sacrament, especially with regard to his teaching on the real presence and the sacrificial nature of the Eucharist. Quasten offers an excellent summary of Chrysostom's Eucharistic teaching:

> ... there is no doubt that he [Chrysostom] is an eminent witness to the real presence of Christ in the Eucharist and its sacrificial character. His statements to that effect are numerous, clear, positive and detailed. He would have this sacrament approached with awe and devotion and calls the Eucharist "a table of holy fear," "an awe-inspiring and divine table," "the frightful mysteries," "the divine mysteries," "the ineffable mysteries," "the mysteries which demand reverence and trembling." The consecrated wine is "the cup of holy awe," "the awe-inspiring blood," and "the precious blood." Moreover, the Eucharist is an "awe-inspiring and terrible sacrifice," "a fearful and holy sacrifice," "the most awe-inspiring sacrifice." Pointing to the altar, he says: "Christ lies there slain," "His body lies before us now." "That which is in the chalice is the same as what flowed from the side of Christ. What is the bread? The Body of Christ." "Reflect, O man, what sacrificial flesh you take in your hand! To what table you will approach. Remember that you, though dust and ashes, do receive the Blood and the Body of Christ."[7]

Noted for his fine preaching, Chrysostom had a flare for the dramatic and used rich images to captivate his audience. To em-

---

5. John Chrysostom, *Homily against Anomoeos*, 5 (*Pat*, 3:479).
6. See *P*, 384–87; *Pat.*, 3:478–79.
7. For relevant references to Chrysostom's writings, see *Pat.*, 3:480.

phasize the reality of the real presence and to bring out the unity of the Eucharist with the sacrifice of Calvary, he projects the earthly characteristics of Christ's body and blood onto the bread and wine: "'Not only ought we to see the Lord, but we ought to take Him in our hands, eat Him, set our teeth upon His Flesh and most intimately unite ourselves with Him....' 'What the Lord did not tolerate on the Cross [i.e., the breaking of His legs], He tolerates now in the sacrifice through the love of you; He permits Himself to be broken in pieces that all may be filled to satiety.' "[8] Such statements flow from the close connection Chrysostom sees between the Eucharistic celebration and the events of Christ's paschal mystery. In his mind, the two cannot be separated.

When referring to the Eucharist, Chrysostom states quite clearly that the bread and wine are changed into the body and blood of Christ. Jesus, as priest and victim, effects this change through the words of institution uttered by a priest over the Eucharistic elements. Even though the Eucharist is offered daily, it remains one sacrifice identical with Jesus' sacrifice on the cross: "There is one Christ everywhere, complete both in this world and in the other; one body. As then, though offered in many places, He is but one body, so there is but one sacrifice.... We offer that now which was offered then; which is indeed inconsumable."[9] Chrysostom offers many vivid descriptions of what takes place during the Eucharist. Quasten has put together a series of quotations from the *Doctor Eucharistiae*:

> Believe that there takes place now the same banquet as that in which Christ sat at table, and that this banquet is in no way different from that. For it is not true that this banquet is prepared by a man while that was prepared by Himself.... Today as then, it is the Lord who works and offers all.... We assume the role of servants; it is He who blesses and transforms.... It is not man who causes what is present to become the Body and Blood of Christ, but Christ Himself who was crucified for us. The priest is the representative when he pronounces those words, but the power and the grace are those of the Lord. "This is my Body," he says. This word changes the things that lie before us;

8. John Chrysostom, *Homily 46 on John*, 3; *Homily 24 on 1 Corinthians*, 2 (*Pat.*, 3:480).
9. John Chrysostom, *Homily 17 on Hebrews* (*Pat.*, 3:480–81).

and as that sentence "increase and multiply," once spoken, extends through all time and gives to our nature the power to reproduce itself; even so that saying "This is my Body," once uttered, does at every table in the Churches from that time to the present day, and even till Christ's coming, make the sacrifice complete.[10]

Chrysostom believes in the change of the Eucharistic elements into the body and blood of Christ, the close identification of the Eucharistic sacrifice with the sacrifice of the cross, and the eschatological orientation of the Eucharistic banquet. His strong positions on these teachings helped to secure their place in the mainstream of the Church teaching.[11]

Observations

The following remarks seek to delve more deeply into Chrysostom's Eucharistic teaching and to offer relevant insights into his contribution to the Church's theology.

1. To begin with, Chrysostom's literalist approach to Scripture, which he gets from his close ties with the Antiochene school of exegesis, greatly influences his understanding of the Eucharist. Because he interprets such texts as John 6:51–66 and 1 Corinthians 11:23–27 literally, he argues for a close identification of the consecrated elements with Jesus' flesh and blood and for the importance of the words of institution for bringing about this important change. Chrysostom takes Jesus' words at face value and does not try to spiritualize them. In the spirit of Antiochene exegesis, he limits himself to the literal meaning of the text and develops his teaching on the Eucharist from there.[12]

2. With regard to how the change takes place in the Eucharistic elements, Chrysostom stands apart from most of the Greek fathers, who generally point to the invocation of the Holy Spirit at the *epiclesis* as important for the change. Although he sometimes speaks of the importance of the *epiclesis*, he also highlights the words of institution

---

10. For relevant references to Chrysostom's writings, see *Pat.*, 3:481.
11. For more Chrysostom's teaching on the Eucharist, see *P*, 384, *Pat.*, 3:479–82; *HD*, 2:178–79, 182–84; *Eucharistie*, cols. 1144–47.
12. See *Eucharistie*, cols. 1144–45.

as the time when the change occurs. In this respect, his teaching on the Eucharist is again clearly derived from his hermeneutical approach to Holy Writ. His literalist attitude shapes not only his belief in the real presence, but also in the manner in which the change in the Eucharistic elements themselves takes place.[13]

3. Chrysostom greatly reveres the Eucharist and stands in awe of it. For him, this sacrament should be approached with reverence and holy fear. Because he sees a close connection between the Eucharist and Christ's sacrifice on Calvary, he recognizes that the sacrament brings human suffering into the very heart of Christian worship. Through the Eucharist, the suffering of the faithful is incorporated into Christ's paschal mystery and given new meaning. For Chrysostom, Christ's paschal mystery transforms suffering into hope in the resurrection and new life in the world to come.

4. Chrysostom believes that receiving the Eucharist establishes a close bond between Jesus and Christians, both as individuals and as a community. He exhorts his hearers to prepare themselves for the table of the Lord and directs them to purify their souls so that they will welcome the Lord in an appropriate manner and obtain as much fruit as possible from consuming the body and blood of the Lord. By preparing themselves well for what they are about to receive, the faithful give further glory to God and are able to participate even more intimately in the sacramental mystery of Christ's sacrificial self-offering.[14]

5. In addition to a deeper unity of Christians with Christ and among themselves, Chrysostom also highlights life in the resurrection as an important fruit of Eucharistic worship. He is much clearer than the other Greek fathers on this point. He takes Jesus at his word that whoever eats his flesh and drinks his blood has life eternal and will be raised up on the last day (cf. Jn 6:54). In addition to the general resurrection of the dead, Chrysostom believes in a special, glorious resurrection reserved for the just as their eternal recompense. Once again, Chrysostom's teaching on the Eucharist flows from his close literal reading of Jesus' own words.[15]

---

13. See *HD*, 2:182.
14. See *Eucharistie*, col. 1146.
15. Ibid.

6. As a preacher, Chrysostom is apt to use vivid metaphors and imagery rather than philosophical concepts to convey his meaning, but his intention is always the same: to identify the consecrated elements with the body and blood of the crucified and risen Lord. His tendency to project descriptions of Christ's earthly body and blood onto the appearance of the consecrated elements stems not from a desire to confuse Jesus' physical, earthly presence with his spiritual, glorious presence in the Eucharist, but to impress upon his readers and listeners the real as opposed to symbolic nature of that presence.[16]

7. Since Chrysostom identifies the Eucharistic sacrifice with that of Calvary, he believes that the sacrifice of the altar is the same as that of the cross. For him, Jesus Christ is the chief priest of this one sacrifice, who acts through his priestly ministers to bring about the Eucharistic change. Although he sometimes speaks of the Eucharist as a commemoration, he repeatedly affirms that Christ is in the same state in the Eucharist as he was during his passion: Jesus is beaten and nailed to the cross; blood and water flow from his opened side.[17]

8. Finally, much of Chrysostom's language revolves around the notion of "the Lord's table" and he refers to the Eucharist very often as a "sacrificial meal," affirming that Jesus' body and blood are "real food and drink." Indeed, he has a very strong sense of the Eucharist as a banquet, especially as a foretaste of the heavenly banquet. The eschatological dimension of his teaching comes through quite poignantly when he speaks about the sacrament's capacity to "increase and multiply" every time the words of institution are uttered over the Eucharistic elements by a priest. The Eucharist, for Chrysostom, is the sacrament of the new creation that ushers in a world renewed by Christ and will reach its completion at the end of time.[18]

---

16. See *Pat.*, 3:480.
17. See *HD*, 2:183.
18. See *Pat.*, 3:481.

Conclusion

John Chrysostom, archbishop of Constantinople, was the great-est preacher and orator of his time, perhaps the greatest the Church has ever known. Although he followed the literalist exegetical method of the Antiochene School, he carefully evaded the doctrinal errors toward which it was prone. He was a bedrock of traditional orthodoxy and rarely parted from the theological mainstream.

Nearly the whole of Chrysostom's literary corpus survives to this day, a tribute to his popularity as a preacher and to the high regard his contemporaries and succeeding generations of Christians had for his thought. No other Greek father has had so extensive a body of writings preserved in so many languages. Some would go so far as to say that Chrysostom was to the East what the thought of Augustine of Hippo was to the West.

Comparisons aside, Chrysostom was a towering figure for his day and holds a prominent place among the great Church fathers of the Golden Age of the patristic era. His teaching on the Eucharist forms an important part of his theological legacy and he has contributed greatly to the Church's understanding of the sacrament.

Reflection Questions

1. How helpful are the literal and spiritual interpretations of Scripture in understanding the Eucharist? Which attracts you more? Are these different approaches diametrically opposed or complementary to each other? Do you like Chrysostom's use of the literal approach in his treatment of the Eucharist?
2. Do you think one should approach the Eucharist with reverence and holy fear? If so why? If not, why not? What, in your opin-ion, would be the opposite of "holy fear"? Can such a phrase be subject to misunderstanding today? How should one prepare oneself to receive the sacrament worthily?
3. Do you think it is better to employ vivid metaphors and imagery rather than philosophical concepts to convey the doctrine of Christ's real presence in the Eucharist? What are the strengths

and weaknesses of each approach? Which approach is more effective? Which do your prefer? Can these approaches be used to
complement each other? If not, why not?

4. Chrysostom draws a close connection between the Eucharist
   and the sacrifice of Calvary. Do you think this close connection
   exists in the minds of most believers today? Do you think it
   should? If so, what can be done to emphasize this dimension of
   the Eucharistic celebration in the hearts and minds of today's
   believers?

5. Do you think of the Eucharist as a foretaste of the heavenly
   banquet? If so, then what does the Eucharist tell you about the
   banquet that is to come? What hopes and dreams does it embody
   for you? What hopes and dreams does it embody for the Christian community? What hopes and dreams does it embody for all
   of humanity?

Jerome

True Sacrament of Passover

The flesh and blood of Christ is understood in two ways; there is either the spiritual and divine way, by which He Himself said: "My flesh is truly food, and my blood is truly drink"; and "Unless you shall have eaten my flesh and drunk my blood you shall not have eternal life." Or else there is the flesh and blood which was crucified and which was poured out by the soldier's lance.

Jerome

What did the early Church's greatest linguist and Scripture scholar have to say about the Eucharist? Jerome (c. 347–420), our next voice from the past, was one of the most learned and versatile of the Church Fathers. Born into a wealthy Catholic family at Strido in Dalmatia, he travelled to Rome in 354 to be trained in grammar, rhetoric and philosophy. He knew three languages (Latin, Greek, and Hebrew), studied exegesis in Constantinople under Gregory of Nazianzus, and was the secretary and counsellor of Pope Damasus in Rome.

Jerome lived much of his life in the secluded desert places of Syria and Palestine, and from 385 until his death headed a monastic community in Bethlehem. Although he had an irascible temperament and became embroiled in heated controversies, he devoted most of his time in to study, writing, and other scholarly pursuits.

Jerome's most noteworthy achievement is his Latin translation of the Scriptures (i.e., the Vulgate), which from the sixth century on would be the standard version used through the Christian West. He was a staunch defender of the Church of Rome and was generally conservative in his theological views. His views on the Eucharist reflect his keen sensitivity to the Scriptures and their reception in the life of the community.[1]

Jerome's Theological Outlook

Jerome was very well educated (he knew Latin, Greek and Hebrew and was called a "man of three languages") and made important contributions to Christian learning. In his day, he was widely known as a translator, exegete, polemicist, preacher, and letter writer. The words of Augustine of Hippo reveal what high regard his contemporaries had for his near encyclopaedic knowledge: "What Jerome is ignorant of, no man has ever known."[2]

Although not noted for creative innovation, Jerome used his great breadth of knowledge to plumb the depths of the Christian tradition and make it available to others. In addition to his Latin translation of the Bible, he translated many works of Origen, the great third-century theologian of Alexandria. He also translated a number of works of Eusebius of Caesarea (d. 339), including *The Chronicles* (which he himself updated to the year 378), and the monastic rules and letters of Pachomius, Theodore, and Orsisius.[3]

As an exegete, he wrote a variety of Scripture commentaries. In the Old Testament, he commented on the Psalms, Ecclesiastes, and most of the Prophets. In the New Testament, he commented on four letters of Paul (Philippians, Galatians, Ephesians, and Titus), the Gospel of Matthew, and revised Victorinus of Pettau's *Commentary on the Apocalypse.*[4]

Jerome entered into polemical debates, where he opposed the errors of Origen and Pelagius and defended Catholic positions regarding virginity, religious life, good works, and devotion to Mary. A large number of his homilies to his monastic community in Bethlehem also survive, as well as an abundance of letters that provide unique insights into the theological controversies of his day. Of particular

---

1. For biographical information on Jerome, see *P*, 462–66; *CH*, 1:400–2; *FLC*, 129–82.
2. See *CH*, 1:400–2; *P*, 466–73.
3. See *P*, 466–69.
4. Ibid., 470.

note is his correspondence with Augustine, his Latin contemporary from North Africa, whose influence on succeeding generations would equal (and eventually surpass) that of Jerome.[5]

Theologically, Jerome was a loyal son of the Church. He avoided philosophical and theological speculation and argued primarily from Scripture and tradition. He had a high regard for the teaching of Rome and often referred to its liturgy, life, and practice when seeking to resolve controversies. He makes his position quite clear to Pope Damasus: "I follow no one as the first except Christ alone, hence I want to remain in communion with you, that is, with the see of Peter. I know that the Church is founded on this rock."[6]

In doctrinal matters, Jerome looked to the teaching of Rome as a guiding rule of faith. In his use of Scripture, he had a high regard for the literal sense, but was deeply influenced by the allegorical approach developed by the Alexandrian school. He liked this approach because it enabled him to preserve the inspiration and inerrancy of the whole of Scripture, allowing him to extract spiritual meanings from texts, the literal meaning of which he could find difficult to accept. To be considered valid, however, these spiritual senses had to be accepted by the Church.[7]

In keeping with his loyalty to Rome, Jerome was staunchly anti-Pelagian, insisting on the necessity of both free will *and* grace for salvation. Unlike most of the other great theologians of his day, however, he believed that the monarchical episcopacy was not divinely established, but a development of ecclesiastical law. With regard to the final judgment, he believed that all those who denied God would suffer eternal punishment. Christians, however, even those who were serious sinners, would be judged mercifully.[8]

Jerome's Teaching on the Eucharist

Jerome was a sacramental realist in his Eucharistic teaching. He justified the real presence through Jesus' words at the Last Supper:

---

5. Ibid., 470–72.
6. Jerome, *Epistle*, 15.2 (*P*, 474–75).
7. See *CH*, 1:401–2; *P*, 473–74.
8. See *P*, 474–75.

We recognize that the bread that the Lord breaks and gives to his disciples is the same body of the Savior, himself having said to them: "Take and eat, this is my body," and that the chalice is that of which he says: "Drink of it all of you, for this is my blood of the New Covenant, which will be shed for many." If then the bread which is descended from heaven is the body of the Lord, and if the wine which he gives to his disciples is his blood…, then we reject the Jewish fables…. It is not Moses who gives us the true bread, but it is the Lord Jesus, who himself is both guest and banquet, the one consuming and also the one being consumed.[9]

This is just one instance of Jerome stating very clearly that the faithful receive the body and blood of Jesus in the Eucharist.[10] In other places, he affirms that the clergy feed the faithful by confecting the body and blood through their holy words and that the *epiclesis* or the invocation of the Holy Spirit over the gifts plays some part in the consecration.[11] He also advises those who are about to receive the body and blood of Christ to prepare themselves accordingly. For married couples, he claims this means abstaining from the conjugal act.[12]

Jerome often uses figurative and typological language to describe the nature of the Eucharist. This approach to the sacrament comes from his Scriptural background and his attempt to point out the various relationships between the Old and New Testaments. He describes a number of Old Testament incidents as shadowy types or prefigurings of the sacrament of the Last Supper. The most prominent of these refers to the Passover lamb and the high priest, Melchizedech:

After the type had been fulfilled by the Passover celebration and He had eaten the flesh of the lamb with His Apostles, He takes bread which strengthens the heart of man, and goes on to the true Sacrament of the passover, so that just as Melchizedech, the priest of the Most High Gods, in prefiguring Him, made bread and wine an offering, He too makes Himself manifest in the reality of His own Body and Blood.[13]

9. Jerome, *Epistle* 120.2.2 (*Eucharistie*, cols. 1152–53 [my translation]).
10. See Jerome, *On Matthew,* 26.26; *Epistle,* 120.2; *Epistle,* 82.2; *On Ezechiel,* 41.8; *On the Epistle to the Ephesians,* 1.7 (*HD*, 2:314).
11. See Jerome, *Epistle,* 14.8; *Epistle,* 64.5; *Epistle,* 146.1; *On Sophonias,* 3.7 (*HD,* 2:314–15).
12. See Jerome, *Epistle* 47.15 (*HD*, 2:317).
13. Jerome, *On the Epistle to the Ephesians*, 4.26.26, no. 1390 (*FEF*, 2:203).

In this passage, two Old Testament rites — that of the Passover (Ex 12:1–14) and that offered by Melchizedech (Gn 14:17–24) — converge in Jesus' celebration of his Last Supper with his disciples. The Passover lamb eaten at the Last Supper is the "type" for Jesus, the Paschal lamb of the New Covenant. Jesus, in turn, blesses bread and wine and shares it with his disciples, in much the same way that Melchizedech pronounced a blessing over them and shared it with Abraham. For Jerome, these two sacrificial offerings of the Old Testament foreshadow Jesus' sacrificial self-offering that took place in an unbloody way on Holy Thursday and in a bloody way on the days immediately following it. For him, the institution of the Eucharist at the Last Supper cannot be separated from the events of Jesus' passion, death, and resurrection. It is not just one symbol among many others, but the full realization of what was prefigured in the Old Testament.[14]

Jerome spells out the relationship between the Last Supper and Jesus' paschal mystery. He often speaks of the Last Supper as an "image" or "type" of the passion, i.e., as something that foreshadows the events of Christ's paschal mystery. In using such language, he does not mean to de-emphasize the close connection between the two, but to bind them together. He speaks of the Last Supper as giving real spiritual food and nourishment to the faithful and making present the real body and blood of Christ offered to God from the cross.

For Jerome, there are two ways of speaking about Jesus' body and blood:

> The flesh and blood of Christ is understood in two ways; there is either the spiritual and divine way, by which He Himself said: "My flesh is truly food, and my blood is truly drink"; and "Unless you shall have eaten my flesh and drunk my blood you shall not have eternal life." Or else there is the flesh and blood which was crucified and which was poured out by the soldier's lance.[15]

In his mind, there is no essential difference between these two understandings of Christ's body and blood, only a distinction in

---

14. See *Eucharistie*, col. 1153.
15. Jerome, *On the Epistle to the Ephesians*, 1.1.7, no. 1365 (*FEF*, 2:192).

mode or manner of being. The unity between the two comes from Jesus' own words, which specifically connect the bread and wine with the offering up of his body and the shedding of his blood.[16] Jerome's distinction, however, also helps to avoid a crude, cannibalistic interpretation of the Eucharist.

Taken together, the above passages show that Jerome believes in Jesus' real presence in the consecrated elements and understands the Eucharistic celebration in terms of banquet and sacrifice. He affirms what is essential about the Eucharist and highlights the witness of the tradition concerning them. In keeping with his conservative character, however, he does not probe much further into the meaning of this sacrament, perhaps in part because he does not wish to subject these mysteries of the faith to needless human scrutiny.

Observations

Jerome's teaching on the Eucharist invites comment from a variety of perspectives. In the light of these, the following observations seek to tease out or underline some of the implications of his understanding.

1. As has been said, in his teaching on the Eucharist, Jerome exhibits his love for tradition and the theological mainstream. He steers away from abstract speculation and seeks to glean from the Scriptures and reliable commentators the Church's authentic teaching on the Eucharist. He uses Scriptural rather than philosophical language in his presentation and is careful not to rely on authors whose opinions have been seriously called into question. For him, the Eucharist is a sacramental mystery given by Christ to the Church for the spiritual nourishment of the faithful. Those who scrutinize its meaning must do so with great care and discernment, using the witness of Scripture and the teaching of the Church as a fundamental point of departure.

2. It is important to read Jerome's teachings on the Eucharist in the specific literary context in which they appear. Jerome dedicates no specific treatise or commentary to the sacrament, but disperses his teachings on the subject throughout his many writings, especially in

---

16. See *Eucharistie*, col. 1153–54.

his letters and Scriptural commentaries. The importance of context should not be underestimated. In one letter, he refutes those wishing to make deacons the same as presbyters, but does so by placing presbyters on seemingly the same footing as bishops when presiding at the Eucharist. Read out of context and without the benefit of his other writings, one might mistakenly argue that Jerome fails to distinguish the powers of the episcopacy and presbyterate. On the contrary, although Jerome considers the episcopacy an establishment of ecclesiastical law rather than a divine institution, he clearly recognizes bishops as successors to the apostles and recognized that they alone had the power to ordain.[17]

3. Jerome's use of typology in his teaching on the Eucharist stems from his interest in the Scriptures and his attempt to demonstrate that the New Testament is the fulfillment of the Old. This approach is based on the notion that people and events of the Old Testament foreshadow what appears in the New. In its attempt to find parallel patterns of meaning between the two Testaments, such interpretations resonate strongly with the allegorical approach to Scripture that Jerome (and most of the other Western Church fathers) found very appealing. At the same time, it is only one of several tools used by him to explain the Church's teaching on the Eucharist.[18]

4. Jerome brings together the offerings of two Old Testament sacrifices to explain the mystery of the Eucharist: the Passover lamb and the bread and wine offered by Melchizedech. For him, each is a genuine but incomplete foreshadowing of the Last Supper. He combines them in a single passage ("juxtaposes," if you will) so that together they might convey a deeper meaning of the Eucharist than what either could possibly achieve alone. Acting in this way, they depict the Last Supper as a mystery pointing beyond itself, a sacrificial meal that itself both foreshadows and makes present Christ's sacrificial death on the cross.

---

17. See Jerome, *Epistle* 146.1; *On the Epistle to Titus* 1.1.5. Cited respectively as no. 1357 (*FEF*, 2:187; M.J. Rouët de Journel, *Enchiridion Patristicum*, 25th ed., no. 1371 [Barcelona/Rome: Herder, 1981], 499). See also *P*, 475.
18. For more on the typical sense and its relationship to patristic allegoresis, see Raymond Brown, "Hermeneutics," in *The Jerome Biblical Commentary* (Englewood Cliffs, N.J.: Prentice-Hall, Inc. 1968), 618–19.

5. In addition to the Eucharist's sacrificial nature, Jerome leaves little doubt that Jesus' body and blood are truly present in the consecrated elements. He does not go into *how* this presence takes place, but is content with merely affirming the teaching generally accepted in his day. This sacramental realism reflects both the general trend of fourth- and fifth-century Latin patrology, but is particularly expressive of the position held in Rome. Since Jerome served for a time as secretary and counsellor of Pope Damasus he reflects in his writings a deep respect for the opinions of Rome.

6. Jerome is also very clear about the relationship between the Last Supper and Christ's passion and death on the cross. When he speaks of "two ways" of understanding the body and blood of Christ, he does not mean two completely different realities, but two ways of expressing the same thing. In his mind, the Eucharist *is* the body and blood of Christ in the form of bread and wine just as the crucified Lord *is* the body and blood of Christ in the flesh. In the former, the body and blood of Christ are present in a spiritual mode; in the latter, they are present in bodily flesh and blood.

7. Jerome is also very strong on the role of the higher clergy in the Eucharistic celebration. The Eucharist cannot take place without the presence of a presiding bishop or priest. No one else may preside at the altar, not even a deacon. They feed the faithful from the altar by confecting the Eucharist through their holy words. Because of this power to consecrate, they possess great spiritual wealth and are to be numbered among the richest and most fortunate of souls.[19] This special role, however, carries with it great responsibility. Priests and bishops have the responsibility of shepherding the flocks they tend by feeding them and by keeping them safe from error.

8. Finally, Jerome is clearly a man of his time. His advice to married couples that they abstain from conjugal relations before receiving the Eucharist is a case in point. As with most of the other Church fathers of his day, he has a high regard for Christian asceticism and the monastic ideal. This manifests itself especially in his deep love for virginity and the life of chastity, which he firmly believes is a nobler and superior state of life than marriage. For this reason, he exhorts

---

19. See Jerome, *Epistle*, 125.20 (*NPNF*, 6:251).

married couples to defer to this ideal by refraining from sexual relations at least before receiving the Eucharist. Although other Church
fathers do not go as far, they all insist on purity of soul as a basic
prerequisite for reception of the sacrament.[20]

Conclusion

Jerome is most remembered for his dedication to scholarship
and the monastic ideal. This commitment to learning and asceticism
counteracted his personal imperfections and character flaws and led
him along the way of holiness. Because of his astounding literary
output, he had a vast impact on succeeding generations, especially
through his Latin Vulgate and Scripture commentaries. Because of
this impact and his deep regard for languages and primary sources,
some historians have gone so far as to see him as a forerunner of
Christian humanism.

In his teachings on the Eucharist, Jerome stands in the mainstream of the Latin patristic tradition. He is a sacramental realist
who believes in the sacrificial nature of the Eucharist banquet. He
does not engage in speculative theology, but is interested in probing
the sources of the tradition to present a clear understanding of the
meaning of the Eucharistic celebration. To do so, he uses the tools of
Scriptural allegory and historical typology to present the Eucharist as
the fulfillment of a variety of Old Testament types or figures.

The Eucharist, for Jerome, is intimately related to Christ's paschal
mystery. It is spiritual food, unbloody sacrifice, and real presence. It
is the central act of Christian worship, "the true Sacrament of the
Passover."[21] Presided over by a priest or bishop, who invokes the Holy
Spirit and utters the words of consecration, it is an action of Christ,
who "… makes Himself manifest in the reality of His own Body and
Blood." [22]

---

20. See *HD*, 2:317.
21. Jerome, *On the Epistle to the Ephesians*, 4.26.26, no. 1390 (*FEF*, 2:203).
22. Ibid.

Reflection Questions

1. Do you believe that when explaining the mystery of the Eucharist one should use only the witness of Scripture and the teaching of the Church for one's fundamental point of departure? What benefits are there to staying within the theological mainstream when trying to explain the Eucharist to someone? Are there any liabilities in such an approach?

2. In what way can the events of the Old Testament be seen as a foreshadowing of the New? Upon what interpretative approach to the Scriptures is such a claim based? Can such an approach be supported today? If not, why not? If so, how would you defend your position? In what sense are the Passover lamb and the bread and wine offerings of Melchizedech each a genuine but incomplete foreshadowing of the Last Supper?

3. Do you agree with Jerome that there are "two ways" of understanding the body and blood of Christ (i.e., a physical and a spiritual mode)? How do these modes differ? How are they the same? What are the strengths of Jerome's distinction? Do you see any weaknesses in it? Do you find it helpful in explaining the mystery of the Eucharist to others?

4. Do you agree with Jerome's strong emphasis on the role of priests and bishops in the Eucharistic celebration? Do you agree that, because of their power to consecrate, they possess great spiritual wealth and are to be numbered among the richest and most fortunate of souls? What are the strengths of such a strong emphasis on the role of priests and bishops? What are the dangers? How would you present the role of priests and bishops in the life of the believing community today?

5. Jerome was a man of his time and was unconsciously shaped by subtle prejudices that affected his understanding of the Gospel. Do you think of yourself as a man or woman of your time? Are you in touch with the subtle prejudices that unconsciously shape your understanding of the Christian message? Do any of these touch your understanding of the Eucharist? If so, how?

Voice Twenty-One

Augustine of Hippo
Bread of Love

O Sacrament of piety! O sign of unity! O Bread of love! Anyone who wants to live has both where to live and whence to
live. Let him draw near; let him believe; let him be embodied,
that he may be made to live.

Augustine of Hippo

What did someone who was arguably the greatest theologian
of the early Church have to say about the Eucharist? Augustine of
Hippo (354–430), our next voice from the past, had much to say
about the sacrament of the altar. He was a towering personality of his
day, whose writings helped shape the direction of Western Christian
theology for centuries to come.

Born of a pagan father and a saintly Christian mother, Augustine
was trained in rhetoric in Carthage and began his professional career
as a teacher of liberal arts in his hometown of Thagaste in Numidia,
North Africa. Although he had been enrolled as a catechumen in
his youth, he rejected Christianity as "an old wives' tale" during his
time in Carthage and gave himself over to sensual excesses, taking a
concubine and having a son with her, who they named "Adeodatus"
(372–90). In his search for truth, Augustine joined the Manicheans
and later became interested in Neo-Platonism. In 384, he accepted
a post in Milan as a professor of rhetoric and was touched by the
preaching and teaching of Ambrose, the city's saintly and learned
bishop. The love, dedication, and prayers of his mother, Monica,
had a lasting effect on his life and also influenced his conversion.
Baptized by Ambrose in 387, Augustine returned to North Africa in
388 and was ordained a priest for the diocese of Hippo Regius in

220

391 and then bishop in 395, remaining there until his death some 35 years later.

Although Augustine was deeply influenced in the patterns of his thought by Neoplatonism, he produced a new and creative theological account of Christianity. He was a prolific author and wrote on a wide variety of topics. His most famous works are his *Confessions* (401), an autobiographical account of his conversion, and *The City of God* (426), a comprehensive Christian theology of history. Other noteworthy works include *On the Trinity* (419), *Enchiridion (Faith, Hope and Love)* (423), *On Christian Doctrine* (426), and his *Retractions* (427). In addition to these writings, his literary corpus includes major treatises against the Arians, the Pelagians, and the Donatists, a number of important Scripture commentaries, about 400 sermons, and over 200 letters. He treats the Eucharist in a number of places in his large literary output, at times in great length and at considerable depth.[1]

Augustine's Theological Outlook

The Neoplatonic philosophy that so influenced Augustine's Christian theology was a systematic restructuring of Platonism developed by Plotinus (205–70) and put forward by his disciple Porphyry (c. 232–301) in the *Enneads*. This "new" form of Platonism said that all of reality emanated from the One, the source of all being. It was based on a hierarchical understanding of existence, with lower, lesser levels of existence emanating from the One. The visible world was seen as the lowest level possible

An effect of Neoplatonism on Augustine's thought was to see reality as hierarchically ordered. But Augustine replaced the notion of necessary emanations with the view that the creation of the cosmos was the voluntary act of an almighty God. Augustine also drew a strict line between the supernatural and natural orders and offset Neoplatonism's subtle denigration of the visible world by affirming the fundamental goodness of all creation. The Neoplatonic influence

---

1. The above biographical information comes from *P*, 487–96; *CH*, 1:402–8; *FLC*, 183–276.

on Augustine can be clearly seen in the precedence he gives to universal ideas and the way they influence every level of his thought, from his doctrine of the Trinity, to his concept of original sin and the Fall of Adam, to his allegorical interpretation of the two "books" of Scripture and Creation.

When it came to theological controversy, Augustine distinguished himself as a very effective polemicist. He combated the dualism of the Manichees and insisted against the Donatists that the efficacy of the sacraments did not depend on the moral state of the minister administering them. He also affirmed the divinity of the Logos in the lingering Arian controversy and maintained against the Pelagians that human beings were wounded by original sin and therefore could not earn salvation through their own efforts. Engaging in these and other controversies forced him to articulate his own position on the doctrines of creation, original sin, the incarnation, grace, redemption, and the sacraments. Although he was not systematic in his presentations, hence the necessity to issue his *Retractions* near the end of his life, his theological ideas left a deep imprint on Western Christianity and would influence it in profound ways for centuries to come.

Augustine's contribution to Western theology is profound and far-reaching. Renowned in his day for his capacity to combine the role of a pastor and theologian, he commented extensively on nearly all the relevant topics of his day to do with doctrine, morality, and exegesis. While he made contributions to such areas as Trinitarian theology, the theology of history, the doctrine of original sin, and the theology of grace, his Scriptural commentaries and sermons offer a wealth of material on the spiritual life, and his numerous letters offer profound insights into the ecclesiastical controversies of his day.[2]

Augustine's Teaching on the Eucharist

Augustine's Eucharistic teaching is multi-layered and not always easy to explain. It should be interpreted within its own historical context and not as evidence from the tradition for doctrines that only developed much later. In the words of Jaroslav Pelikan: "It is incor-

---

2. For more on Augustine's theological outlook, see *P*, 517–34.

rect ... to attribute to Augustine either a scholastic doctrine of transubstantiation or a Protestant doctrine of symbolism, for he taught neither — or both — and both were able to cite his authority."[3] Even those who say that Augustine believed in the real presence admit that some of his expressions are difficult to explain. Nor is there any clear evidence that he believed in the continuing presence of Christ in the consecrated elements.[4]

The difficulty in explaining Augustine's Eucharistic teaching comes from a variety of reasons. For one thing, the mystery of the Eucharist itself eludes the grasp of even the most sophisticated theological formulas, since it involves the spiritual presence of a corporeal reality. Augustine's understanding of a sacrament as "a sacred sign" (*sacrum signum*),[5] moreover, is much broader than typically understood today and can be easily misread or taken out of context. In addition, he has a penchant for allegorical explanations that lend themselves to many levels of meaning and often use figurative language that can shift in meaning from one context to another.[6]

Given the above, it is fair to say that Augustine sometimes refers to the Eucharist as a sign or figure of the body of Christ. In one such instance, he clearly depicts the Eucharist as a sign: "For the Lord did not hesitate to say. 'This is My Body,' when He wanted to give a *sign* of His body."[7] At another time, he indicates belief in the real presence: "He took earth from earth, because flesh comes from the earth, and he received his flesh from the flesh of Mary. He walked here below in that flesh, and even gave us that same flesh to eat for our salvation."[8] It seems that Augustine views such interpretations as complementary rather than contradictory. The Eucharist for him both pointed to something and yet manifested what it signified. It both prefigures and makes present that to which it points.

---

3. *CT*, 1:305.
4. See Ibid.; *P*, 529.
5. Augustine of Hippo, *The City of God*, 10.5, no. 1744 (*FEF*, 3:98–99). For other classical definitions, see also Ludwig Ott, *Fundamentals of Catholic Dogma*, trans. Patrick Lynch (Rockford, Ill.: Tan, 1974), 325.
6. See *HD*, 2:408.
7. Augustine of Hippo, *Against Adimantus,* 12.3, no. 1566 (*FEF*, 3:46).
8. Ibid., *Expositions of the Psalms*, III/18 (New City Press, NY 2002), p. 474.

Elsewhere, Augustine draws a clear connection between the Eucharist and Jesus' sacrifice of his body and blood for the forgiveness of sins. In Sermon 227, for example, he speaks thus to the newly baptized:

> You ought to know what you have received, what you are about to receive, what you ought to receive every day. That bread which you can see on the altar, sanctified by the word of God, is the body of Christ. That cup, or rather what the cup contains, sanctified by the word of God, is the blood of Christ. It was by means of these things that the Lord Christ wished to present to us with his body and blood, which he shed for our sake for the forgiveness of sins. If you receive them well, you are yourselves what you receive. You see, the apostle says, *We, being many, are one loaf, one body* (1 Cor 10:17). That's how he explained the sacrament of the Lord's table; one loaf, one body, is what we all are, many though we be. In this one loaf of bread you are given clearly to understand how much you should love unity. I mean, was that one loaf made from one grain? Weren't there many grains of wheat? But before they came into the loaf they were all separate; they were joined together by means of water after a certain amount of pounding and crushing.[9]

Here, Augustine unites the Eucharist to Christ's sacrificial death on Calvary. He affirms Jesus' real presence in the sacrament and emphasizes its unifying role for the members of Christ's body, the Church. He also asserts that the sacrament mediates to the faithful the forgiveness of sins made possible by Christ's death on the cross and should be received daily. In similar passages, Augustine makes it clear that Christ instituted the Eucharist as a memorial of his passion and death in order to give his own flesh and blood as food and drink. He explains that Christ is truly present under the appearances of bread and wine, that this change takes place through the words of institution, and that it does not result from the dispositions and faith of the communicant.[10]

---

9. Augustine of Hippo, *Sermons*, III/6 (New City Press, New York 1993) trans. Edmund Hill, no. 227, 254. The term "pounding and crushing" is *"contritionem"* in Latin, a pun on contrition.
10. For relevant texts, see nos. 1480, 1519, 1520, 1587, 1604, 1652, 1633, 1815, 1820, 2101 (*FEF*, 3:20, 30–31, 54, 59–60, 68, 73–74, 117–19, 220).

The Eucharist, for Augustine, is required for the health of the soul and should be received by the faithful often for spiritual nourishment; it can also be offered for the faithful departed (but not for the unbaptized). Those who receive it worthily become one with Christ's body and blood. As a sacrament, it signifies and assures the unity of the Church. It is a solemn remembering of the sacrifice of Calvary, which prefigures the sacrifices of the Old Law, announced beforehand in the prophecy of Malachi (1:11), and anticipated in a special way in the sacrifice of Melchizedek. It is a sacrificial meal offered in prayer, atonement, adoration, and thanksgiving as the one true sacrifice of the New Covenant.[11]

Observations

Augustine's teaching on the Eucharist invites commentary from a variety of perspectives. The following remarks, while in no way exhaustive, offer some important insights into the nature and scope of his teaching.

1. For one thing, the influence of Neoplatonism on Augustine's philosophy sustains his allegorical approach to the Books of Scripture and Creation and has a significant role in shaping his interpretation of the Eucharist, the sacrament par excellence of the New Creation. It also supports the notion of participation by which lower realities are able to share in the life of higher ones. By taking part in the Eucharist, Christians are able to participate in the life of the Risen Lord; they also have a point of reference for interpreting both past and future events. Augustine's use of Neoplatonic thought forms enables him to see the Eucharist in a threefold sense. It is the point toward which many Old Testament prophecies converge, a bloodless foreshadowing of Christ's sacrificial death on Calvary, and an earthly anticipation of the heavenly banquet.

2. Augustine's teaching on the Eucharist was directly affected by many of the doctrinal controversies in which he was directly

---

11. For relevant texts, see nos. 1516, 1519, 1524, 1593, 1600, 1604, 1652, 1716, 1717, 1744, 1745,1824, 1866, 1930, 1977 (*FEF* 3:29–30, 32, 57, 59–60, 73–74, 90–91, 98, 99, 119, 134, 152, 168).

involved. By affirming that elements of the material world become the body and blood of Jesus, he counteracts the threat of Manichean dualism which saw the soul as belonging to the realm of light and the body to the realm of darkness. By insisting that the Holy Spirit makes the Eucharist an abundant conduit of God's grace and on the necessity of receiving it, he offsets the Pelagian emphasis on human effort as the operative agent in human salvation. By claiming that the Eucharist does not depend on the holiness of the minister, but instead on the proper convergence of word, matter, and intention, he counters the excessive claims of Donatist purism.

3. Since Augustine has a very broad understanding of what constitutes a sacrament great care should be taken not to project onto his Eucharistic teaching concepts unfamiliar to him. Although he has a very clear idea of a sacrament as a sign that points to divine realities, he does not possess the language for distinguishing between what the scholastics would later call the sign (i.e., *sacramentum tantum*), the sign and mystery (*sacramentum et res*) and the mystery itself (*res tantum*). His lack of this kind of terminology is partly the result of his respect for the nature of Christian mystery and his understanding, derived from Neoplatonism, that language is capable of revealing in a single word a wide variety of complementary (and perhaps even contrasting) meanings. But it is also the result of his very different way of approaching the nature of Christian truth and of formulating the distinction between a sacramental sign and the reality to which it points.

4. Augustine's teaching reflects the longstanding position of the Church in North Africa that the Eucharist is a "sacrament of unity." This position goes back to the time of Cyprian of Carthage (d. 258) and reflects the need of the Church to have something to help it stand firm against the forces of division that would undermine its authentic teaching. In Augustine's day, participation in the Eucharist was restricted to those members of the baptized community who were in good standing with the Church. It served as a mark of both correct belief and correct practice, that is, of orthodoxy and orthopraxis, and separated the members of the local Church from those who did not hold firmly to the accepted teachings and practices of Catholic Christianity.

5. Augustine believed that the Eucharistic elements became the body and blood of Christ, but often wrote of it in terms of a spiritual presence. Part of his reason for doing so was to disassociate himself from the concept of the Eucharist as a "bloody meal" and to find a way of speaking about a real presence under a different mode of expression.[12] To speak of a "spiritual presence" is more than mere symbolism and in no way implies that the Eucharistic body and blood is somehow different from the very person of Christ himself.

6. Augustine was interested in how Jesus' real body could be present in the Eucharist in the form of bread and wine. He believed that through the words of consecration the power of the Holy Spirit transformed the Eucharistic elements into the living flesh of Jesus' glorified life. The Spirit is the one who vivifies the bread and wine, and who allows those who worthily partake in the Eucharist to be inwardly healed and spiritually renewed. By eating the body and blood of the glorified Christ, believers enter into deep communion with the Lord and anticipate for a time their own share in the resurrection.[13]

7. Augustine's teaching of the real presence is bolstered by his belief that even sinners and heretics received the body and blood of Christ (albeit unworthily) and that it was also spiritually profitable to small children. In making such claims, he asserts that the Eucharist is the body and blood of Christ and goes beyond the perceptions of the communicants. While the fruitfulness of the sacrament depends on the faith and dispositions of the recipients, he makes it quite clear that the consecrated elements themselves are the real body and blood of Christ independently of the spiritual and moral mindset of the faithful.[14]

8. Finally, Augustine presents the Eucharist as a sacrifice, i.e., an action of self-offering that brings someone into a close, intimate union with God. Christ offers himself as a sacrifice to God from the cross. The Church shares in this sacrifice, because it comprises the various members of his body. The Eucharist is the offering of the Church par excellence and is an act of worship rendered to God alone. It is a true sacrifice, which points to and makes present the one

---

12. See *HD*, 2:410–11.
13. Ibid., 2:414.
14. Ibid., 2:413.

sacrifice of Calvary, and in which Christ, along with the members of his body, is both priest and victim.[15]

Conclusion

Augustine of Hippo was a man of many talents: bishop, theologian, pastor, philosopher, preacher, autobiographer, polemicist, poet, letter-writer — and so very much more. He was a creative thinker who fostered the development of Christian theology in a way that was both continuous with the past and responsive to new modes of thinking. The synthesis he effected between Neoplatonism and Christian thought would have a lasting impact on Western civilization for centuries to come.

Augustine was a bold and probing thinker, who allowed his restless yearning for God to guide him in his search for understanding. He sought truth wherever it revealed itself: in creation, in the Scriptures, in the events of history, in himself, in others, in the Church and its sacraments, even in the midst of heated controversy. For Augustine, God's voice could be heard everywhere, if one but took the time to open one's heart to Christ, who reveals himself as the way, the truth, and the life.

In his teaching on the Eucharist, Augustine displays the very best of Latin patristic thought. With his thought steeped in figurative language and allegorical interpretation, he affirms Christ's real presence in the Eucharistic elements in the context of a sacrificial meal. He does so, while allowing for different levels of meaning to penetrate the mystery of this ritual action and permitting the unifying force of the Spirit to gather the members of Christ's body together in adoration of the Father. The Eucharist, for Augustine, fulfills the Old Testament prophecies and is a sacrament of the New Creation. It points to Calvary and to the empty tomb of the Risen Lord. It is food for the soul, nourishment for the pilgrim, a foretaste of the heavenly banquet.

---

15. Ibid., 2:415–16.

Reflection Questions

1. Do you like Augustine's multi-layered understanding of the Eucharist? If so, what do you like about it? What are its strengths? What are some of its possible weaknesses? Do you like his explanation of the Eucharist as the point toward which many Old Testament prophecies converge, a bloodless foreshadowing of Christ's sacrificial death on Calvary, and an earthly anticipation of the heavenly banquet? Would you add any other layers to this presentation?

2. Augustine uses his teaching on the Eucharist to offset the dangers of Manichean dualism, Pelagian self-justification, and Donatist purism. Can the Eucharist be used to offset similar threats to the faith today? If so, what might those threats be and what role would the Eucharist play in dealing with them?

3. Do you believe that the Eucharist is a "sacrament of unity"? Do you believe that participation in this sacrament should be reserved only for those members of the baptized community who were in good standing with the Church? If so, what would this mean in practical, concrete terms? If not, then what would you suggest should be the visible expression of unity for the Catholic faith?

4. Do you believe that the Holy Spirit transforms the Eucharistic elements into the living flesh of Jesus' glorified life? Do you believe that by eating the body and blood of the glorified Christ, we enter into deep communion with him and anticipate our own share in the resurrection? How does such a presentation of the Eucharist affect your understanding of the phrase "receiving Holy Communion"?

5. In what sense do the members of the Church share in Christ's sacrifice on Calvary? Do they do so through their participation in the Eucharist? Do they share in this sacrifice as both priest and victim? What does such an understanding of the Eucharist tell us about our relationship with Christ? What does it tell us about our relationship with others? In what sense is the Eucharist a sign of unity?

Voice Twenty-Two

Leo the Great

Proclaiming the Real Presence

> Participation in the Body and Blood of Christ effects noth-
> ing else but that we become that which we consume, and we
> carry Him everywhere both in spirit and in body, in and with
> whom we have died, have been buried, and have risen.
>
> *Leo the Great*

W hat did the great popes of the early Church have to say about the Eucharist? Pope Leo the Great (d. 461), our next voice from the past, led the Church of Rome during a time of great political turmoil and is remembered as a great defender of the Roman people. In 452, he met Attila the Hun at Mantua and convinced him to drop his plans of attacking the vulnerable and defenseless city of Rome. Three years later, he met with Genseric, king of the Vandals, and gained strong assurances that the people of Rome would be spared the death and devastation that this army normally left in its wake. A staunch defender of Christian orthodoxy, Leo stood firm against theological errors and devised the Christological formula that was eventually accepted at the Council of Chalcedon (451). His views on the Eucharist flow from his theological outlook and are in keeping with the traditional teaching of the Latin fathers.[1]

Leo's Theological Outlook

Leo's theology shines through his writings, the vast majority of which are sermons and epistles. He developed his Christology, his

---

1. The above information comes from *P*, 417–19; *CH*, 1:317–18.

understanding of Christ, to deal with the threat of Monophysitism, the view of Christ that saw him as having only a divine nature. This doctrine had been developed by Eutyches, Archimandrite of Constantinople, and it claimed that in the Incarnation Christ's humanity had been absorbed into his divinity. In a letter to Flavian, Patriarch of Constantinople, Leo explained in very succinct terms that Christ's human and divine natures were not intermingled, but remained separate and worked in close concert with one another. This letter, known as the *Epistola dogmatica ad Flavianum* (or simply "The Tome of Leo"), set the stage for the Christological definition made at Chalcedon.[2]

In this epistle, Leo asserted that Christ is one Person with two distinct natures: one human and one divine. He maintained that the uniqueness of each nature was preserved at Christ's birth and that they continue to exist without any mixture. He also asserted that Jesus was born "true God and true man" and that "each nature does what is proper to it with the mutual participation of the other." This close cooperation of the two natures allows for the so-called communication of idioms, whereby the traits of Jesus' human nature can be ascribed to him as God and the traits of his divine nature can be ascribed to him as man.[3]

Leo was also a staunch defender of papal primacy. He held that the bishop of Rome was the one true successor of Peter the Apostle, whose primacy extended to all churches throughout the world. The dignity of this office, he maintained, did not depend on the personal worthiness of the person holding it, but in the see of the bishop of Rome, in which the power and authority of Peter inheres. Leo affirmed the rights of ecclesiastical authority in all matters concerning faith, but recognized the Emperor's right to call Councils and to make certain ecclesiastical nominations. He requested the protection of the state to keep order in the Church and especially to combat heresy.[4]

---

2. See *P* 418–20. For the text of Leo's Tome, see Leo the Great, *Letters*, 28 (*NPNF*, 12:38–43).

3. See *P*, 420. For an extended analysis of Leo's thought, see Aloys Grillmeier, *Christ in the Christian Tradition: From the Apostolic Age to Chalcedon (451)*, trans. J.S. Bowden (New York: Sheed and Ward, 1965), 460–77.

4. See *P*, 421.

Regarding the sacraments, Leo normally limited the celebration of baptism to Easter and Pentecost and affirmed the mediatory power of the Church to forgive mortal sins. In conjunction with the latter, he opposed the common practice in some dioceses of publishing the secret, privately confessed sins of public penitents without their consent. His teaching on the Eucharist, faithful to the tenets of Latin theology, is realistic in its interpretation of Jesus' words of institution.[5]

Leo's Teaching on the Eucharist

Leo proclaims the real presence of Christ in the Eucharist. He assumes all Christians will receive communion at Easter and encourages them to prepare for it by avoiding sin and adopting appropriate penitential practices. The real presence, for Leo, is the glorified body and blood of the Risen Lord. He does not speculate about the nature or mode of this presence, but is generally content with the testimony of the Scriptures and with adding his voice to the growing chorus of belief in the presence of Jesus' body and blood in the consecrated elements.[6]

One striking characteristic of Leo's teaching is the way he uses the Eucharist in his arguments against heresy. In a sermon on the importance of fasting, he urges his listeners to restrain themselves not only from food, but also from the errors of the mind. Believers, he insists, should be firm in their faith: "When the Lord says: 'Unless you shall have eaten the flesh of the Son of Man and shall have drunk His blood, you shall not have life in you,' you ought to so communicate at the Sacred Table that you have no doubt whatever of the truth of the Body and Blood of Christ."[7] Those who argue with the truth and doubt the real presence of Christ in the Eucharist, receive it unworthily and without effect: "For that which is taken in the mouth is what is believed in faith; and in vain do those respond, 'Amen,' who argue against that which is received."[8] In the text of the sermon, Leo mentions specifically the errors of Eutyches and Nestorius and

---

5. Ibid., 420–21. See also *HD*, 3:363.
6. See *HD*, 3:362–63, 370–71.
7. Leo the Great, *Sermons*, 93.1 (*FEF*, 3:280).
8. Ibid.

affirms that Jesus Christ is One, True God and Man.[9] Receiving the Eucharist, for Leo, is the ultimate affirmation of the Catholic faith. To partake of it without avowing the real presence or the truth of Christ's humanity and divinity is ineffectual and will produce no tangible fruit in the life of the communicant.

Leo's teaching on the Eucharist also has strong moral overtones. In a sermon on the ascension of Christ, he speaks of how believers should receive the sacraments: "We fittingly celebrate, therefore, the Lord's Passover with the unleavened bread of sincerity and truth. Once the leaven of our past malice has been purged out, the new creature can satisfy its thirst and feed upon the Lord himself."[10] The implication here is that believers should prepare themselves for the Eucharist by humbling themselves through penance and other spiritual practices that purify the soul. The effects of such a sharing in the sacrament are astounding. In a sermon on the passion, he states his position very clearly: "Participation in the Body and Blood of Christ effects nothing else but that we become that which we consume, and we carry Him everywhere both in spirit and in body, in and with whom we have died, have been buried, and have risen."[11] Leo could not be any clearer. At the Eucharist, believers become what they eat. By sharing in the sacrament of the Lord's Last Supper, they share in Christ's Paschal mystery and participate in his passage from death to new life.

The Eucharist, for Leo, is also a mystical gift of spiritual food that affirms the reality of Christ's humanity. In a letter to the clergy and people of Constantinople soon after the Council of Chalcedon, he speaks of the Monophysites as having lost sight of this basic truth of the Catholic faith:

> In what density of ignorance, in what utter sloth must they hitherto have lain, not to have learnt from hearing, nor understood from read-ing, that which in God's Church is so constantly in men's mouths, that even the tongues of infants do not keep silence upon the truth of

---

9. Eutyches, the main proponent of Monophysitism, affirmed that Jesus had only one nature, for his humanity had been completely absorbed into his divinity. Nestorius, the founder of Nestorianism, affirmed that Jesus' divinity and humanity had remained completely separate and functioned as two distinct persons.

10. Leo the Great, *Sermon 2 on the Ascension*, 1–4 in Michael L. Gaudoin-Parker, ed., *The Real Presence through the Ages* (New York: Alba House, 1993), 53.

11. Leo the Great, *Sermons*, 63.7 (*FEF*, 3:278). See also, Ibid., 53.

Christ's Body and Blood at the rite of Holy Communion? For in that
mystic distribution of spiritual nourishment, that which is given and
taken is of such a kind that receiving the virtue of the celestial food
we pass into the flesh of Him, Who became our flesh.[12]

One again, Leo uses the Eucharist in his efforts to dampen the
influence of the Monophysite heresy on the life of the faithful. At the
same time, he emphasizes the close connection between the Catholic
belief in the humanity of Jesus and the doctrine of the true presence
of Jesus' body and blood in the consecrated bread and wine. To receive the Eucharist according to authentic Catholic belief, a person
must believe that Jesus was *both* God *and* man. To believe otherwise
would make a mockery of the sacrament and of the transformation it
seeks to bring about in the lives of believers.

Observations

Leo's teaching on the Eucharist invites comment from a number
of perspectives. The following remarks seek to distil and analyze
some of the more significant elements of his thought.

1. To begin with, Leo highlights the faith dimension of the Eucharistic celebration. The testimony of Scripture is very clear on what
happens there, and he feels no need to probe the mystery of what
takes place there any further. For Leo, there is no room for doubt
when one approaches the altar of God. In his letters and sermons, he
affirms the faith of the Church and refuses to water it down. At the
Eucharist, bread and wine become Christ's body and blood. This is
the faith of the Church, and this is what he preaches and teaches. He
encourages the faithful always to be firm in their faith.

2. Leo is not an innovator, but a bearer of the theological tradition
he hopes to pass on to others. As Pope, he values highly his role as an
authoritative defender of the faith. What he achieved on a political and
material level for the people of Rome against the barbarian hordes of
Attila and Genseric, he sought to do on a moral and spiritual level for
Christians throughout the world.

---

12. Leo the Great, *Letters*, 59.2 (*NPNF*), 12:58.

3. Leo exhorts his listeners to discipline their minds as they do their bodies with penitential practices. They must be careful not to give in to the laziness of mind and spirit that leads to doctrinal errors such as those propounded by Eutyches and Nestorius. The Eucharist, Leo believes, encourages this kind of right thinking by putting them in touch with the body and blood of Christ himself. Leo believes that the person who approaches the Eucharist with humility, sincerity, and a desire for truth will be led along the way of truth by Jesus, "the Way, the Truth, and the Life" (Jn 14:6).

4. In the light of the above, Leo uses Christ's presence in the Eucharist as an argument against heresy, specifically, as we have seen, against Monophysitism. According to Catholic belief, Jesus' body and blood are truly present in the consecrated Eucharistic species. Such a belief implies that Jesus was fully human when he walked on earth and was not simply absorbed into his divinity as a drop of fresh water is absorbed by the ocean. Leo's use of the sacrament in this way affirms the traditional Christian principle of *lex orandi, lex credendi*. He uses the prayer of the Church to guide his determination of what he believes. One reason why the Monophysite beliefs of Eutyches are wrong is because they do not reinforce the implied beliefs of Christian liturgical worship.

5. According to Leo's understanding, those participating in the Eucharist become what they consume. They are incorporated ever more deeply into the divinized humanity of Christ. Receiving the Eucharist has a deifying or divinizing effect on the communicant. Rather than losing one's humanity in Christ's divinity, Christ's divinized humanity elevates those who eat Christ's body and drink his blood by allowing them to share in his human and divine Sonship. Leo describes the effects of the Eucharist on the communicant in a way that closely resembles the understanding the *theosis* (that is, the divinization) of humanity in Eastern Christian thought (see 2 Peter 1:4). To become what one eats is another way of speaking about God becoming human so that humanity might become divine.

6. Leo emphasizes the importance of approaching the Eucharist with the appropriate interior dispositions. Believers should prepare for their reception of the sacrament by avoiding sin and do-

ing penance. They should root out all malice from their lives and clothe themselves with sincerity and truth. Only when they humble themselves by purifying their souls with penance and other spiritual practices will they be able to get the most out of their celebration of the sacrament. Leo is well aware that the Eucharist is not a magical ritual that produces an effect independent of the interior dispositions of the communicant. While he firmly believes in the real presence, he understands that Jesus will not transform a person's life against his or her own wishes. For him, properly preparing for the sacrament is a sign of one's willingness to undergo the inner conversion of heart that the reception of Jesus' body and blood signifies.

7. Leo also emphasizes the mystical dimensions of the Eucharistic celebration. Through the "mystic distribution" of Jesus' body and blood, believers gain access to spiritual nourishment that puts them in touch with the life of the Risen Lord. The Eucharist, for Leo, brings Christ's paschal mystery into the midst of the believing community. By partaking of the consecrated bread and wine, believers eat the celestial food that enables their flesh to pass into his. As such, the Eucharist is a mystical celebration of humanity's redemption. When they eat and drink of Jesus' body and blood, believers become one with the humanity of their saving Lord, are imbued with his life, and are elevated to the status of divine Sonship.

8. Finally, Leo's Eucharistic teaching both flows from his other theological concerns and is the sustaining source that enables him to resolve them. If the prayer of the Church leads the community of the faithful to formulate sound doctrine, it must also be viewed as the source from which the Church's theological reflection flows and is sustained. When thrown in the midst of a heated controversy about the nature of Christ, such as with Monophysitism, Leo's genuine concern for orthodoxy leads him to examine his faith in the rituals that guide his worship and gives him life.

Conclusion

Leo the Great was the greatest pope of the fifth century and probably one of the greatest in all of history. Remembered as "the guardian of orthodoxy" and "the savior of Western civilization," he gained such accolades primarily because of his extraordinary accomplishments in the political arena and his theological contributions to the Church's understanding of the mystery of Christ, the God-Man.[13]

Leading the Church of Rome during a period of great turmoil and unrest, Leo was a decisive ecclesiastical administrator, a discerning theologian, and an eloquent preacher. He placed his many talents not only at the service of the Church of Rome, but of Christian churches throughout the world. As the successor of Peter, he was very much aware of his power and authority and was not afraid to use it. It is no small tribute to his theological brilliance and his judicious exercise of this authority that, having read his now famous "Tome" on the relationship between the human and divine in Christ, the fathers of Chalcedon responded: "Peter has spoken through Leo."[14]

Leo's teaching on the Eucharist is rooted in the dual testimony of Scripture and Christian worship. It affirms the real presence of Christ in the consecrated elements and brings out the moral, spiritual, and even mystical dimensions of the sacrament. Leo uses the Eucharist to offset the dangers of heresy, especially the threat of Monophysitism. He exhorts the faithful to discipline the mind by steering clear of the laziness of thought that denigrates Christ's full humanity or posits a radical break between his two natures. He also teaches that those who receive the Eucharist worthily become what they consume. It would be difficult to find a more eloquent way of describing the redemptive and divinizing effects of this supreme act of Christian worship.

Reflection Questions

1. Do you consider it important to restrain yourself from the errors of the mind? What ideas do you consider a threat to your faith? How do you restrain yourself with regard to them? What concrete steps do you take in your day-to-day life to ensure that you remain firm of faith?

---

13. See *CH*, 1:317; *P*, 417.
14. See Henry Denzinger, *The Sources of Catholic Dogma*, trans. Roy J. Deferrari (St. Louis and London: B. Herder Book Co., 1957), 58 n.1.

2. Do you believe that the Eucharist encourages right thinking by putting one in direct contact with the body and blood of Christ? If so, does this occur automatically or does it depend on the dispositions with which one approaches the sacrament? What dispositions should one have when receiving the Eucharist?

3. Do you believe in *lex orandi, lex credendi*, the idea that the prayer of the Church guides, and should guide, our belief? If so, then how does the present prayer of the Church guide your faith? What truths would it have you affirm? What would it have you deny? What does it tell you about the way you should put your faith in action?

4. Do you believe that receiving the Eucharist has a deifying or divinizing influence on the communicant? If so, then what concrete effects should one expect to be manifested in a person's life? What changes should you expect to experience in yourself? What changes should you expect to see in others?

5. Do you believe that the Eucharist brings Christ's paschal mystery into the midst of the believing community? Do you believe that, through it, believers gain access to spiritual nourishment that puts them in touch with the life of the Risen Lord? Do you believe that the Eucharist is a mystical celebration of humanity's redemption by Christ?

Voice Twenty-Three

Gregory the Great
Holy Sacrifice of Christ

Search into your own hearts and drive out this deadly aver-
sion. But if you are still earthly minded, you will perhaps be
seeking for earthly food. Behold how even earthly food has
been changed for you into spiritual nourishment. To take
away this distaste from your soul, the matchless Lamb has
been slain for you in the supper of the Lord.

Gregory the Great

What did the other great pope of the early Church have to say
about the Eucharist? Pope Gregory the Great (d. 604), our next voice
from the past, represents a bridge between the Eucharistic theology
of the early Church and the deep private and devotional turn it took
in succeeding centuries. Born at the tail end of Late Antiquity and
the dawn of the Middle Ages, he came from a noble Roman family
of high senatorial rank and was Prefect of Rome from 572–73. In
575, he retreated to St. Andrew's, a monastery under the Rule of
Benedict established by him on his family estate, where he intended
to live the rest of his life in solitude. The call to ecclesiastical service, however, foiled his well-laid plans for a life of contemplation.
He was the papal representative to the court of Constantinople from
579–85 and was elected pope and bishop of Rome in 590.

Gregory led the Church during a time of great upheaval. Despite
poor health and scarce resources, he embarked upon a comprehensive program of Church reform. Among his many accomplishments
were his successful efforts to gain the allegiance of the Germanic
tribes, to bring back Arian Christians to the Catholic fold, to evan-
gelize the Anglo-Saxons of Britain, and to root out the remaining

pagan enclaves of Italy. He also reformed the Latin Mass, renewed the liturgical music of his day, and was a staunch supporter of Benedictine monasticism. Gregory was beloved by the Roman people. He engaged in numerous charitable works for their general welfare and, on several occasions, convinced the Lombards to spare them when they marched on Rome and were about to enter its gates.

Along with Ambrose, Jerome, and Augustine, Gregory is considered one of the four great Latin Church fathers. He was thoroughly Augustinian in his outlook and wrote almost exclusively on pastoral and moral concerns. His teaching on the Eucharist is rooted in his desire to address these general practical interests.[1]

Gregory's Theological Outlook

Primarily a pastor and administrator, Gregory does not make any major contributions to the history of theology. For the most part, he is content with following the thinking of St. Augustine and applying it to the daily challenges facing him as the leader of the church of Rome.

In addition to numerous letters and homilies, his major works include the *Pastoral Rule*, a moral commentary on the book of Job (*Moralia in Job*), and a collection of *Dialogues Concerning the Life and Miracles of the Italian Fathers*. His *Sacramentarium Gregorianum* reformed the Latin Mass and gave the Eucharistic canon a shape it would maintain for centuries. Gregory's practical application of Augustine's thought helped shape the theological outlook of the Latin West. Throughout the Middle Ages and beyond, Augustine was admired as the theologian par excellence of the Western Church and Gregory was seen as his primary disciple and principal promulgator.

On specific points of doctrine, Gregory either slightly varies Augustine's thinking or moderates his more rigorist tendencies for general pastoral use. He wrote on such topics as the knowledge of Christ, the sacraments, Church governance, purgatory, the communion of saints, and angelology. He believed the Pope was the head of the universal Church, preferred the name "Servant of the servants of God" (*Servus servorum Dei*), highly respected the teachings of the

---

1. The above information comes from *P*, 556–62; *CH*, 1:320–22.

first four Ecumenical Councils, and even considered these teachings to be on the same level as Holy Scripture. He taught the indissolubility of marriage, asserted the validity of baptisms and ordinations by heretics, continued the pastoral teaching on penance promoted by Augustine and Pope Leo I, and permitted the veneration of the images and relics of the saints. On more speculative doctrinal points, he wrote against the belief that Christ's knowledge was defective in certain areas, and taught that angels were created simultaneously with the material world, dividing them into nine choirs, the lowest of which were created to minister to humanity. One of Gregory's most lasting doctrinal influences was his affirmation of the existence of purgatory, a teaching that would permeate the medieval outlook and remains a part of Catholic teaching to this day.[2]

Gregory's Teaching on the Eucharist

In addition to his belief in purgatory, Gregory emphasizes the special intercessory powers of the holy sacrifice of the Mass. The clearest example of his teaching appears in the fourth book of the *Dialogues*:

> This Sacrifice alone has the power of saving the soul from eternal death, for it presents to us mystically the death of the only-begotten Son. Though He is now risen from the dead and dies no more, and "death has no more power over him," yet, living in Himself immortal and incorruptible, He is again immolated for us in the mystery of the holy Sacrifice. Where His Body is eaten, there His Flesh is distributed among the people for their salvation. His Blood no longer stains the hands of the godless, but flows into the hearts of His faithful followers. See, then, how august the Sacrifice that is offered for us, ever reproducing in itself the passion of the only-begotten Son for the remission of our sins.[3]

The Eucharist, for Gregory, was a mystical presentation of Christ's sacrifice on Calvary, enabling those who participate in it to benefit from the saving mystery of Christ's Paschal mystery. In the Eucharist, Christ becomes a victim and offers his body and blood for

---

2. See *P*, 562–64; *CH*, 1:320–22.
3. Gregory the Great, *Dialogues*, 4.60 (*FC*, 39:272–73).

the salvation of the world. These intercessory powers extend even to the souls in purgatory: "The holy Sacrifice of Christ, our saving Victim, brings great benefits to souls even after death, provided their sins can be pardoned in the life to come. For this reason the souls of the dead sometimes beg to have Masses offered for them."[4] For Gregory, "the benefits of the holy Sacrifice are only for those who by their good lives have merited the grace of receiving help from the good deeds others perform in their behalf."[5] The souls in purgatory benefit from Masses said specifically for their eternal repose, a practice that would gain popularity during the Middle Ages and imprint itself on the spiritual psyche of Catholics for centuries to come.[6]

If the understanding of the Mass as a holy sacrifice was already deeply rooted in the patristic tradition, Gregory dramatized its importance with vivid detail. As he says in his *Dialogues*: "[w]ho of the faithful can have any doubt that at the moment of the immolation, at the sound of the priest's voice, the heavens stand open and choirs of angels are present at the mystery of Jesus Christ. There at the altar the lowliest is united with the most sublime, earth is joined to heaven, the visible and invisible somehow merge into one."[7] The Mass makes present the sacrifice of Christ's body and blood on Calvary, a voluntary offering of Jesus, the God-Man, that opened up the heavens and reestablished humanity's contact with the divine. For Gregory, the sacrifice of the Mass cancels the lesser sins of the faithful on earth and the souls in purgatory. It also releases those in purgatory from the temporal punishment due to sin. In his presentation (which became the traditional and commonly accepted one), there is a close connection between the doctrine of purgatory and the intercessory powers of the sacrifice of the Mass. In the words of J. Tixeront: "The doctrine of purgatory, becoming more and more explicit during this period, naturally leads to a growing sense of the efficacy of the Mass as an expiatory and propitiatory sacrifice and a means of helping the souls of the departed."[8]

---

4. Ibid., 4.57 (*FC*, 39:266).
5. Ibid., 4.59 (*FC*, 39:272).
6. See *CT*, 1:356.
7. Ibid., 4.60 *FC*, 39:273).
8. See *HD*, 3:373; *CT*, 1:355–56.

If Gregory contributed to making the holy sacrifice of the Mass a commonly accepted teaching of the Catholic faith, he was less specific regarding the doctrine of the real presence. Although he accepts the presence of Christ's body and blood in the consecrated species, he does not develop his thought, but is content instead with echoing Augustine's teaching of the *real spiritual presence*. Gregory simply presumes the presence of Christ's body and blood in the sacrament, and does not expound upon his assertions. He clearly emphasizes the sacrificial dimensions of the Mass more than (but not to the exclusion of) the doctrine of the real presence.[9]

On other points regarding the Eucharist, Gregory remains close to the tradition and exhorts the faithful to prepare their souls for the Eucharist through acts of penance and conversion of their hearts. He believes that the Eucharistic sacrifice obtains not only the remission of lesser sins for the living and dead, but also spiritual and even temporal blessings that the living may need. To demonstrate his point, Gregory includes in his *Dialogues* many miracle stories of people who received both spiritual and temporal help through the intercessory powers of the Mass.[10]

Observations

Gregory's teaching on the Eucharist invites comment from a variety of perspectives. The following remarks seek to probe his insights and to find meaningful points of reference for his readers today.

1. To begin with, Gregory emphasizes very strongly the link between the Eucharist and the sacrifice of Calvary. This connection is so close that the words of the priest change bread and wine into Christ's body and blood and open up the heavens to allow humanity to commune once more in fellowship with the Holy Trinity. Jesus Christ is both priest and victim of this holy sacrifice. Gregory underscores the *real* sacrificial dimension of the Eucharistic celebration. The celebration is not merely a symbol of Christ's sacrifice on Cal-

---

9. See *CT*, 1:356.
10. See *HD*, 3:363, 371, 373–74. For some examples of miracle stories pertaining to the sacrifice of the Mass, see Gregory the Great, *Dialogues*, 4.57–62 (*FC*, 39:266–75).

vary, but a true participation in it which brings with it extraordinary powers of intercession.

2. Gregory asserts that the sacrifice of the Mass presents the sacrificial death of God's only-begotten Son to the faithful in a mystical way. To speak of the Mass as a mystical presentation underscores the sacramental dimension of the ritual (the Latin word *sacramentum* parallels the Greek *mysterion*). Gregory here is not referring to an actual mystical experience on the part of those participating in the Mass, but to the manner in which Christ's bloody sacrifice on Calvary transcends time and space and becomes present in the liturgical ritual. In later centuries, the phrase "the bloody sacrifice of Calvary made present in an unbloody manner" would be used to describe the same theological truth.[11]

3. These powers of intercession extend to both the living and the dead. Theologically, these powers come from Christ who, as the one, true mediator between God and humanity, intercedes for the faithful in a unique and powerful way. All Christian intercession is made through, with, and in the person of Jesus Christ the one high priest. To the living, the intercession of Christ at Mass offers the remission of lesser sins and specific spiritual and temporal assistance in living the Christian life. To the dead, they offer remission of these same sins, as well as the relief of temporal punishment due to sin.

4. At the sacrifice of the Mass, Christ's powers of intercession extend to the other members of his body, the Church. This self-offering of Christ's body involves not only the living, but also those in paradise with God, as well as those in need of purgation. This all-inclusive dimension of the prayer of Christ's body emphasizes the close bonds of fellowship among the living and dead. During the Middle Ages, Gregory's strong emphasis on the intercessory powers of the Mass made it a vehicle whereby the members of the faithful could commune with their dead ancestors and receive consolation that their prayers at Mass were united with the intercessions of Christ himself.

---

11. See *Council of Trent*, Ses. 22, chap. 2 in Henricus Denziger and Adolfus Schönmetzer, *Enchiridion Symbolorum*, no. 1743, 32 ed. (Freiburg in Breisgau: Herder, 1963), 408–9. See also, *Catechism of the Catholic Church*, no. 1367 (Vatican City: Libreria Editrice Vaticana, 1994), 344.

5. Gregory's stance toward the real presence reflects the general trend of Latin theology to reaffirm Christ's presence in the consecrated elements, but to generally steer clear of speculative attempts to explain the mode of Christ's existence present there. As a follower of Augustine, he leans toward an understanding of a real spiritual presence in the bread and wine, but does not say much in terms of an explanation regarding that presence. Such a non-speculative approach is in keeping with Gregory's strong pastoral and administrative bent. He assumes Christ's presence in the consecrated elements, but is more interested in the effects receiving these gifts will have on the believer than in trying to explain how it comes about. In Latin theology, the debate on the nature of the real presence does not become controversial until well into the ninth century.

6. For Gregory, the intercessory powers of the Eucharistic sacrifice have real, tangible effects in everyday life. His *Dialogues* are full of miracle stories of ordinary people whose lives have been dramatically affected by the power of Christ acting through the Mass. The purpose of these stories was to build up the faith of the faithful by demonstrating to them that the Lord cares for his people in myriad ways and protects them from harm's way. Many of them are tales of people being saved from the forces of evil manifested through demonic, human, or natural means. Such tales of redemption are intended to highlight the salvific dimension of the Eucharistic sacrifice.

7. The reception of Gregory's teaching on the Eucharist in succeeding centuries contributed to developments which he himself may not have accepted. His emphasis on the sacrificial and intercessory dimensions of the Mass became embedded in the mindset of popular devotion and spiritual practice of the Middle Ages and beyond. The result was an understanding of the faith that focused on the saying of Masses said for specific intentions for the spiritual and temporal needs of the faithful both the living and dead. While this emphasis was a valid development rooted in genuine insights into the connection between the Eucharistic celebration and the one sacrifice of Calvary, it sometimes led to an unhealthy "privatization" of the Mass and its redeeming fruits.

8. To speak of the "privatization" of the Mass means that those attending the Eucharist thought of themselves as relating to the litur-

gical action primarily as individuals and only secondarily (if at all) as the body of Christ and the communion of saints. As a result, the fruits became increasingly seen as within the sphere of the particular person or persons for whom the Mass was being celebrated, instead of the people of God as a whole. While Gregory was not directly responsible for this shift in emphasis, his focus on the intercessory powers of the sacrifice of the Mass contributed to it. Furthermore, some of the positions associated with the Medieval "privatized" Mass that gained a degree of support from Gregory's theology contributed to the debates at the time of the Reformation. Some of the difficulties that arose are being resolved through ecumenical dialogue. The tension between individual and community has been felt within each of the Christian communions since then. For the Roman Catholic Church it was not until the liturgical movement of the twentieth century and the eventual renewal of the liturgy at the Second Vatican Council with the publication of *Sacrosanctum Concilium* (4 December 1963) that the proper balance between the needs of the individual and the Church as a whole was restored.

Conclusion

Gregory the Great filled a spiritual and political vacuum in Rome during a period of decline. He laid the foundation for developments in the Western world that would become basic to medieval Catholicism. Although he was not a speculative thinker and did not contribute to the development of Latin theology in a way similar to Augustine and the other great Latin Fathers, his pastoral and administrative sensibilities helped forge the structures of an institution that would guide the Church through the tumultuous centuries ahead.

Gregory was an Augustinian at heart and put the teachings of his master to good, practical, use. His major works focused on the pastoral and moral concerns of the Church and were intended to lead the faithful to a deeper relationship with God through Jesus Christ, their mediator, high priest, and saving victim. He used his authority as the Pope of the universal Church to promulgate his administrative and pastoral agenda and, for the most part, succeeded well. To no small degree, the medieval papacy was inspired and shaped by Gregory's understanding of his papal office and his efforts to extend his influence through the Latin West and beyond.

While affirming the real presence, Gregory's teaching on the Eucharist focuses on the sacrificial and intercessory dimensions of the Mass. He describes the Eucharist as a mystical presentation of Christ's sacrificial death on Calvary, an act of self-offering which restores humanity's relationship with God through the intercession of Christ, the one, true mediator. For Gregory, the fruits of the Eucharist extend to the spiritual and temporal welfare of all believers, both living and dead. He offers many stories and miraculous accounts of believers who were assisted by God through the intercessory powers of the Eucharist. For this reason, he encourages the faithful to foster a deep reverence for the Mass as a "Holy Sacrifice." His emphasis on this dimension of the Eucharistic celebration imprinted itself on the devotional life of the faithful and influenced the nature of the Church's liturgical worship for centuries to come.

Reflection Questions

1. Do you believe that the Eucharist is a true participation in Christ's sacrifice on Calvary and brings with it extraordinary powers of intercession? What are these powers of intercession like? Are they general or specific? Toward whom are they directed? How are they invoked?

2. Do you believe that the intercessory powers of the Eucharist extend to both the living and the dead? To what extent do they flow from Christ as the one, true mediator between God and humanity? What graces can the Eucharist obtain for the living? What graces can it obtain for the dead?

3. Do you believe that the intercessory powers of the Eucharistic sacrifice have real, tangible effects in everyday life? If so, what are these tangible effects like? A miracle? A providential turn in circumstances? A change of heart? Have you experienced any such effects in your own life?

4. Do you think of the celebration of the Eucharist primarily as an individual or as a communal action? Is it solely a communal action? Is it solely an individual action? When celebrating the Eucharist, how can one maintain a proper balance between the needs of the individual and of the believing community?

5. Do you think Gregory's understanding of the Eucharistic celebration is compatible with the vision proposed by the Second Vatican Council? What are the areas of convergence? Are there any areas of divergence? Are there any differences in emphasis? Do you see anything in Gregory's understanding of the Eucharist that needs to be retrieved by Christians nowadays?

Conclusion

Scientists tell us that each human voice gives off a distinctive recordable print that cannot be duplicated. Anyone who has sung in a choir or listened to a performance of choral singers knows it can also blend with other voices in spirited chants and other forms of inspiring song. Much the same holds true for the voices from the distant past presented in this book. Even though they span a period of over 500 years (roughly 95–604 C.E.), each of them arose out of a distinct set of circumstances in the history of the post-apostolic Church and responded to a unique set of pressures that threatened the emerging orthodoxy from within and/or without. Listening to them from across the centuries, however, also enables us to experience them resonating with each other and harmonizing in significant theological and pastoral ways. The result confirms something very important about the faith of the post-apostolic Church. Taken either alone or as a whole, all of the representative voices presented in this volume affirm the centrality of the Eucharist for the life of the believing community.

Throughout this book, we have made a determined effort to allow these voices on the Eucharist to speak for themselves. By listening to them and questioning them in appropriate ways, some of us may have come across striking similarities with our own beliefs. Others may have seen some stark differences; still others may have uncovered various mixtures of likeness and difference. Regardless of what might have been found, looking to the past in this way should encourage us all to probe the foundations of our faith and ask ourselves why we believe what we do about the Eucharist. Our purpose in this book was not to project later, deeply held views back upon an earlier, less sophisticated age, but merely to permit these writers of the post-apostolic ages to speak in a way that could be heard and responded to today in practical and relevant ways. Although every such act of historical translation necessarily involves an interpretation of the past in the light of our present-day assumptions, we have made great efforts to insure an open, authentic dialogue with these important voices of early Christianity's emerging orthodoxy.

In the final analysis, the Eucharist itself provides the common medium through which we hear, interpret, and respond to these voices from the distant past. Just as the air around us carries the sound of a voice from one person's lips to the ears of another, so the Church's celebration of the Eucharist offers the necessary environment of faith that allows these voices to come to the fore. "Faith comes through hearing," the Apostle Paul tells us, "and what is heard is the word of Christ" (Rom 10:17). Each of these voices seeks to speak the word of Christ to their own contemporaries and to all who are willing and able to hear. The faith they proclaim is about Christ's presence in the Eucharist, and about its enormous and transforming effects as it draws all who share in it into the very life of God, where each person is united to all others. Although their lifeblood no longer passes through their veins and sinews and their earthly voices have long since fallen silent, they have bequeathed to us a testimony of faith that never ceases to inspire. It remains for us to make their "living faith" a part of our own Christian experience.

Acknowledgments

Parts of this book were previously published as: "Clement of Rome on the Eucharist," *Emmanuel*, 109 (no. 4, 2003): 245–55 [Voice One]; "Ignatius of Antioch on the Eucharist," *Emmanuel* 110 (no. 1, 2004): 14–21 [Voice Two]; "Eucharist in *The Martyrdom of Polycarp*, *Emmanuel* 110 (no. 3, 2004): 196–204 [Voice Three]; "Christian Eucharist in *The Didache*," *Emmanuel* 109 (no. 5, 2003): 338–45 [Voice Four]; "Justin Martyr on the Eucharist," *Emmanuel* 109 (no. 3, 2003): 132–41 [Voice Five]; "Irenaeus of Lyons on the Eucharist," *Emmanuel* 110 (no. 2, 2004): 100–108 [Voice Six]; "Clement of Alexandria on the Eucharist," *Emmanuel* 110 (no. 6, 2004): 495–503 [Voice Seven]; "Tertullian on the Eucharist," *Emmanuel* 110 (no. 4, 2004): 292–301 [Voice Eight]; "Hippolytus of Rome on the Eucharist," *Emmanuel* 111 (no. 1, 2005): 14–22, 34 [Voice Nine]; "Origen on the Eucharist," *Emmanuel* 111 (no. 2, 2005): 114–22 [Voice Ten]; "Mingling Water with Wine: Cyprian of Carthage on the Eucharist," *Emmanuel* 111 (no. 3, 2005): 218–26 [Voice Eleven]; "Athanasius on the Eucharist," *Emmanuel* 111 (no. 4, 2005): 326–34 [Voice Twelve]; "Cyril of Jerusalem on the Eucharist," *Emmanuel* 111 (no. 6, 2005): 485–93 [Voice Thirteen]; "Hilary of Poitiers on the Eucharist," *Emmanuel* 111 (no. 5, 2005): 406–14 [Voice Fourteen]; "Ambrose of Milan on the Eucharist," *Emmanuel* 112 (no. 5, 2006): 388–96 [Voice Fifteen]; "Basil the Great on the Eucharist," *Emmanuel* 112 (no. 1, 2006):4–13 [Voice Sixteen]; "Gregory Nazianzus on the Eucharist," *Emmanuel* 112 (no., 2, 2006): 116–25 [Voice Seventeen]; "Gregory of Nyssa on the Eucharist," *Emmanuel* 112 (no. 3, 2006): 209–17 [Voice Eighteen]; "John Chrysostom on the Eucharist," *Emmanuel* 112 (no. 4, 2006): 303–11 [Voice Nineteen]; "St. Jerome on the Eucharist," *Emmanuel* 112 (no. 6, 2006): 485–93 [Voice Twenty]; "Augustine of Hippo," *Emmanuel* 113 (no. 1, 2007): 4–12 [Voice Twenty-One]; "Leo the

Great on the Eucharist," *Emmanuel* 113 (no. 2, 2007): 116–23 [Voice Twenty-Two]; "Gregory the Great on the Eucharist," *Emmanuel* 113 (no. 3, 2007): 218–26 [Voice Twenty-Three].

Unless otherwise stated, all quotations from Scripture come from *The New American Bible* (New York: Catholic Book Publishing Co., 1970). In keeping with the book's popular tone, footnotes have been kept to a minimum. The strictly historical material in the book is not original to the author. Those interested in pursuing particular points of interest can begin by looking to such works as Jean Daniélou, *A History of Early Christian Doctrine Before the Council of Nicea*, 3 vols. (London/Philadelphia: Darton, Longman & Todd/The Westminster Press, 1970–77) and W.H.C. Frend, *The Rise of Christianity* (Philadelphia: Fortress Press, 1984). As far as the Eucharist is concerned, helpful insights appear in *The Eucharist of the Early Christians*, trans. Matthew J. O'Connell (New York: Pueblo Publishing Company, 1976) and Daniel J. Sheerin, *The Eucharist*, Message of the Fathers of the Church, vol. 7 (Wilmington, DE: Michael Glazier, 1986).

A special word of thanks goes to Rev. Paul Bernier, SSS, editor of *Emmanuel Magazine*, for his help in first publishing these essays. Special thanks also go to Callan Slipper of New City, London, for his invaluable editorial help in putting them into book form and to Gary Brandl of New City Press, Hyde Park, NY, for his assistance in preparing the book's American edition.

ALSO AVAILABLE

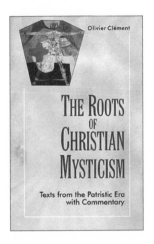

The Roots of Christian Mysticism
Texts from the Patristic Era with Commentary

Olivier Clement

"There are some books so good that all one wants to say is: go out, buy it and read it — it is marvelous! And so it is with this fine translation."

—Andrew Louth
Fairacres Chronicle

"Clement has provided a helpful contribution to all who are interested in the study of spirituality."

—*America*

ISBN 1-56548-029-5
382 pp., paperback

Also available

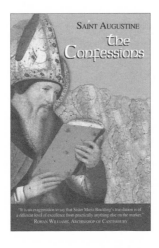

The Confessions

Saint Augustine
Translation by
Maria Boulding, O.S.B.

"Boulding's fresh new translation of this classic captures the essence of Augustine's struggle to integrate faith and understanding as his heart seeks to rest in God."

—Publishers Weekly, RBL

"Augustine's Confessions has been much translated: but it is no exageration to say that Sister Maria Boulding's version is of different level of excellence from practically anything else on the market."

—Rowan William
Archbishop of Canterbury

ISBN 978-1-56548-084-1
416 pp., paperback